A World on Edge

The End of the Great War and
the Dawn of a New Age

DANIEL SCHÖNPFLUG

Translated by Jefferson Chase

PICADOR

First published 2018 by Metropolitan Books, New York

First published in the UK 2018 by Macmillan

This paperback edition first published 2019 by Picador
an imprint of Pan Macmillan
20 New Wharf Road, London N1 9RR
Associated companies throughout the world
www.panmacmillan.com

ISBN 978-1-5098-1851-8

1 3 5 7 9 8 6 4 2

A CIP catalogue record for this book is available from the British Library.

Printed and bound by CPI Group (UK) Ltd, Croydon, CR0 4YY

Visit **www.picador.com** to read more about all our books
and to buy them. You will also find features, author interviews and
news of any author events, and you can sign up for e-newsletters
so that you're always first to hear about our new releases.

Memories, thank God, cannot be photographed . . . No, to be honest, even if I had all the material in the world in front of me, notes from the First World War, letters, passports, family photographs, love letters and everything that attaches itself to an eventful life like mussels to a ship's keel, I still wouldn't have used it as people would expect here . . . Yes, I love the half-light, but please don't confuse the half-light with blurriness and anything washed-out.

—George Grosz

Contents

A World on Edge

PROLOGUE

And now the Torch and Poppy Red
We wear in honor of our dead.
Fear not that ye have died for naught;
We'll teach the lesson that ye wrought
In Flanders Fields.

—Moina Michael

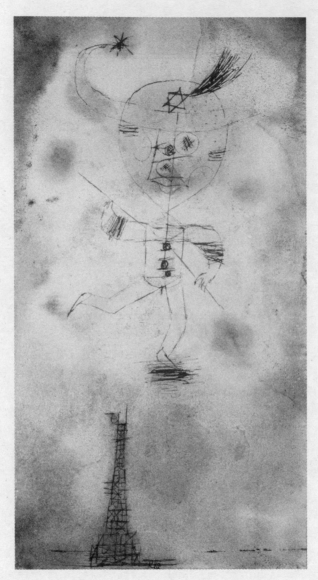

Paul Klee, *The Comet of Paris*, 1918

IN THE EARLY hours of November 11, 1918, the German Kaiser dangles at the end of a long noose strung between two skyscrapers in New York. Confetti flutters through the sunlight and swirls around the lifeless German monarch. Obviously this isn't Wilhelm II in the flesh but merely his likeness, a larger-than-life cloth puppet complete with moustache and spiked "Pickelhaube" helmet. Long white paper streamers tossed from the upper stories catch on the point and sway majestically, high above the street.

The armistice between the Allies and the German Empire took effect at 5 a.m. Eastern Standard Time. After four years of relentless fighting, the Germans—called "Huns" since the beginning of hostilities—have been brought to their knees. The Great War has been won—at the cost of more than sixteen million lives worldwide. New Yorkers learn the news from the morning papers and take to the streets by the thousands. A sea of people swells below the skyscrapers, decked out in suits and bowler hats, in their best Sunday attire, in olive drab and nurses uniforms. They walk shoulder to shoulder, arm in arm, saluting, embracing. Church bells peal, salutes are fired, marches and fanfares join with millions of laughing, singing, and chanting voices to form a din like crashing surf. Honking their horns, drivers steer through the crowds at walking speed, while those inside wave flags enthusiastically above the cars. The cheering city erupts in a spontaneous festival with hand-painted posters, self-proclaimed tribunes, musical bands and people dancing with abandon in the streets. All work comes to a standstill on this day of victory, which—so they believe—will soon lead to peace throughout the world.

Moina Michael had recently taken a leave of absence from her job as a housemother and instructor at a women's teaching college in Georgia, and for several weeks has been working for the YWCA. In the buildings of Columbia University in Manhattan, this solidly built woman of almost fifty helps young women and men prepare for overseas service. The most capable among them are to cross the Atlantic to become civilian workers behind the front lines, helping soldiers get needed supplies—or so they think. Two days before the end of the war, Michael happens to get hold of a copy of the *Ladies' Home Journal* featuring the war poem "In Flanders Fields" by Canadian lieutenant John McCrae, which begins with the lines: "In Flanders fields the poppies blow / Between the crosses, row on row." The page in the magazine is ornately decorated with heroic soldier figures hovering, as though ascending to heaven, above a graveyard covered in red poppies. A rapt Michael reads the poem to its conclusion, where McCrae conjures up the image of a dying soldier whose ever-weakening hands pass on the torch of battle to the survivors. The words and images echo inside her, as if the poem were written just for her, as though the voices of the dead were speaking directly to her. *She* is the one who is meant. *She* must extend her hand and grasp the sinking torch of peace and liberty. *She* must become an instrument to keep the faith. *She* must ensure that the memories of millions of victims never fade. They can't have fought in vain. Their deaths cannot have been senseless.

Michael is so moved by the poem and the mission she suddenly envisions that she takes a pencil and jots down verses of her own on a yellow envelope. The lines center on the poppy. Swearing a vow in rhyme, she pledges to pass on the lesson from the fields of Flanders to future generations: "Oh! you who sleep in Flanders Fields, / Sleep sweet—to rise anew! / We caught the torch you threw / And holding high, we keep the Faith / With All who died."

While she's writing down these words, a group of young men approach her desk. They've collected ten dollars as an expression of thanks for her help in furnishing their YMCA quarters. As she accepts the check, everything comes together. Her thoughts cannot remain mere words, no matter how well rhymed. Her poem must become reality. "I shall buy red poppies—twenty-five red poppies," she tells the dumbfounded men. "I shall always wear red poppies." She shows them McCrae's poem and, after a bit of hesitation, recites her own. The men are enthusiastic. They, too, pledge to wear red poppies, and Michael sets off to procure some. But while the great metropolis has all manner of artificial flowers, its selection of the bright red *Papaver rhoeas* so lauded in verse proves rather deficient. As a result Moina spends the final hours of the war scouring New York for fake poppies. At last she finds some at Wanamaker's, a gigantic New York department store selling everything from notions to automobiles, and boasting a tea room with much crystal on display. There she buys one large poppy for her desk and two dozen four-petaled blossoms, all made of paper. Back at the YMCA, she pins the latter to the lapels of the young men she thinks will soon be fulfilling their duty in

France. Such are the humble beginnings of an amazingly successful symbol. Within a few years, poppies will come to stand throughout the English-speaking world for the memories of those killed in the First World War.

The enormous significance of this symbol emerged from an extraordinary moment in history, a time when people around the world were celebrating and reflecting and swearing revenge. The poppies point back to the past and forward to the future all at once. On the one hand they are an admonition to confront the most recent chapter of history and never to forget it. In this sense, they are part of a global culture of commemoration, which will ultimately see ceremonies held, monuments erected, and the names of the fallen chiseled in stone at government buildings and military bases. On the other hand, Moina Michael's idea also looks ahead. For her, the blood that was shed and the masses who sacrificed their lives and health impose a responsibility upon the future. Her naïve hope, born of spontaneous inspiration and her own deep religiosity, is that flowers will blossom on the soldiers' graves. For her as well as for many of her contemporaries, the end of the war poses the urgent question of how the future will unfold. The armistice conjures visions of a better life, but also unleashes fears. It gives birth to revolutionary ideas, desires, and dreams—but also to nightmares.

In his 1918 *The Comet of Paris*, the Swiss-born German artist Paul Klee trained his eye on precisely this state of suspension between the past and the future, reality and projection. The watercolor and ink drawing made by the soldier at the Royal Bavarian Aviation School depicts not one, but two comets: the first one green with a long, curved tail and the second in the form of a six-pointed star. Both orbit the head of an acrobat with a pole balancing on an invisible wire high above the Eiffel Tower. It is one of the many Klee works from this time featuring stars above cities, and here as so often elsewhere, the artist was working as an "illustrator of ideas." In this picture, faraway Paris—the capital not only of Germany's enemy but also of art itself—is depicted as a modern Bethlehem. Meanwhile, the comet is a cipher for the unexpected, a portent of great events, of profound change, possibly even catastrophe. Comets have always been viewed as such, and the symbolism is especially potent in the fragile, fraught atmosphere of the early twentieth century. The comet stands for the brief illumination of unimagined possibilities on the horizon, for futures yet unknown. The little sister of the comet, the shooting star, invites viewers to make wishes. But a meteorite falling to earth—another closely related celestial phenomenon—provides a terrifying example of destructive power. Not long before, in 1910, the Earth had crossed the paths of the Great Daylight Comet and Halley's Comet, events that made more fearful earthlings start preparing for the end of the world. These events, together with reports of the Richardton meteorite, which fell in North Dakota on June 30, 1918, may have inspired Klee.

Klee's high-wire aerialist is suspended halfway between the man-made wonder of the Eiffel Tower and these simultaneously promising and threatening heavenly bodies. He belongs to neither of the two spheres completely and is constantly in danger of losing his balance and falling, as the stars swirl around his head, causing him to appear more intoxicated than exhilarated. His rolling eyes seem to intimate that the lights around his forehead are making him dizzy, increasing the danger that he will plummet to the ground.

With *The Comet of Paris*, Klee came up with an ironic allegory for life in the year 1918, which teetered between enthusiasm and defeatism, hopes and fears, high-flying visions and cold, hard realities. Anyone inclined to believe that comets were a harbinger of the future could see November 11 as the fulfillment of prophesies. It was a day when old Europe both lay in ruins and celebrated its survival. A day that sparked revolutions, shattered empires, and shook the world order. The events of that November had all the force of a giant meteorite. Rarely had history seemed more undecided, more open to human intervention. Rarely had people felt such an urgent need to transform lessons learned from the past into plans for the future. In turn they conceived new political ideas, new societies, new art and culture, and entirely new ways of thinking. A new man, the man of the twentieth century, born in the flames of war and freed from the shackles of the old order, was proclaimed. Like the proverbial phoenix, Europe—and the entire world—was set to rise from the ashes.

The people depicted on the following pages were all high-wire artists; their subjective views on the events of the time have been reconstructed from how they depicted themselves in their autobiographies, diaries, and correspondence. The truth of this book is the truth of those documents. Sometimes that truth will collide with that found in history books. At times our eye-witnesses are clearly lying. They watched their dreams light up the firmament and were astonished to see them burn out so quickly, cooling off into cosmic rock and smashing into the ground as reality set in. Each of them is inching ahead atop a fine line stretched above the abyss. Some of them, like Moina Michael, succeeded in retaining their balance, while others crashed to earth, as was the case with Kaiser Wilhelm II, for whom, at least in effigy, the thin wire turned into a hangman's noose.

The events and memories documented by contemporaries also illustrate the almost unbearable tension that charged the days immediately following the First World War. Visions, desires, and dreams did more than inspire those who crossed the great fissure between the nineteenth and twentieth centuries. They also set them at odds with one another. Some plans for the future were diametrically opposed to others. Some—at least according to many of the new preachers of salvation—even ruled others out and could only be realized if their opponents were destroyed. For this reason, instead of bringing about the peace so passionately longed for, the bitter struggle for a better future only brought new violence and claimed millions of new victims.

— One —

The Beginning of the End

Whether to right or left, forward or backward, uphill or downhill—you must go on, without asking what lies before or behind you. It shall be hidden; you were allowed to forget it, you had to, in order to fulfill your task!

—Arnold Schönberg,
Jacob's Ladder, 1917

Paul Nash, *We Are Making a New World*, 1918

NOVEMBER 7, 1918. The sun has already set over the Belgian landscape as a column of five black government automobiles sets off from the German Supreme Army Command in Spa. Sitting inside the last car is Matthias Erzberger, a corpulent fellow of forty-three years, with metal-rimmed glasses, a carefully trimmed moustache, and hair parted fussily down the middle. The government of the German Reich has dispatched the minister without portfolio with a three-man delegation into enemy territory on a historic mission. His signature will end a war that has lasted over four years and touched nearly the entire globe.

At 9:20 p.m., amid a fine rain, the vehicles cross the German front line near the French town of Trelon. Before the lead row of German trenches, where artillerymen were subjecting French troops to deadly fire just hours before, is no man's land. The cars crawl forward, feeling their way through the gloom, toward the enemy lines. The lead vehicle is flying a white flag, and a bugler plays calls at regular intervals. The prearranged cease-fire holds. No shots are fired as the German delegation passes through contested territory on their way to the first French trenches, a mere 150 meters away. There Erzberger is given a cool but respectful reception. The French forgo the customary blindfolds for enemy negotiators, and two officers accompany the car to the village of La Chapelle, where French soldiers and civilians rush up and greet the German representatives with applause and cries of *"finie la guerre?"*

Erzberger's delegation continues his journey in cars provided by the French. Wherever the moon breaks through the clouds, its pale light falls upon an apocalyptic panorama. Picardy, for four years a major theater of war, has been transformed into a realm of death. Shattered artillery and the wreckage of military vehicles line the streets, rusting away alongside the decomposing carcasses of dead animals. Barbed wire twists its way across the fields. The ground is pockmarked by thousands of explosions, contaminated by tons of live munitions, rendered rancid by the stench of countless bodies and poison gas. Rainwater collects in the trenches and shell craters. All that remains of the forests are broken, charred tree trunks whose jagged silhouettes stand out against the night sky. The column of vehicles passes through villages and towns razed by the retreating German troops. A shaken Erzberger later writes of the village of Chauny: "Not a single house was left standing. There was one ruin next to another. In the moonlight, the remnants extended up into the air. There was no sign of life."

The route the French leadership has chosen for the German emissary takes him through the most war-ravaged parts of northern France—a landscape that looks as though it has been blasted by a meteor and will be demarcated a "red zone" on later maps. The horrific sight is intended to soften up Erzberger for the armistice negotiations. It's hoped that the spectacle of fields that experts doubt will ever again be arable will impress upon him how much harm the Germans have done to the French. The civilian Erzberger has likely seen images of the devastation in

photographs, newspapers, postcards, and weekly newsreels—
publicizing such destruction has been a central element of French
war propaganda. Perhaps he's also familiar with some of the
many paintings by contemporary artists depicting this new
landscape. Britain's Paul Nash, for instance, turned his experience
into an iconic work with a pallid sun rising over a forest that
has been blown to bits. The title of the painting is *We Are Making
a New World*, which can be read equally well as an expression of
sarcasm or of hope. Nevertheless, seeing those desolate waste-
lands with Erzberger's own eyes, witnessing this terrible legacy
of the Great War, was an entirely different experience. "That
drive," Erzberger will write in his memoirs, "shook me more
than the one I had taken three weeks earlier, to the deathbed of
my son."

United States Army Captain Harry S. Truman has long ago
gotten used to the sight of the landscapes of war. In a letter to his
sweetheart, Bess, he describes them:

> Trees that were once most beautiful forest trees and stumps
> with naked branches sticking out making them like ghosts. The
> ground is simply one mass of shell holes . . . I am sure that this
> desolate country was cultivated and beautiful like the rest of
> France and now, why Sahara or Arizona would look like Eden
> beside it. When the moon rises behind those tree trunks I spoke
> of a while ago you can imagine that the ghosts of the half-
> million Frenchmen who were slaughtered here are holding a
> sorrowful parade over the ruins. It makes you hope that His
> Satanic Majesty has a particularly hot poker and warm corner
> for Bill Hohenzollern when his turn comes to be judged and
> found wanting.

Truman, a farmer from Missouri placed in command of an artillery battery, is stationed 150 kilometers east of the ruins of Chauny, which Matthias Erzberger will drive through on the night of November 7, 1918. In the Argonne forests, where Truman has been deployed since the end of September, the final battles are raging between the Allied forces and the German Reich. The French commander in chief, Marshal Ferdinand Foch, has chosen the tree-covered hills in the triangle between France, Germany, and Belgium as the arena for a decisive last offensive. The Siegfried Line, one section of the German Hindenburg Line, fell during the first few days of that assault, and the French army and the American Expeditionary Forces, the largest military contingent the United States has ever sent abroad, is marching with determination eastward toward the Rhine. In his dugout near Verdun, Truman writes: "The outlook I have now is a rather dreary one. There are Frenchmen buried in my front yard and Huns in the back yard and both litter up the landscape as far as you can see. Every time a Boche shell hits in a field over west of here it digs up a piece of someone. It is well I'm not troubled by spooks."

In contrast to the Kaiser, the heir to the throne, Wilhelm von Preussen, doesn't sport any facial hair. In what might be an attempt to distinguish himself from the towering figure of his father, the skin under the crown prince's nose is clean-shaven. Compared with the Kaiser's imperious appearance, including a proud mustache shaped like an eagle diving toward its prey, Wilhelm, even when older, will look a bit boyish, even a bit naked. Still, lack of facial hair does have its advantages. Unlike thousands of German soldiers, among them a certain Adolf Hitler, the man born in Potsdam's Marble Palace and the oldest son of the Hohenzollern dynasty doesn't have to shave anything off when the introduction of gas warfare makes wearing gas masks a must—and facial hair a potentially deadly obstruction. At the age of thirty-six, Wilhelm von Preussen heads Army Group German Crown Prince, which at that point still consists of four armies. But that doesn't mean he's in command. His father, who hasn't allowed young Wilhelm much participation in the running of the state, has scrupulously taught him to leave all decisions up to chief of the General Staff, Count Friedrich von der Schulenburg, whom the crown prince often semi-ironically refers to as "my boss."

By the summer of 1918 the German spring offensive has stalled, the army group is in constant retreat, and in the face of unrelenting enemy attacks, the crown prince has come to doubt that Germany will emerge victorious. He will write: "We had the feeling we were taking the brunt of the enemy's swirling offensive . . . and could persevere more or less by sacrificing all our strength . . . But for how long?" A bit later, after visiting the First Foot Guards, commanded by his brother Prince Eitel Friedrich, nicknamed Fritz, he finally concedes that Germany's struggle against the Allied forces has been in vain. The usually cheerful Fritz looks gray and bent with care as the two greet each other. There are only five hundred men left in his regiment, the soldiers' provisions are miserable, and the gunners have "shot themselves out." While the German machine guns are able to fend off attacks by American infantry, carried out in mobile columns instead of long rows, that is, in "a fashion not in keeping with war," they have enormous difficulties dealing with the

Allies' latest military hardware. American tank brigades, for instance, simply overrun the German trenches, which are manned by no more than one soldier every twenty meters, and then fire at the Germans from behind. Unlike Wilhelm and Fritz's troops, the Americans seem to have inexhaustible reserves of manpower and heavy machinery. Each American attack is accompanied by bombardments even more intense than those at Verdun or the Somme. The brother princes grew up with stories of military heroism, of fields of honor where the fate of whole empires was decided and commanders led their troops brandishing drawn sabers while egret plumes fluttered atop their helmets. Now they find themselves surrounded by the reality of cold logistics and bloodred corpses.

Forced to acknowledge the enemy's superiority, Wilhelm is feeling more and more helpless. Fatigued and badly equipped with worn-out weapons and dwindling ammunition, his remaining soldiers—the ones who haven't preferred being captured to being killed—struggle to resist the enemy. But every offensive increases Wilhelm's sense that there is nothing he can do. "The air quivered with fire," he will recall. "There were dull sounds of impact, a yelling and rolling that never quit." By the end of September, the crown prince knows the game is over: "The minds of these men, who had bravely risked their lives a thousandfold for the fatherland, were bewildered by hunger, pain, and deprivation—where now was the line between what they could do and what they were willing to do?"

ALVIN C. YORK only joined the US infantry after a considerable moral struggle. A tall, red-headed, broad-shouldered country boy, York came from Pall Mall, a village in the Tennessee mountains, and was a pious Methodist who took the Bible at its word. For him, the Fifth Commandment—"Thou Shall Not Kill"—was a sacred argument against military service. When York received his draft notice, he was deeply torn between his calling as a Christian and his duty as an American. He repeatedly pored over scripture looking for guidance. He prayed and consulted with his pastor before writing "I don't want to fight" across his draft card and mailing it back. But this rather terse application for conscientious objector status was rejected, and York ultimately accepted the inevitable, hoping he wouldn't be assigned to a combat unit. He completed basic training in Camp Gordon, Georgia, and then traveled via New York to Boston, where at 4 a.m. on the morning of May 1, 1918, he shipped out. York, who had never been away from his mountain home, was now crossing the vast Atlantic on his way to fight in faraway Europe. Homesick, seasick, and afraid of German submarines, he found the voyage little short of torture. "It was too much water for me," he would write in his diary.

After a stop in England, York reached the French port of Le Havre on the English Channel on May 21. Weapons and gas masks were handed out. "That brought the war a whole heap closer," he recalled. In July, his unit was deployed on relatively quiet sections of the front so they could accustom themselves to combat conditions. York's first battle came days after General John J. Pershing launched the St. Mihiel offensive on September 12—a bloody conflict that ended with an American victory of world-historical significance. It was the first time the American Expeditionary Forces had taken independent action; up to that point the American forces in Europe had taken orders

from the French. St. Mihiel was thus emblematic of America's
new self-confidence.

In early October, ten days after the launch of Marshal Foch's
Grand Offensive, York's unit was redeployed to the Argonne.
Now he, too, saw the devastated forests, which looked to him
"as if a terrible cyclone done swept through them." York's life was
already hanging by a thread as his unit moved up to the front
line in the Argonne. German artillery bombarded the roads, and
German planes strafed the marching troops with machine-gun
fire. The men spent the day of October 7 near the village of
Chatel-Chéhéry lying in "little holes by the roadside," and York
saw his comrades "blown up by the big German shells." Order-
lies ran past with stretchers carrying wounded men who cried
out in pain. The road was littered with corpses with open mouths
and blank eyes, but no one bothered with them. The constant
rain was beginning to fill York's hole in the ground.

At 3 a.m. on October 8, orders are issued to commence what
will be York's most dangerous mission. At 6 a.m. they are to
attack from nearby Hill 223 and take a stretch of rail tracks used
by the Germans to get fresh supplies. York and his unit spring
into action, don their gas masks, and set off tramping through
the rain and the mud. At 6:10 a.m., slightly behind schedule, the
attack begins. A trench mortar is supposed to pin the Germans
back, but the valley the American soldiers are marching through
turns out to be a "death trap" raked by machine-gun fire from
concealed positions above, and the first waves of attackers go
down "just like the long grass before the mowing machine at
home." Those who manage to survive lie as flat as possible behind
every available cover, whether a swell in the ground or sometimes even their fallen comrades. The soldiers can't lift their

heads for all the bullets. When in the face of such concentrated fire it becomes apparent that a frontal attack would be suicide, York's commanding officer comes up with a new plan. He orders the surviving soldiers from three squads—seventeen men, including York—to crawl back, then push their way through thick underbrush on the left toward the crackling barrels of the machine guns.

A stone's throw away from those guns, the American soldiers happen upon a clearing where a dozen German soldiers are eating breakfast. They have put down their helmets and guns. Both sides are surprised by the encounter and freeze for a moment, thunderstruck. But the Americans have guns in their hands, while the Germans are sitting in their shirtsleeves chewing their food. What's more, the latter believe they're seeing the vanguard of a much larger American force. So they put their hands up to surrender. In the meantime, German machine gunners have spotted the Americans and swiveled their barrels toward the clearing. York watches six of his comrades die: "Corporal Savage was killed. He must have had over a hundred bullets in his body. His clothes were 'most all shot off." The Germans and the Americans throw themselves on the ground, the US captors seeking shelter among their prisoners. York is lying barely twenty meters from the German machine-gun nest. With bullets flying all around, the hunter from the Tennessee mountains entrusts his fate to his good eye and steady hand. Every time a German sticks his head up from the concealed blind, York shoots him cleanly.

In the end, a German officer jumps from his trench with five soldiers, running at York with fixed bayonets. When they're a few meters away, York shoots them down one after another with his pistol, starting with the ones in back. "That's the way we shoot wild turkeys at home," he writes. "You see we don't want the front ones to know that we're getting the back ones, and then they keep on coming until we get them all."

By this point, York has killed more than twenty German soldiers and is yelling at the rest to give up. A German major offers to get his comrades to surrender. He blows his whistle, and the Germans emerge from their trenches, throw down their weapons, and raise their hands. York has them line up in two rows, ordering the remaining men in his unit to keep them under guard. The group begins marching to the American lines, braving a double danger. There are other German positions nearby, and it's possible that American troops might mistake the rows of marching German soldiers for a counterattack. But York succeeds in getting everyone, including a few more soldiers he takes prisoner along the way, back alive to where the captive enemy soldiers are counted. There are 132 of them in all, captured almost single-handedly by the former pacifist.

DURING THE FINAL offensives on the western front, which will cost more than a million soldiers their lives, health, or liberty, the wheels of international diplomacy continue to turn, exploring the possibilities of ending the war. This process has been going on for a while. On October 4, the German government sends a telegram to President Woodrow Wilson requesting negotiations for an armistice. It is a tactical maneuver designed to give the more conciliatory American head of state a leading role in the peace process. The hope is to create a counter to the European Allies, particularly France, which insists on punishing its archenemy Germany harshly for aggression. Months before, on January 8, 1918, in a speech to the US Congress, Wilson listed fourteen points formulating America's war aims and the basis for a future peaceful world order. These included open covenants of peace, freedom of navigation upon the seas, equality of trade conditions, reductions in national armaments, and a final adjustment of all colonial claims. Borders in Europe and the Middle East were to be reestablished with the withdrawal of German troops, and a new territorial order was to be stabilized. A league of nations guaranteeing all its member states' independence and sovereignty was to be founded. Later Wilson added that Germany would have to adopt a parliamentary system of government, which he understood to mean the Kaiser would have to abdicate his throne. The Fourteen Points initiative, for which the US president would win the 1919 Nobel Peace Prize, was never cleared with America's European allies. Having paid a price of its own in the Great War, the United States now considered itself entitled not merely to be counted among the world's great powers but to lead the way.

Wilson had left it up to the Allied military leadership to work out the specifics of the armistice, which is why November 1 found Marshal Foch presenting his own ideas to the representatives of Germany's major enemies. The armistice, Foch insisted, would have to be tantamount to a capitulation. That was the only way he could accept an end to the war without the final battle to the death he had set his heart on. Otherwise the Germans, by using the protection of the Rhine, could take advantage of a cease-fire to regroup or at the very least put pressure on the negotiations. Landscapes played a central role in Foch's thinking, though not the ghostly remnants of forests as painted by Nash, but rather what Berlin sociologist Kurt Lewin had recently called "directive landscapes." Lewin illustrated how the strategies of military conflicts imposed boundaries and directions, zones and corridors, "fronts" and "rears" upon nature, and this was exactly how Foch saw landscapes. In his headquarters, which looked more like the central office of a large company or an engineering firm than a field command, the marshal of France managed space and allocated human and material resources to different areas. Thinking as always in terms of military logistics, Foch demanded that Allied soldiers cross the Rhine so German forces wouldn't be able to recover. For him war was about advantages in numbers and probabilities. The question: Would the Allies be able to end a strategic and tactical war—that is, a "modern" one—with a modern, logistic peace? His answer: If they didn't, they would imperil the future they hoped to be able to shape after so many hard-won battles.

By November 4, the Allied representatives agreed to the terms of peace they would seek to dictate. They reflected most of Foch's ideas and were immediately relayed to Washington. That very day, the German armistice commission's request to take up negotiations arrived in Paris. Foch issued instructions for how the German delegation was to be received. A few days later, in the night between November 6 and 7, he received a radio telegram telling him the names of the German envoys.

THE 129TH ARTILLERY Regiment, which included Truman's battery, has been tasked with protecting advancing Allied troops from German fire. In early November he writes to his beloved Bess that in five hours he fired 1,800 shells at the "Huns." At the start of the offensive, they had to be on their guard. As soon as they began bombarding enemy gunners, they made themselves visible and ran the risk of being shelled or gassed. It was a strange war, one determined by technology, tactics, strategy, ballistics, and logistics, in which they almost never saw the enemy face-to-face. But German resistance had begun to dwindle in late October, as an incident with two downed pilots attests. Truman writes: "[The Germans] don't seem to have had the energy to come back yet . . . One of their aviators fell right behind my Battery yesterday and sprained his ankle, busted up the machine, and got completely picked by the French and Americans in the neighborhood. They even tried to take their (there were two in the machine) coats. One of our officers I'm ashamed to say, took the boots of the one with the sprained ankle and kept them." The pilot, Truman adds, managed to save his life by shouting *"La Guerre fini"* (sic).

Still, the offensive demands the utmost of Truman's men, who must be constantly ready to follow the rapidly advancing front, with heavy artillery that has to be pushed and pulled through muddy terrain, in part by horses and in part by human muscle power. The night marches take their toll on the men. "Every one of us was almost a nervous wreck and we'd all lost weight until we looked like scarecrows."

Yet the more tangible German defeat seems, and the longer Truman's regiment advances against the invisible enemy without suffering major losses, the more the war that the United States entered in April 1917 seems to him to be "a terrific experience." He has grown accustomed to living in makeshift quarters—as an officer he has access to a stove, a telephone, and a mobile kitchen. At one point he even remarks that he's gotten so used to sleeping on the ground that after the war he'll probably have to lie down in the cellar. In the final weeks of the war, with victory on the horizon, the tone of Truman's letters becomes increasingly upbeat and his thoughts turn ever more to the United States. If he makes it back home, he writes, he'll be happy to spend the rest of his life trotting behind a mule in a cornfield. He even finds the time to send Bess a couple of dried flowers as a souvenir, accompanied by a few gallant words.

Truman's letters from the final days of fighting are reminiscent of Charlie Chaplin's film about the Great War, *Shoulder Arms*, which premiered on Broadway on October 20, 1918. The movie, which was commissioned as part of a drive to solicit war donations, has the small man with the funny moustache clowning around in what appear to be the same trenches in northern France where Truman spends the last weeks of the conflict. By the end of the film, the hero succeeds in freeing a pretty girl from German captivity. Along the way, he encounters the Kaiser himself, takes him prisoner, and marches him off at gunpoint. The Tramp ending the Great War—a "terrific experience."

LATE IN THE afternoon on November 7, Marshal Foch climbs aboard a special train in Senlis, northeast of Paris, accompanied by his chief of staff, General Maxime Weygand, three general staff officers, and representatives of the British fleet under Admiral Rosslyn Wemyss. It's a short trip, with the train stopping in a forest clearing just beyond the town of Compiègne. What follows is a long night of waiting. The other train, which Erzberger and his delegation boarded after midnight at the ruined station in Tergnier, doesn't arrive until the next morning at 7 a.m.

Two hours later, at 9 a.m. on November 8, an icy atmosphere

reigns at the initial meeting in a carriage of Foch's special train that has been repurposed as an office. The German delegation enters first, taking their designated seats at the negotiating table. The French group follows, led by Foch, whom Erzberger describes as a "small man with hard, energetic features, which immediately made it clear that he was a man accustomed to issuing commands." In lieu of handshakes, the two sides greet each other with military salutes or, in the case of the civilians, cursory bows. The delegations introduce themselves, and Erzberger, Alfred von Oberndorff, Detlof von Winterfeldt, and Ernst Vanselow are requested to present their authorization to carry out negotiations on Germany's behalf.

Foch opens the proceedings with feigned ignorance. "What brings you gentlemen here?" he asks. "What do you wish from me?" Erzberger answers that his delegation would like to hear what the Allies would propose to reach an armistice, to which Foch replies drily that he has no proposals to make. Oberndorff responds, saying that now is not the time to quarrel over the word "proposal," adding that if it suits Foch better, the Germans would like to know what conditions the Allies would set for an armistice. Foch insists that he has no conditions to set, whereupon Erzberger reads out the final note from Wilson explicitly authorizing Foch to do precisely that. Finally the marshal lays his cards on the table, saying that he is only authorized to reveal the conditions if the German side first officially asks for an armistice—i.e., sues for peace. Under no circumstances does he want to spare the Germans this humiliation.

Erzberger and Oberndorff formally declare that they are in fact asking for an armistice in the name of the German Reich. Only then is Weygand allowed to read out the most important sections of the Allies' decision of November 4. "Marshal Foch sat there at the table with stony calm," Erzberger will write. Britain's representative, Wemyss, tries to look similarly indifferent, but he betrays his inner turmoil by constantly playing with his monocle and his large, horn-rimmed glasses.

The members of the German delegation listen to the terms being read out with pale, solemn faces, as Weygand will later remember, while tears run down the cheeks of the young navy captain Vanselow. In return for a cease-fire, they are told, the Allies demand not just the immediate withdrawal of German troops from all occupied parts of Belgium, France, Luxembourg and Alsace and Lorraine. They also want a French occupation (at Foch's insistence) of the left bank of the Rhine and the establishment of demilitarized zones around Mainz, Koblenz, and Cologne. Furthermore, they stipulate that Germany hand over most of its weaponry, aircraft, warships and trains, and that the peace treaty the Reich concluded with defeated Russia in 1917 be annulled.

"A heartbreaking moment," Weygand will recall. After the conditions are read out, General von Winterfeldt tries to get the other side to soften its stance. The Allies could at least extend the deadline for signing the agreement so that he could consult with his government, and they could surely agree to a temporary cease-fire while the German side evaluated the terms. Foch refuses on both counts and issues an ultimatum. Germany has until 11 a.m. on November 11 to sign the armistice agreement, after which, and only after which, a cease-fire would be declared. That same day, Foch sends orders by telegram to all of his field commanders instructing them to keep up the intensity of their offensives. The idea is to achieve "decisive results" while the cease-fire negotiations are still in progress. There is nothing to negotiate, he stresses to Erzberger. The Germans can take the offer as it stands or leave it. The only concession he makes is to allow "private" conversations between ranking members of both delegations. Erzberger hopes that he can at least persuade the Allies to make concessions regarding deadlines and the amount of military hardware Germany will be required to hand over with the argument that he's trying to prevent mass starvation and a complete breakdown of social order in the Reich.

At the end of the meeting, a Captain von Helldorf is sent with the list of Allied demands back to the German headquarters in Spa. The private conversations begin that afternoon and last two days, while the hours set by the ultimatum tick away. At 9 p.m. on the evening of November 10, fourteen hours before the deadline, encoded telegraphic orders from the Reich chancellor reach the forest clearing. They authorize Erzberger to accept all Allied conditions. Nonetheless, the German delegation seems to have convinced the other side on at least a few isolated issues. They succeed in getting the Allies to agree to a final round of negotiations. Between 2 and 5 a.m. on November 11, six hours before the ultimatum expires, a few last changes to the settlement are agreed to. They don't actually soften the final document, but neither are they merely cosmetic. Germany will have to hand over only 1,700 airplanes instead of 2,000, and only 25,000 machine guns instead of 30,000. Germany needs the guns, Erzberger proposes, to keep revolutionary forces at bay—an argument that Foch scoffs at. The demilitarized zone on the right bank of the Rhine is also reduced from forty to ten kilometers, and German troops will have thirty-one days and not twenty-five to withdraw from the river's left bank. In response to the threat of starvation in Germany, the Allies promise that for the duration of the cease-fire, initially set at thirty-six days, they will keep their adversary supplied with food.

At 5:20 a.m. on November 11, 1918, shortly before the pale, late-autumn morning has broken, the two sides put their signatures to the final page of the armistice. The ultimate version with all of the last-minute changes is still being drawn up. After screwing the top back on his fountain pen, Erzberger points out that some of the provisions of the agreement he has just signed will be nearly impossible to put into practice. He concludes with the pathetic declaration: "A people of 70,000,000 suffers but does not die." Foch's only comment is a dry *"très bien!"* The two delegations then go their separate ways, again without handshakes.

TOLD LIKE THIS, the end of the Great War seems almost like a chamber play, as if in the autumn of 1918 world history had been shrunk to pocket size and concentrated on a handful of actors and settings in the small area between Paris, Spa, and Strasbourg, which at that point was still a German city. In reality, of course, the great global war didn't fit quite so neatly inside a single train carriage.

Between 1914 and 1918, the European contest of strength between the Entente powers of France, Great Britain, and Russia, and the Triple Alliance of the German Reich, the Austro-Hungarian Empire, and (until 1915) Italy, had grown into a global confrontation. It was fought out not just in Europe, but in the Middle East, Africa, East Asia, and on the world's oceans. Seventy million soldiers from five continents fought in the war, and the ten million who lost their lives weren't all Europeans. Eight hundred thousand Turks, 116,000 Americans, 74,000 Indians, 65,000 Canadians, 62,000 Australians, 26,000 Algerians, 20,000 Africans from German East Africa (Tanzania), 18,000 New Zealanders, 12,000 Indochinese, 10,000 Africans from German Southwest Africa (Namibia), 9,000 South Africans, and 415 Japanese also died in the Great War.

From the perspective of the actors whose voices have thus far been heard in this book, the caesura of November 1918 was an all-too-clear divide between war and peace. But in fact the machinery of war, once it had reached running temperature, could not be halted by a single document. The signatures at Compiègne sealed only one of four cease-fire agreements in 1918 between various warring parties. And these were but a first step in establishing the peace. It would take a series of further agreements, the last of which was signed in 1923, for the war to finally end; until then military actions and confrontations continued in a number of places. On the western front, the cease-fire was followed by Allied troops advancing to the Rhine and occupying not just its left but its right bank in 1923. Hungary and Romania continued to do battle in the Balkans. On the Baltic coast, Latvia fought for its independence from the newly formed Soviet Union. And if that weren't bad enough, huge numbers of people died in a global epidemic of the Spanish flu, which cost more lives than all the battles in all the theaters of war combined.

Over the course of this period new wars would break out between Ireland and England, Poland and Lithuania, Turkey and the Armenian Republic, and Turkey and Greece. In Eastern Europe and Asia, moreover, the Russian Revolution unleashed

a bloody civil war between supporters and enemies of the Bolsheviks, which would last until 1922.

MARINA YURLOVA CAME from a family of Cossacks and grew up
in a village in the Caucasus Mountains. At the age of only fourteen, she cut her hair and disguised herself as a man to fight by
her father's side in the tsar's army. By age seventeen, she was lying
in a hospital bed in Baku. She had been shelled while driving an
army truck, and all she remembered afterward were fragmentary scenes of detonations, shrapnel and screams. She spent
months in the hospital in a semicoma. Her physical injuries
soon healed, but the psychological aftereffects of the explosion
refused to subside. Her entire body trembled, her head twitched
uncontrollably from side to side, and when she opened her mouth,
all that came out was unintelligible stammering. She kept reliving the devastating images of the moment that could have been
her final one, when she could have gone from being a warrior to
a casualty of war.

It was in Baku that Marina learned that the tsar for whom she
had risked her life had abdicated, and as the months passed, she
saw for herself that the October Revolution had ushered in a new
age. While being transported to a different hospital, she observed
a group of rebel soldiers massacre a gray-haired general of the old
Russian army. One after another, the uniformed men stabbed the
officer in the belly with bayonets, even though he had probably
collapsed dead after the first thrust. Marina had seen a lot of violence and death in three years of war but "nothing . . . could equal
a murder like this." Later, she watched from the window of a
Moscow ward as revolutionary soldiers assembled and heard

enraged speeches against the tsar, and it dawned on her that the old order had ceased to exist. "I had a vague feeling that the end of the world had come," she recalled. "My old nurse used to tell me that according to some prophesy she had heard, the world was due to finish within two thousand years after Christ." Apparently the old woman was right, Marina thought, finding the idea strangely comforting.

As a war invalid, Marina didn't immediately have to choose a side in the battle for the future that began in Russia in 1917. But in her heart she had no doubts as to where she stood. Her family had served the tsars for generations. That thought at least was clear in her head, even though it continued to twitch. The electric shock therapy she received in Moscow improved her condition somewhat. But aside from the thrice-daily sessions, no one paid any attention to a woman injured in the war with the German Reich, which had concluded anyway with the Treaty of Brest-Litovsk on March 3, 1918. Emotionally numb, Marina accepted the fact that her bedsheets were growing grayer by the day from dust and cigarette smoke. Through grimy windowpanes, she saw the outlines of a new regime forming in Moscow. She was horrified when she heard that Tsar Nicholas II and his family had been executed that July. Did she also hear the news that on November 3, the Bolsheviks had unveiled a statue of Robespierre in Alexander Gardens, or that it had collapsed four days later because it was made of such poor-quality concrete?

ON OCTOBER 23, 1918, Thomas E. Lawrence left Damascus—at least this is what he claims in his autobiography. His entry into the Syrian metropolis through the imposing city gate on the first day of that month had possessed all the trappings of a victory parade. At around 9 a.m., in the glittering morning sun, he had ridden through the town clad in the white vestments of a prince of Mecca. Dervishes whirled before his horse, while Arabian warriors trailed behind him, crying shrilly and firing rifles in the air. The entire city had turned out to glimpse the man who embodied the Arab revolts against the Ottoman Empire: Lawrence of Arabia. The defeat of the Turkish troops and their German allies in the Middle East was sealed.

But by late October, the British officer Lawrence no longer sees the taking of Damascus as a day of victory. He's utterly exhausted from his superhuman efforts and has seen horrible massacres, but what weighs down his soul more than such blood-drenched memories is the knowledge that the freedom for which he and his Arab friends have fought is an illusion. European statesmen, military leaders, and diplomats have long since drawn up plans for the Middle East after the collapse of the Ottoman Empire, to divvy up the region among themselves. The Arab people play only a marginal role in their plans.

IN THE FINAL days of the war, Rudolf Höss is also in Damascus—at least that's what he'll later claim in his autobiography. The eighteen-year-old soldier hails from Mannheim in southern Germany. His strictly Catholic father wanted him to go into the priesthood, but Herr Höss died during the second year of the war, and then his son lost his bearings and his interest in school. Wanting to get away from home, he volunteered to serve. The war took the young Catholic to the Promised Land. Amid the sacred sites of Palestine, which he knew from the Bible, Höss experienced the pitiless warfare the German Reich waged together with the Turks against the British Empire and its Arab allies.

Höss underwent his "baptism by fire" in the desert sands when his unit encountered enemy groups of English, Arab, Indian, and New Zealand fighters. For the first time he experienced the power that comes from holding a weapon in one's hands and deciding whether others live or die. He didn't dare look his first kill in the eye, but soon he got used to killing. He felt at home in his strictly regimented unit and enjoyed the bond that fighting created between the men. "Strangely, I had immense trust in and deep respect for my cavalry captain, my military father," Höss will write. "It was a much more profound relationship than to my real father."

What Höss will also later remember, along with the violence and the camaraderie, is an experience that shook his religious faith. In the Valley of Jordan, he and his comrades chanced upon a long row of peasant carts full of grayish-white moss with bright red spots. The German soldiers searched the carts thoroughly to make sure that they didn't contain concealed deliveries of weapons for the English. Through an interpreter, Höss asked what the peasants were doing with all the moss and learned that they were taking it to Jerusalem. Later someone confided that the plants were sold there as "moss of Golgotha" to souvenir-seeking Christian pilgrims who believed the red spots were the blood of Jesus. Höss is revolted by this example of commerce. It's the beginning of his turn away from the Catholic Church.

BY THE TIME Marina Yurlova is transferred to Kazan, the capital of Tatarstan, far to the east of Moscow, the Romanov dynasty has fallen, the Great War has grown into a new, all-encompassing conflict, and civil war has broken out across Russia. At a train station in Moscow, the invalids witness a gunfight between the Bolshevik Red Army and the "White Army" of troops loyal to the royal family. The Red soldiers who defend the station against an attack by the tsarists are so underfed, and their uniforms so ragged, that they don't resemble a regular army at all. But for Marina, their grim determination to win or die trying makes these "yellow ghosts" the epitome of the revolution. She can't help but respect them.

The train to Kazan on which Marina is put in November 1918 makes slow progress. Waiting for her at the end of the journey is another hospital ward with hard beds and threadbare sheets. The bed next to hers is occupied by a handsome young man who has just turned twenty. His face is rosy, and his gray eyes sparkle under his dark curls. It takes Marina a second to notice what is unusual about him. His body doesn't move. He doesn't have any arms or legs. All he can do is turn his head. His eyes follow Marina with a mixture of pain and pride in his one remaining capability.

The revolution arrives in Kazan as well. The Bolsheviks are determined to mobilize all the forces at their disposal against the tsarists. Marina is horrified to discover her name on a list of hospital patients to be drafted into the service of the Red Army. She's supposed to go back to war despite her twitching head, her shot nerves? An order publicly posted by the Red Army instructs her to report to the University of Kazan.

This is the moment when the logic of the revolution imposes itself on Marina. There is no room in the Bolsheviks' principles for people to be exempt from the battle between the great ideologies solely because they've been badly injured. One is either a passionate supporter of the new Russia or an enemy to be liquidated. That's how the newly minted Red Army soldier who is haranguing the patients sees the world. Neutrality, he proclaims, is "an inexcusable position." Nor does he have any time for the notion that soldiers shouldn't get mixed up in politics. "Whom do you stand for?" he bellows at the pathetic little group of the wounded. "What government do you believe in?" He turns to Marina. "What do you believe in?" Before she can speak up, the man answers his own question. "A Cossack . . . ! In the Tsar's name, the Cossacks terrorized the peasants and workers!" Marina begins what she hopes will be an impassioned refutation. "Brothers!" she exclaims and extends her arm to underscore her words. But before she can make a plea to come together to fight in the name of the motherland, her shell-shocked nerves fail her. Marina collapses, unconscious.

Two

A Day and an Hour

Hurray, the war is over!
Hurray, the fight is won!
Back from the life of a rover,
Back from the roar of the gun.
Back to the dear old homeland,
Home with the peaceful dove;
Don't let us sing anymore about war,
Just let us sing of love.

—"Peace Song" by the Scottish singer
Harry Lauder, December 1918

Briton Rivière, *St. George and the Dragon*, 1909

INSIDE HER CRAMPED office on the rue de Lille in Paris, at just a few minutes after 11 a.m. on November 11, 1918, the journalist Louise Weiss is startled by a series of unexpected noises. At first it's nothing but the sound of chairs scraping across floors, and doors and windows being thrown open. Then come voices, shouts, and the ringing of bells. The staff of *L'Europe nouvelle* pours across the courtyard onto the street. Has the hour come at last?

At the start of the Great War, Louise Weiss was twenty-one years old. After passing her university exams with flying colors, she traveled with her siblings to the peaceful Breton village of Saint-Quay. The summer landscape seemed lovelier than ever. But one day she found herself standing alone on a platform, stunned and enveloped in locomotive smoke as a troop train carried her beloved older brother off to join the war against Germany. Only then did Louise realize a new era had begun. Would she, too, have been willing to make such a sacrifice? She sensed her answer would be no. But her brother hadn't been asked if he was willing or not.

French losses in the early battles along the German border sent a wave of refugees to the still passable west of the country. For Louise it was a matter of course that she would volunteer to help. Overcoming her natural shyness, she asked the priest in

Saint-Quay to provide a workspace, begged some money from her uncle, and convinced Mother Hertel, who ran a local moving company, to place a truck at her disposal. With it she drove around the village, picking up mattresses, bed linens, chairs, pots, firewood, coal, and other essentials. No sooner had she started making collections than the first families arrived.

Providing for the refugees grew more difficult with every day, but Louise kept finding generous donors. The next arrivals had even greater needs: soldiers wounded in the Battle of the Marne in September 1914. Louise managed to have them billeted in a villa belonging to an unmarried woman named Mademoiselle Vallée. The troops, who included several Moroccans and Senegalese, caused quite a stir in the Breton village. Nonetheless, the villagers donated everything the soldiers needed and more; the majority of the men recovered and moved on, having expressed their gratitude in a heartfelt speech.

After a couple of detours, Louise made her way back to Paris, where she worked as a secretary in a senator's office. This was hardly a glamorous job for a young woman with a university degree, but at least it was in Paris, where she could meet interesting people and absorb the current political scene. Louise keenly followed the tumultuous events and began writing her first articles. One day the journalist and publisher Hyacinthe Philouze turned up at the senator's office in search of some juicy news. Philouze had a dubious reputation as a political opportunist whose various publishing projects were always on the verge of bankruptcy. When the senator was out, Louise and Philouze got to talking. In the course of the conversation, he told her about a friend who had come into a small fortune following the death of an army buddy and who didn't know how to invest it. Did Louise really want to spend the rest of her life working as a secretary for some doddering old senator? Maybe she had an idea for something sensible that could be done with the money? How about a weekly political newspaper, Louise shot back, to spread democracy in the world, and to advance the cause of independence for the peoples of the Habsburg monarchy? It could be called *L'Europe nouvelle*—the new Europe.

"I like it!" cried Philouze. "That's a wonderful idea!" When she offered more details, he exclaimed: "It's a deal!" Much to the surprise of everyone who knew him, Philouze proved true to his word: Louise Weiss left the senator's office and moved into the editorial spaces of the new paper she had helped conceive. Officially her title was copyeditor, but in reality she served as editor-in-chief, responsible for the paper's overall content. The first edition appeared in January 1918. It must have also been around this time that Louise had her hair cut short. Henceforth she would wear it that way, its wispy curls playing around her round face with its defiant, stiff upper lip.

On this day, November 11, 1918, she is studying articles for the next *L'Europe nouvelle*, a special issue devoted to the topic on everyone's mind: the end of the war. Perhaps she's drafting the open letter to Georges Clemenceau in which she will congratulate the French prime minister on his impressive victories but point out that, with the end of the conflict, the national aspirations of various peoples must be taken into account. Or maybe she's reviewing an extensive report on the situation in Central and Eastern Europe, where old monarchies have collapsed, or editing a long article that describes how the idea of a "community of nations," already being debated by the Allies in London, might be realized. It is essential, argues the author Jules Rais, to quickly establish the foundations of a better future atop the ruins of old Europe. The danger is too great that the hatred spawned by all the years of war will lead to further conflict. There is also the threat that economic competition among European states will doom all attempts to establish a permanent peace. Concerted efforts will be needed to ensure this doesn't happen, first and foremost through education. Young people must be taught foreign languages and sent on exchange programs to learn about other cultures. Rais also proposes an international system of state credit whereby big countries would help smaller ones procure loans at favorable rates. Many countries have taken on massive debts to finance the war, and this mutual support could strengthen commonality of interest as well as form the basis for a new European solidarity and a lasting peace.

As Louise pores over the copy, sentence by sentence, the commotion outside increases. She knows what it means: the armistice has been signed. Four days too soon. The issue she's working on isn't set to go to press until November 15, and she hasn't finished editing it. Instead of joining her enthusiastic colleagues in the general celebration, Louise Weiss shuts her office windows to block out the tolling of the bells and din of voices from the huge crowd of people.

AT 10:30 A.M. the same day, Harry Truman is still asking himself how the Germans might react to Allied proposals for an armistice. Apparently he doesn't know that some four hours earlier, with the ink still drying on the cease-fire agreement, Allied Supreme Commander Foch sent a telegram to all active war zones. "Hostilities will cease on the entire front November 11 at

11 a.m. French time," it reads. Crossing the front line is forbidden. The state of territorial gains and losses at that moment is to be maintained. No contact with the enemy is permitted.

The telegram takes several hours to reach all parts of the front, and until its arrival Truman seems to have hoped the war against Germany would continue. In a letter to Bess, he writes: "It is a shame we can't go in and detonate Germany and cut off a few of the Dutch [common slang for German] kids' hands and feet and scalp a few of their old men but I guess it will be better to make them work for France and Belgium for fifty years." With grim satisfaction, Truman calculates that during the final offensive he must have fired ten thousand rounds of ammunition at "the Hun," concluding, ironically, that this must have had "a slight effect." He isn't alone in wanting to continue the bombardment right to the final minute of the war. A nearby battery, he writes, "seems to want to get rid of all of its ammunition before the time is up."

TRUMAN'S ISN'T THE only position on the front where the fighting lasted to the absolute bitter end. The final hours and minutes of the war claim many lives. At 9:30 a.m., a miner from Leeds named George Ellison is shot dead while on patrol. At five minutes to eleven, several hundred kilometers northwest of Compiègne, in the Ardennes, a German bullet kills a shepherd named Augustin Trébouchon. Two minutes before the armistice comes into force, Canadian Lawrence Price loses his life near Belgium's Canal de Centre.

At long last, the hour hand on the clock reaches eleven. The day and the hour appointed by the military leaders and diplomats in that forest not far from Paris has arrived. The armistice becomes international law, bringing with it one of those rare moments of global simultaneity. For the rest of their lives, millions of people all over the world will be able to remember exactly what they were doing at 11 a.m. on November 11, 1918.

Foch leaves the historic clearing in the woods near Compiègne soon after the agreement is signed. He describes the moment when war gave way to peace in solemn terms: "An impressive silence followed fifty-three weeks of uninterrupted battle." Full of emotion, he praises the Allied armies for winning "the greatest battle in history and saving the most sacred cause: freedom in the world!" He adds: "Be proud! With immortal glory you have adorned you flags! Posterity shall show you its gratitude." Back in Paris, Foch immediately presents himself to the French president at the Élysée Palace. Then he makes his way back home where his wife is waiting. It takes him a while to push through the crowds of people gathered to congratulate him, who are celebrating and weeping with joy. When he finally arrives home, he's forced to make an impromptu speech. His apartment is covered in bouquets of flowers sent by everyone from important celebrities to people he doesn't even know. He repeatedly has to interrupt his lunch and go to the window to greet the masses who have congregated in the street below.

Two days before, on November 9, Arthur Little already feels euphoric, confident the war is over. A battalion commander in the US 369th Infantry Regiment, he has taken a day's leave from the front for a very special excursion. Driving in a borrowed car, he travels to a tank unit stationed some eight kilometers outside the small city of Langres. There, he contacts the commanding officer, explains the reason for his visit, and is invited to lunch. Afterward, a certain Sergeant Little is summoned. A young man appears, salutes Arthur Little, and begins to give a report. Suddenly, in mid-sentence, he falters. With astonished eyes, he stares at the older man, and a couple of seconds pass before he recovers enough composure to speak. "Oh, father! I'm so glad to see you. They told me you'd been killed!" The two men wrap their arms around each other.

Together they drive to Langres to send a telegram to Sergeant Little's mother in America. They enjoy a large dinner, go to the theater, and spend the night at a YMCA hostel. The young man has come directly from the battlefield and hasn't slept in weeks. As soon as his head hits the pillow, he sinks into a deep slumber. His father has to catch a train early the next morning, but he leaves his son in bed, sure that nothing bad can happen to him anymore. It's November 10, 1918. Little knows it's extremely unlikely his son will be returning to battle.

With this happy certainty in mind, Arthur Little rejoins his battalion, which is no ordinary unit. The American soldiers who serve in it come from a branch of the New York National Guard that was reconstituted in federal service as the 369th Infantry Regiment. And although Little is white, most of the soldiers are African Americans from Harlem. These soldiers struggled with racism before and after deployment. They had been barred from taking part in a parade of the Rainbow Division of the New York National Guard, with organizers claiming that "there was no black in the rainbow." Only a very few were given command positions. Only due to a shortage of manpower were they deployed to France, where the American military leaders generally regarded them as unreliable and assigned them menial tasks like unloading ships, digging trenches, and burying casualties. Nor were they allowed to fight alongside white American troops. When the regiment was placed under French command, however, the situation changed. The French were used to deploying black soldiers from their African colonies and didn't hesitate for a moment to give the African Americans rifles or send them to the frontlines. And the men from Harlem wasted no time in showing they were every bit the equal of their white brothers-in-arms. They were fierce warriors who inspired fear in their German enemies, and their battalion became known as the "Harlem Hellfighters." It was a title of respect, and some of the men in the unit became legends.

The greatest of the unit's heroes was Henry Johnson. Small in stature, he had worked as a porter at the train station in Albany before the war. During training and his first months of active duty, he was known only for his big mouth. But one night, while he was keeping watch, a German commando made out the position Johnson had taken up with a comrade and attacked. The other soldier immediately took a bullet, leaving Johnson all on his own. Determined to hold his position and save his comrade's life, he killed more than twenty Germans with his rifle, a few grenades, a pistol, and a knife, forcing the enemy to retreat. Johnson, who was wounded all over his body, became America's first black war hero. Even the *Saturday Evening Post* reported the deeds of the man nicknamed "Black Death."

Another man whose fame extended well beyond the ranks of the Harlem Hellfighters was a black officer named James Reese Europe, the director of the regimental band. Before the war, he had been the leader of a popular New York ragtime outfit called the Society Orchestra, which played his syncopated, "hot" arrangements of marches, dance numbers, and popular songs. The Society Orchestra was one of the first bands to feature the saxophone and specialized in foxtrots, a musical style that scandalized the white middle classes but brought Harlem nightclubs to a boil. Europe was one of the earliest black musicians to make a record for the Radio Corporation of America. He joined the war effort as a lieutenant—highly unusual for a black soldier—and led a military band with more than forty instruments. No sooner had he arrived in the town of Brest than he came up with a jazz version of the "Marseillaise" that really got French feet moving. That was only the beginning. After five months on the frontlines, an experience that acquainted Lieutenant Europe with the ugliest side of trench warfare and inspired him to compose the ragtime song "On Patrol in No Man's Land," the military leadership decided that the war effort needed jazz more urgently than forty extra black and Puerto Rican soldiers. The Harlem Hellfighters Band was redeployed to Paris. For several months it performed in theaters, concert halls, parks, and hospitals. The effect on the French was unbelievable. Parisians had never heard jazz before, and audiences were captivated by ragtime's driving rhythms, off-beats and syncopation, the blue notes and glissandi of the melodies, the triumphant saxophones and nasal sound of muted trumpets. Whenever and wherever the band appeared, the French were electrified by the spectacle of black people on stage, playing without any sheet music, improvising solo passages, their bodies relaxed, their eyes half-shut, moving their arms and legs in time with the music and sometimes twitching convulsively. This was an expression of a new lifestyle and the harbinger of a new era—a truly twentieth-century one. It was modern in a pleasantly different sense than machine guns, submarines, and tanks.

Far away from the musicians in Paris, November 11, 1918, finds the fighting members of the Harlem Hellfighters in a camp in the Vosges, where they are recovering after 191 straight days of combat. Arthur Little describes the moment when the war ends as one of quiet satisfaction. A French interpreter comes by with two bottles of champagne. Toasts are made. Everyone is relieved, if not quite relaxed. There is no equivalent of the madness then erupting in New York, London, or Paris. As Little recalls, peace comes as a moment of calm and brightness when the burden of responsibility, which as a commanding officer he has felt for weeks, drops from his shoulders. The men from Harlem are amused to see the people of Alsace take to the streets in their traditional garb and celebrate liberation from German occupation by drinking great quantities of Riesling. Colonel William Hayward—the regiment's white commanding officer—sums it up best: "The day Christ was born was the greatest day in the history of the World, and this day is the second greatest day."

BY CONTRAST, IN Berlin, on this "second greatest" day in history, Käthe Kollwitz receives the "terrible news" of how the Compiègne negotiations have ended. She records her gloomy impressions in her diary. At this point, the sculptor and graphic artist—the daughter of a bricklayer from Königsberg—is fifty-one years old and married to Dr. Karl Kollwitz. The two of them live in her home city, in the working-class district of Prenzlauer Berg. A round-faced woman with straight hair kept in a knot, she is horrified when she reads of the "terrible ceasefire conditions" in the newspaper. That evening, as celebrations continue in Paris, New York and London, a "deathly silence" pervades the streets of Berlin. Fear begins to spread, and people stay home. Now and again, gunshots echo through the deserted streets.

AT 11 A.M. on November 11, 1918, artillery captain Harry Truman leans back in his quarters with a broad grin on his face, eating some blueberry cake. But as his French comrades begin passing around a bottle of wine and break into song, he can't help feeling somewhat disappointed. He is satisfied with the outcome of the war and how he has handled his part, as he writes Bess: "You know I have succeeded in doing what it was my greatest ambition to do at the beginning of the war. That is to take a Battery through as Battery commander and not to lose a man." But his aspirations for military glory are by no means fulfilled. As a child he read Homer and Napoleon's memoirs and dreamt of going to West Point and achieving heroic deeds that would make the French emperor look like a "sucker." Now, despite what he's accomplished in the Great War, he's still a long way from realizing those boyhood dreams: "My military ambition has ended with my having arrived at the post of centurion. That's a long way from Caesar, isn't it? Now I want to be a farmer." He reacts with resignation when it becomes clear that he has no hope of promotion now that the war is over: "I've almost come to the conclusion that it's not intended for me ever to be very rich, nor very poor, and I am about convinced that that will be about the happiest state a man can be." Maybe, he thinks after the armistice is announced, he can at least become the commandant of an occupied German city. Or perhaps even become a congressman and be nominated to the House Armed Services Committee once he returns to the United States.

VIRGINIA WOOLF HAS known that the end was coming since October 15, 1918, when Herbert Fisher—Virginia's cousin and for the past two years Britain's minister of education—told her over a cup of tea, "We've won the war today." Fisher had picked up this advanced bit of good news directly from the War Ministry. Moreover, unlike the Kaiser himself, he knew Wilhelm II would soon be abdicating.

Woolf was thirty-six years old and had just published her first novel, which received good reviews but was selling poorly. She tried to combat the nagging worry that she was nothing more than a dilettante nursing a conviction that any "work" other than writing would be a "waste of life." Virginia and her husband, Leonard, lived in Richmond, a quiet hamlet on the Thames west of London. Theirs was a harmonious marriage, though she had made it clear from the start that she felt no physical attraction for him. How strong their connection was emerged shortly after their wedding when Woolf suffered a serious mental breakdown. After a phase of extreme agitation in which she was bubbling with ideas, talking nonstop, and ultimately making no sense, she succumbed to her delusions and began hearing voices. Severe depression followed, during which she didn't want to get out of bed, speak, eat, or go on living. The inner darkness that had come over her was so profound she tried to overdose on medication. Leonard took her to a series of doctors, but none could help, after which he drew up a strict regimen for her that included regular work hours, proper nutrition, and regular sleeping times. He even kept track of her monthly period.

The Woolfs had bought a small, hand-driven printing press with which they hoped to start a small literary publishing company. Perhaps Leonard thought that working on a modest project might help Virginia exorcise her demons. The first work to appear in that imprint, in 1917, was a thin brochure containing two short stories, one ("The Mark on the Wall") by her and one ("Three Jews") by him. It was a good thing they were concentrating on short stories: because of the limited type that came with the press, they could only print two pages at a time. They also began looking for other authors but were very critical, turning down a manuscript entitled *Ulysses* by an unknown writer named James Joyce. The text was not only much too long for their press—they also found it unsavory because it contained so much farting and excrement.

In any event, as she acknowledged in her diaries, Britain's minister of education wasn't visiting the important writer Virginia Woolf but rather a member of the family. And when Herbert arrived at his cousin's house, it wasn't as a statesman from 10 Downing Street, where news from all over the world came racing through every ten minutes and "the fate of armies does more or less hang upon what two or three elderly gentlemen decide." In Virginia's company Herbert could be amiable and informal. Nonetheless, his presence made a strong impression on her. He seemed like a connection to the real world, to the truth and to life. She even described him as "one who was in the very centre of the very centre." How natural and close to home the events of the world seemed when he touched upon them in broad conversation. For example, when he described the preparations for armistice negotiations and the need to talk Ferdinand Foch out of his vindictiveness and his desire for a final battle, Herbert made it sound as though he'd spoken with the French general himself. And how convincing he seemed when he opined that the Germans had a greater number of "brutes" among them than other peoples since they had been "taught to be brutal." For one afternoon, thanks to Fisher, Virginia felt in touch with what was going on in the world, yet at the same time she became painfully aware how restricted her social circles were in village-like Richmond.

In truth, the Great War had never really made it to Richmond. Sure, there were shortages of certain basic necessities, and domestic help was hard to come by. On her visits to London, Virginia had experienced the threat and terror of bombs dropped by German zeppelins. But even if German aircraft did occasionally fly over the hamlet, Richmond had little to fear. There the war seemed so remote it had little effect on villagers.

On their walks the Woolfs would talk about the coming peace and how people would soon be so prosperous they would forget the war ever happened. Both doubted that the inhabitants of Richmond would be euphoric for long about the fact that the British had liberated the Germans from their pompous monarch and given them freedom. In the final weeks of the war, Virginia registered the progress of the diplomatic negotiations, which the newspapers brought into her house. But all the headlines had little impact on her otherwise eager mind. Was "the whole thing too remote and meaningless?"

As a result, as the celebratory cannon shots are fired in Richmond at 11 a.m. on November 11, the Woolfs feel no enthu-

siasm. Virginia writes in her diary: "The rooks wheeled round, &
were for a moment, the symbolic look of creatures performing
some ceremony, partly of thanksgiving, partly of valediction
over the grave. A very cloudy, still day, the smoke toppling over
heavily towards the east; & that too wearing for the moment a
look of something floating, waving, drooping." Sirens also
sound to mark the hour history was being made.

How was she supposed to write amid all this commotion?
The servant girls burst in. "Nelly has four different flags that she
wants to hang out toward the street. Lottie says that we have to
do something, and I can see she's near tears. She insists upon pol-
ishing the door knocker and to call out over the street to the old
fireman who lives across the way. Oh God! What noise they
make." Woolf herself feels quite melancholy. "All the taxis are
honking and the schoolchildren . . . gather around the flag. The
atmosphere is like that at a wake. Now there's a harmonium playing a hymn, and a huge Union Jack is being raised on a pole." So
this is peace.

This is peace? The next day, the Woolfs take the train to
London. In the face of the historical significance of the moment,
they feel a bit restless, but they soon regret their decision to make
the trip. "A fat, slovenly woman in black velvet & feathers
with the bad teeth of the poor insisted upon shaking hands with
two soldiers . . . She was half drunk already, & soon produced
a large bottle of beer which she made them drink of; & and
then she kissed them." The British capital is teeming with
such wretched, flag-waving, intoxicated figures, and the sky
opens up and drenches the revelers with autumnal down-
pours. In her diary, Virginia writes that "there was no centre,
no form for all this wandering emotion to take." By "centre," is

she referring to her cousin, Minister of Education Herbert Fisher? Probably not directly, even if she has previously used this term to describe him. She complains that the government had not provided any rituals for such an extraordinary day: "There seemed to be no mean between tipsy ribaldry & rather sour disapproval." Respectable people can only react with dismay at the unpleasant spectacle of the heaving masses, the closed shops, and the rain.

NGUYEN TAT THANH had spent months washing mountains of dishes in the basement of the posh Carlton Hotel, deep below the bustling streets of London's Haymarket district. Uniformed servers on the ground level would place the dirty porcelain inside a dumb waiter and send it down to Nguyen and his coworkers. They would throw out the scraps of food, separate the dishes, glasses, and cutlery, carefully wash them in large tubs, then dry and polish them with cotton towels.

Nguyen left his homeland, the French colony of Indochina, before the start of the war and worked much of the next six years as a galley mate on a steamship line. In this way he managed to see half the world. He had gotten used to getting up at 4 a.m. to scrub kitchens and heat their ovens. Every time his ship set sail, he would have to climb from the hot, smoky kitchen down to the ice-cold supply deck to collect the day's food and haul it back up to the galley. His once delicate frame grew muscular and wiry from lugging around heavy sacks of coal and food, but his face, with its high forehead, intense eyes, and full lips, remained fine and expressive.

Nguyen had come to London in 1917 to improve his English.

Before and after his long shifts washing dishes at the Carlton, he could often be seen sitting in Hyde Park with a book and pencil. The books not only enriched his vocabulary but gave him ideas, including some he could apply to everyday life. For instance, one morning he decided not to throw away the scraps of food but to arrange them neatly on a plate and take them back up to the kitchen. When the much-feared French head chef Auguste Escoffier asked him what he was doing, he replied: "These things shouldn't be thrown away. You could give them to the poor." Escoffier smiled and replied: "My young friend, listen to me! Leave your revolutionary ideas aside for a moment, and I will teach you the art of cooking, which will bring you a lot of money. Do you agree?" From that day on, Nguyen was frequently allowed to work in the confectionery, where he learned how to create exquisite pastries. At least this is what Nguyen will later write in his memoirs.

On November 11, 1918, T. E. Lawrence is dining in London with Charles ffoulkes, the director of the Imperial War Museum, and their old mutual friend Edward Thurlow Leeds, now working for military intelligence. The three of them are enjoying the tranquility of the Union Club dining hall. From their table they have a view of the massive crowds celebrating on Trafalgar Square. The three friends have much to talk about after four years of a war that has made their shared interest in medieval armor and weaponry appear like a ridiculous idiosyncrasy.

But had not the painter Briton Rivière imagined victory as Saint George, lying next to his dead horse, utterly exhausted after overexerting himself to slay the dragon? Rivière had created this

image of the spent hero in shimmering armor before the Great
War, but it now seemed an amazingly prescient vision of this
particular day and hour. The victors and vanquished of the
conflict that engulfed the entire globe are equally fatigued—and
are sprawled side by side in a state somewhere between life and
death. In 1914, national and imperial rivalries, foolish leadership,
and a rigid system of alliances had plunged the world into war.
By 1918 all that was left of the once high-minded goals of that
struggle were the victors' hopes of recouping some of their enormous costs from their bankrupt enemies' assets. Saint George
can also be seen as the embodiment of the condition many soldiers found themselves in at 11 a.m. that day. They are so exhausted
from fighting, so overwhelmed by the inhumanity of the war and
the omnipresence of death, that even those on the winning side
lack the strength to be triumphant. They care little about the
ideas of the commanders, diplomats, and statesmen for which
they fought. All they want is to return to the safety and comfort
of their homes and forget what now lies in the past. Some don't
even feel like celebrating.

EVEN BEFORE THE armistice, Alvin York is transferred from the
bullet-riddled Argonne Forest to a completely different setting.
After an uninterrupted tour of duty lasting several weeks, he and
a group of comrades are granted furloughs and take the train
to Aix-les-Bains in the foothills of the French Alps. The pris-
tine lakeside spa with its whitewashed buildings overlooking
Lac du Bourget is the exact opposite of the wasted landscapes of
northern France. York and his comrades settle into the upscale
Hôtel d'Albion with its fluttering flags. They race motorboats

across the lake, whose calm waters reflect the mountains, and accept invitations to dine with the spa town's grateful residents.

Since the day he almost single-handedly cleared out the nest of German machine gunners and took more than one hundred prisoners, the man from Tennessee has been more convinced than ever that God is watching over him. His comrades have offered rational reasons for the extremely unlikely chain of events that made him into a hero, but for York there's only one explanation: on October 8, 1918, God sent him a sign. After letting himself be drafted, York had been plagued by doubts about his decision. Could there be any excuse for him as a Christian going to war and killing others? In the end, though, God heard his prayers and used him as His instrument. A heavy burden of guilt dropped from York's shoulders.

Nonetheless, on November 11, Sergeant York is not in the mood for celebration. For him the Great War ends in an idyllic lakeside resort, and all the death and destruction seem infinitely far away, almost unreal. The news from the train carriage in Compiègne reaches the spa around midday. "It was awful noisy," he will write. "All the French were drunk, whooping and hollering. The Americans were drinking with them, all of them. I never done anything much. Jes went to church and wrote home and read a little. I did not go out that night. I had jes gotten back there and were all tired. I was glad the armistice was signed, glad it were all over. There had been enough fighting and killing. And my feelings were like most all of the American boys. It was all over. And we were ready to go home. I felt they had done the thing they should have done, signing the armistice." The celebrations in Aix-les-Bains last several days, but York never joins in. His desire to exorcise everything he witnessed and experienced in the past weeks is so great that he doesn't dare let himself go.

IT TAKES A while for Louise Weiss's curiosity to get the better of her, but eventually the journalist goes downstairs for a firsthand look at the Parisian "frenzy." Once on the street she is swept away by a crowd "hooting with joy and hatred"—a sea of humanity crested with thousands of French and American flags. Soldiers are carried through the streets, as captured weapons are brandished for display. The delirium of fanfares and people kissing and dancing with joy contrasts sharply to the group of mourning women standing off to the side. Louise finds it all horrible and, what's even worse, stupid. As much as she had hoped for victory, this celebration of aggression, this apotheosis of massacre, seems positively barbaric.

Louise retreats to the back room of a café. A group of celebrants storm in and surround a soldier with a shattered lower jaw and wounded eye that have been poorly stitched back together. One of the revelers blows a bugle. Champagne corks pop. Louise nearly chokes on her croissant. She feels isolated and loses herself in memories of Milan Štefánik.

It was in the first years of the war when the two of them met. At a dinner hosted by a mutual friend in Paris, a small man with stooped shoulders and a receding hairline joined the table and introduced himself with a slight accent. The first thing Louise noticed about him was how precisely he handled his cutlery with his pale, neatly manicured hands. After a few minutes, Louise asked him: "And what are you doing in Paris?" He looked at her with his clear blue eyes and replied: "I am 'doing' the independent grand duchy of Bohemia." Louise knew enough history and geography to place him as either a Czech or a Slovak. Štefánik was impressed, as was she when she learned that this man had indeed come to Paris to fight for his homeland's independence from the Habsburg Empire. Louise immediately fell in love with Štefánik and his ambitious project. It was the beginning of an unusual amorous relationship she would characterize in her memoirs as a "complete spiritual agreement in a climate of inhuman asceticism." From that moment on, Louise knew that she would follow this man and support his cause with all her strength.

On November 11, as Louise sits with mixed emotions in a Paris café, Milan is in Siberia somewhere between Irkutsk and Vladivostok, stuck in a battle for control of the Trans-Siberian Railway. This is the main conduit for a massive movement of some fifty thousand Czech troops. Initially, the Czechoslovak Legion had fought on the side of the Allies, particularly Russia. But that changed with the October Revolution and Russia's departure from the war. Since then, Czech units have been following a crazy plan to traverse Asia to China, cross the Pacific, return to Europe via North America, and link up with the Allied troops in France. But Siberia is bitterly cold, and the situation is pure chaos. The Czechs, who increasingly consider themselves enemies of the Bolsheviks, can never be sure whether the Russian units they encounter are friends or foes. The distances are immense; the railway signals, all broken. Many of the Czech units that manage to reach the safety of the Pacific coast have to turn right back to help their comrades trapped in the interior of the country. For weeks they've been living in railway cars, some of which are said to be crammed with gold plundered from the Bolsheviks. The train stations are stained red from the massacres carried out by various sides. Milan Štefánik is stuck in the middle of all this. Will Louise ever see him again?

When Marina Yurlova again opens her eyes, the first thing she sees are gray walls. Little by little, images from the past come back: Kazan, the hospital, being drafted, the bellowing of the Red Army officer. The good news: she's alive. The bad news: she is evidently in a prison. All she can make out in the dank, dimly lit space are a cot, some dirty straw, a stove, a tiny barred window, and an iron door. She passes out again before she can make a closer inspection. She only wakes up when a key grates in the lock of her cell door, and a wan little man steps in with a paraffin lamp. He orders her to get up, sets two bowls on the cot, and shuts the door behind him without a further word. One of the bowls contains some sauerkraut and boiled potato skins with fungus growing out of them like gray worms. The other bowl is full of foul-smelling water. There's also a piece of hard, dark bread. Marina doesn't know how long it's been since she's eaten, but she's not touching this meal.

Time crawls by. Is it hours or days? All at once, Marina is awakened from her stupor by the sharp crack of a gunshot. She hears shouted commands, another shot, and the cry of a dying man. There's no doubt: prisoners are being executed in the courtyard. Was it not just the end of the war that awaited her here in Kazan, but the end of her own life as well? The prison guards say nothing, and she can see no clue in their expressionless faces as to her fate. Still, it's a somewhat comforting sign that they at least keep bringing her bowls of food, together with a chamber pot.

After some time, the executions seem to cease. Silence descends upon the building. Is she the last soul left alive here? Have they simply forgotten her? To judge from the tiny sliver of sky visible from her window, it's early afternoon when the noises suddenly strike up again. Powerful explosions rock the building. Smoke pours in from under the door, and through her tiny window Marina can see flames. The explosions have such force that they can only come from bombs. This goes on for hours. It isn't until morning that the massive blasts give way to the quieter exchange of rifles.

The blood freezes in Maria's veins when a key again turns in the lock. "Who are you, there in the corner?" a voice yells. The first thing she notices is that the accent isn't Russian. The soldier entering her cell isn't wearing a Russian uniform, either. "I'm a Cossack," she says in a thin voice; "my home is in Caucasia." "Follow me," orders the soldier. She walks out into the sunny courtyard, where more soldiers are waiting. Ragged-looking men and women are stepping from the darkness of the prison into the unfamiliar bright light. The soldiers try to explain in broken Russian, and Marina is able to piece together what happened. Her liberators are Czechs who had earlier fought with the Russians against Austria and have now joined up with tsarist White Russian troops. Under the command of Vladimir Kappel, they have captured the city of Kazan and freed the prisoners taken by the local Bolsheviks. For once, it's an advantage that Marina is a Cossack. "You may go where you wish," the Czech soldiers announce. The former prisoners don't have to be told twice. They rush to the prison gate and vanish in the crowd of onlookers. Marina remains standing, undecided. "Will you go with us?" the Czech soldiers ask. Marina nods and follows them.

Where else does she have to go? Her homeland doesn't exist anymore, not in the new Bolshevik Russia. Absent any alternatives, she becomes a soldier again and is assigned to guard a munitions factory. The domes and minarets of Kazan stand out against the setting sun, and Marina falls asleep on the bare floor of a barrack.

When she wakes up, she can hear shots. Once again the war has her in its grasp. The Bolsheviks are counterattacking. Someone presses a rifle into Marina's hand. She receives an order. She obeys. She shoots. She comes under fire. In the end, an enemy bullet rips into her shoulder, and she's back in the hospital. But the White Russian resistance in Kazan is broken, and she has to abandon her bed faster than she was admitted to it. Together with thousands of refugees on foot and in wagons, Marina leaves the city along a road that leads through a seemingly endless plain. There she comes under Red Army fire from above. Word goes round that there's a rail station in Chelyabinsk. But Chelyabinsk is almost a thousand kilometers east, Marina's arm has gone numb, and supplies have run out. Finally, a truck takes Marina and a small group of Czech soldiers to the western terminus of the Trans-Siberian Railway. With the butts of their rifles, the Czechs force the civilians waiting in a freight car out of the train to make room for themselves. The hours drag on. Finally the train starts rolling, east, toward Siberia. Seven thousand kilometers of track lie ahead of them.

AT 11 A.M. on November 11, at precisely the moment when the guns fall silent on the western front, Matthias Erzberger and the German delegation climb back aboard their train, which starts rolling north. Only thirty minutes have passed since he received the final version of the armistice agreement. The blinds on the windows of his compartment are drawn. The news about the outcome of the negotiations has traveled quickly, and people gather at the stations to greet the train with both cheers and jeers. Once back in Tergnier, the negotiators wait until sunset before continuing their journey in the German cars they left there. They drive through the night to the frontline, which they reach at 2 a.m. and which they can now, with the guns silent, cross without risk to their lives.

By 9 a.m., Erzberger is at the German headquarters in Spa, where nothing is as he left it. A soldiers' and workers' council has formed in the Belgium resort and is attempting to arrest the army supreme command. Officers have had their epaulettes torn from their shoulders, and rank-and-file soldiers have stopped saluting their superiors. Erzberger quickly realizes that the unbelievable news that reached him in Compiègne is true. The Germany of November 12 is no longer the country he knew at the start of his mission on November 7. The Kaiser has fled to the Netherlands, and revolution is fully under way. Shortly after Erzberger's arrival in Spa, Quartermaster General Wilhelm Groener calls a meeting in which he praises Erzberger for the result of the negotiations. Field Marshal Paul von Hindenburg also uses the occasion to thank him for "the uncommonly valuable service" Erzberger has rendered to the fatherland.

Later, Erzberger receives two envoys from a workers' council in Hanover who are on their way to Brussels to "proclaim world revolution." The revolutionaries have even commandeered a locomotive to this end. They're convinced that General Foch has been shot dead and that all the hostilities are over. Erzberger informs them that only a few hours ago he saw Foch very much alive and that fighting between the revolutionaries and German loyalists is still going on in Brussels. The council envoys are completely crestfallen, but they thank Erzberger for clearing up their misconceptions and agree to travel with him to the Reich capital that day to return the locomotive. The rebels and the diplomat may be going in the same direction, but they have completely different agendas. The two revolutionary workers want to get back to Berlin to witness the radical socialist Karl Liebknecht made Germany's new chancellor. Erzberger, on the other hand, wants to assess the situation in Berlin with his own eyes and determine whether the armistice he concluded in the name of the German Reich is still worth the paper it was written on.

A DAY AND an hour. Arbitrarily specified in an agreement by negotiators who could have chosen another day, a different hour—the moment when the armistice comes into force seems to synchronize millions of lives. But the same moment also stands for vastly different experiences. While some people fall into one another's arms with joy, and others look toward the future with total despair, the war goes on in many parts of the world, where people remain unaware that a historic document has been signed in Compiègne. A day and an hour. And yet, even though people see the historical juncture from very diverse perspectives, at 11 a.m. on November 11, 1918, for just an instant, the entire world seems to sync up. Then the moment passes, and history once again falls apart into countless individual, asynchronous stories.

At 4:30 a.m. on November 17 the Harlem Hellfighters are ordered to break camp in the Vosges and march east. As Arthur Little will recall, the thought of leaving their trenches and heading toward the German frontlines feels odd. Will there really be no more enemy fire? Little shows up far too early at the troops' point of rendezvous and stands shivering in the cold. A liaison officer has to remind him that now, with the war over, he's allowed to start a fire. Together they wait in silence, holding their hands over the flames, until the eastward march commences. The soldiers' first steps take them through no man's land and then past the abandoned German trenches and positions. In Cernay, the regiment lines up behind the band, which blows the signal "forward march." It's the last leg of the long journey from Harlem to the Rhine.

The troops make their way through small abandoned towns, basically intact, that only a short time ago provided quarters for German soldiers. After a short night in some provisional accommodations, the Hellfighters continue east, reaching Ensisheim on November 18. Here the troops encounter other people for the first time. The inhabitants are well prepared for the arrival of the Americans. They've decorated their houses with flags and hung pictures of President Wilson in the windows. Girls in embroidered Alsatian dresses, their hair elaborately plaited, toss flowers onto the street to form a carpet of blossoms over which the 1,500 soldiers of the American regiment tread. Many a man in uniform gets kissed for the first time in months. Banners have been hung over the streets, reading "Greetings to Our Deliverers," "Vive la République!" and "God Bless President Wilson!"

After decamping from Ensisheim, Little calls a halt in the village of Balgau. When he wakes up the following morning, November 19, a long line of civilians has formed in front of his quarters. "What do they want?" he asks his orderly. "Passes, sir," he's told. Little quickly has a makeshift office established to handle the villagers' requests. He's astonished to learn what the locals had to put up with under German occupation. They needed official permission to take their cows to pasture, to go to the market in the neighboring village, or to visit the cemetery, and they don't realize that things are now different. On November 20, Little, who has been appointed military governor of the town, has the local crier promise the townspeople "friendliness" and "protection." The lines outside his office get shorter, and the villagers retrieve their silverware and supplies from where they had hidden them from the Germans.

That same day, Little receives a set of orders marked "urgent." His heart skips a beat when he reads them. French general Georges Pierre Louis Lebouc is offering the black Americans the chance to be the first Allied unit to reach the Rhine. The orders are to be carried out immediately, and Little springs into action. He puts together a reconnaissance group of reliable men and mounts his horse, skipping dinner, to ride out to Nambsheim—a short distance from the Rhine. The small troop presses on toward the river that will soon once again form the eastern border of France. They ask some Alsatian foresters the best way, but the woodsmen shake their heads in warning. There are still Germans on the riverbank, evacuating their troops using a ferry attached to a rope across the water. Would the arrival of US soldiers rekindle hostilities? Little doesn't want to risk squandering his head start. After all, his orders stated that they were for "IMMEDIATE EXECUTION." He pushes on with the reconnaissance troop. Within minutes they come upon a clearing with an open view of "the wonderful swift running water of the Rhine." Little's men dismount, shake hands and congratulate themselves. Caught up in this historic moment, Little improvises a short speech. Seeing the Rhine with his own eyes reminds him of great explorers. He and his men have no reason to feel inferior to de Soto, Drake, Frobisher, or even Columbus, he says before ordering them to set up a monitoring post.

Only now do Little's men notice that on the far bank of the river, the final German soldiers are getting off the ferry and heading home. In a few hours, however, they will learn that another black American unit reached the river a bit before they did. Thus it is Colonel Hayward and not Major Little who will receive General Lebouc's thanks for establishing the "black watch on the Rhine."

Three weeks later, on December 13, an opulent ceremony begins on the plain of Münchhausen, sixteen kilometers northeast of Mülhouse. The entire French-American division has assembled there, ten thousand men standing at attention in the clear air of this mild winter's day. The low-lying sun sends its rays across the plain as bugles sound fanfares. Dressed in a blue uniform, General Lebouc trots up on a cream-colored horse. With his chin angled toward the sky he rides up and down the ranks of the units, greeting the Americans with the words *"mes chers amis."* Finally he dismounts and orders the standards of all the units brought forward. In the name of the 369th

Infantry Regiment, Little, too, approaches the general. Lebouc pins the Croix de Guerre to all the standards and kisses the commanding officers on both cheeks. A bit later, the regiments withdraw, one after another, causing the ground to tremble as they tramp off.

After hours of marching, the soldiers return to their camp, but no one complains about having spent the entire day on his feet. Little understands why. "Our men had tried to make history to honor their race," he will recall, "and their efforts were recognized." Under French command, the soldiers from Harlem were able to show that they were good for more than just unloading ships and digging trenches and graves. Now, having completed the long march from Harlem to the Rhine, they can prepare to return from the Rhine back to Harlem. Will America welcome them with the respect they had not been shown when the country sent them off to war? Would the sacrifices made by the black soldiers in war be rewarded in peacetime?

THE ALLIES REACH the largest city in Alsace, Strasbourg, on November 21, 1918, putting an end to a turbulent time in which the city on the Rhine was the scene of demonstrations, plundering, and revolutionary unrest. Five days later, Foch rides into Strasbourg on horseback. Upon arriving, he stops to salute the statue of General Jean-Baptiste Kléber. In his right hand, Foch carries a saber once owned by that French revolutionary war hero. For the French, this day marks the end of a humiliation that has gnawed at the national soul ever since France was defeated by Prussia in 1871, and Germany annexed Alsace and Lorraine,

declaring them "Reich states." The Allies' victory restores the
two *départements* west of the Rhine to France.

A FEW DAYS later, Louise Weiss arrives in Strasbourg. She and
her family are taking a journey into the past—both her parents
are from Alsace, and the *"désannexion"* is a matter dear to their
hearts. They are carrying large packages of food, soap, fabric, and
candles for their relatives who stayed behind. There's hardly any
room to sit inside their car. Louise has been forced to dress up in
traditional garb—a dress, apron, sash, and hairband that once
belonged to Gretel, her father's former wet nurse. Gretel had been
wearing these clothes in 1871, when, with the Germans laying
siege to Strasbourg, she had saved Louise's father, then a small
child, from starvation by packing him inside a basket and smug-
gling him through enemy lines.

When they reach the former border between France and
Alsace in the Vosges Mountains, Louise's father stops the car. He
gets out and bends down to pick up some pebbles of his native
soil. He places one in the hands of each of his children. They
gather in a circle, solemn and silent, stamping their feet to keep
warm. Louise's father decides to take a detour over the Vieil
Armand, the hotly contested mountain ridge that cost thirty
thousand German and French soldiers their lives. By the time
they arrive, the sun has set behind the mountains. In the misty
darkness, they can only imagine the skeletons of the bullet-riddled
pine trees and the cratered ground with the remnants of tents
and barbed wire blown by the wind.

In Strasbourg, the Weiss family's cousins welcome them with
kisses. Together they visit familiar places like the house in which

Weiss père was born on rue de la Nuée-Bleue and the Gothic cathedral. As she once did as a child, Louise lays her cheek on the cool stones of the cathedral wall so she can follow the ascending line of the building's exterior into the pinnacle's spire and all the way up to the heavens.

The afternoon after their arrival in Strasbourg, the famous journalist Louise Weiss is invited to the official celebrations commemorating the liberation of Alsace. She takes her seat several rows behind President Raymond Poincaré and Prime Minister Georges Clemenceau on the grandstand that has been erected on the place de la République. A never-ending parade begins. Soldiers, "drunk with enthusiasm," march past the grandstand with sabers drawn, "so close that you could almost think they were begging for a caress." They are followed by local Alsatian representatives who pass by in traditional costumes, swinging banners and blowing fanfares—not marching, but rather dancing with pride and joy. Their colorful black and red silk ribbons and their gold-embroidered caps sparkle in the sun. A tear trickles down the president's cheek, and Clemenceau the "Tiger," as he's nicknamed, has to press his eyes shut, so overcome is he by emotion. The procession lasts for hours, and in contrast to the victory celebrations in Paris, Louise appreciates its power, comparing it to a "torrential river" and a "flow of lava." Still, she can't help but ask herself: was this triumph worth the lives of two million French people?

Months later, she will again pose this question when her family travels to Arras, in northern France, where Louise was born. For her parents, this trip, too, is a pilgrimage to a place of family history and to memories of happy bygone days. But the once pretty town lies in ruins. The church spire, the train station, and the house where Louise was born have been blasted to rubble. Louise removes a bit of shrapnel from the piles of stone and wooden boards that used to be her home. The shrapnel was precisely where her cradle must once have stood.

A poor, provisional excuse for a street leads from Arras to the former battlefields outside the gates of the city. Louise surveys the war-ravaged landscape. Rusting artillery barrels still point up to the heavens, while mildew coats tarpaulins left in muddy craters and weeds sprout everywhere between twisted scraps of metal and filthy barbed wire. On the nearby hills, a seemingly endless graveyard of roughly hewn, identical gray crosses stretches toward the horizon, above a carpet of red poppies. "Red like blood?" Louise wonders. "Is this an appeal? Or an accusation?" Louise senses that the images of destruction in the city of her birth, the fields of death, and the spectacle of the poppies bind her more closely than ever to her mother country. And in that moment, confronted by such scenes, Louise Weiss—the cosmopolitan founder of *L'Europe nouvelle* and the advocate of the freedom of all peoples—feels like a Frenchwoman in every fiber of her being.

— *Three* —

Revolutions

In place of a type-true people, born of and grown on the soil, there is a new sort of nomad, cohering unstably in fluid masses, the parasitical city dweller, traditionless, utterly matter-of-fact, religionless, clever, unfruitful, deeply contemptuous of the countryman and especially that highest form of countryman, the country gentleman. This is a very great stride toward the inorganic, toward the end.

—Oswald Spengler, *The Decline of the West*, 1918

Our erstwhile Eden is no more
We now have something else in store
For each must now take spade in hand
And learn anew to tend the land
To plow the earth and sow new seed
And rid the fields of stubborn weeds
Together we must bend our backs
And march ahead and forge new tracks:
For only sweat and sacrifice
Will let us reclaim paradise.

—Ratatösker, "Future,"
Simplicissimus, November 24, 1918

George Grosz, *Explosion*, 1917

ON THE EVENING of Sunday, November 10, 1918, hundreds of flares explode over Wilhelmshaven, on the North Sea, illuminating the sky with flashes of light and scattering red, green, and white stars, while cannons from the port garrison thunder away. Sirens wail deafeningly. Seaman Richard Stumpf breaks off what he's doing and heads for shelter. After all, what can this be other than an air-raid alert or a warning of an imminent attack by the British fleet? A rumor soon spreads that the fireworks are celebrating the unification of Communist parties from different countries into a Third International: the world revolution has finally begun. At first people believe this, and uncertainty and fear spread throughout the small city until finally a broadsheet informs the ships' crews and inhabitants what's really going on. Stumpf reads, with increasing horror, about the Allies' conditions for an armistice, which apparently have been leaked to the press even before the agreement has been signed. Enraged he cries out, "This is what you get for your God-damned brotherhood of nations!" Then he withdraws to a quiet corner, overcome by emotion.

After the final shell has exploded and the sirens have been switched off one by one, all is calm again in Wilhelmshaven, but inside Stumpf a tempest is raging. In his view it borders on madness to subject an industrious, undefeated nation to such conditions. It's like they're spitting right in his face. Is this the peace the local navy men and dock workers risked their lives for?

Stumpf has been stationed aboard the SMS *Wittelsbach* since March. The vessel has remained berthed in Wilhelmshaven for over a year as a so-called support ship, a floating barrack. Serving on board the *Wittelsbach* is tedious; the time is spent on dull, pointless drills, chores like mending socks and washing shirts, and selling thread, soap, and pepper to earn a little extra money. By the fall of 1918, Stumpf had long stopped believing in victory and had adapted his morning prayers to his circumstances: "Lord, bring us peace, bread, and happiness." Starting in October more and more rumors circulated that the German fleet had suffered horrible losses and that "German submarine warfare . . . has lost its sting."

Earlier that autumn, Stumpf had noticed that following four years of war at sea in which dreary confinement alternated with deadly peril, many of his brothers-in-arms had become extremely agitated. "Bolshevik ideas" have turned the heads of many of his comrades. Would their morale hold up for the final battle their superiors kept talking about? Given the men's "dismal mood," Stumpf didn't think it would. More frequently he pondered the prospect of defeat, not just for the German fleet, but for the whole German Reich. "Can the fleeting period between 1870 and 1914 really have been our one shining historical moment?" he wondered.

Nonetheless, Stumpf still supported the existing political order. "Not because I've been indoctrinated with love for the Hohenzollerns," he insisted: he was simply convinced that "the roots of our prestige and all of our strength lie in the imperial system"—and he held on to that belief even in the final weeks of the war. His image of the enemy also still reflected German propaganda. "If we bend to the desires of the cold-hearted plutocrats across the channel and on the other side of the ocean, and send the Kaiser off to hell, I would be ashamed for all time of ever having been German."

But there were increasing signs that the sailors' discouragement would soon lead to mutiny. A specific situation had precipitated the crisis. English and American naval units had set off with the intent of engaging the German fleet in the Heligoland Bight off the north coast. Meanwhile the Allies had let it be it known in the international press that if Germany were defeated, it would have to hand over its entire fleet. To prevent the latter, on October 24, 1918, German naval command ordered its ships to make an all-out effort to repel the enemy in one last decisive battle. By this point, the enemy naval forces were so superior that the order was tantamount to scuttling the fleet. Was it possible that thousands of men were being sent to their deaths merely to preserve a handful of officers' outmoded concepts of honor? A few days later, when units stationed in Germany's Baltic Sea ports were supposed to ship out, rebellions flared up in Kiel and Wilhelmshaven. First, the stokers abandoned their posts and shut down the engine rooms of the gigantic steam-driven warships. The crews of other ships stayed ashore instead of following orders to take up positions for the battle at hand. To make things worse, a heavy fog settled over the Baltic, making it senseless to try to set sail.

Stumpf felt "deeply sad that things had come to this." At the same time, he noted with a hint of schadenfreude: "Now where is the almighty power of the proud captains and naval commanders? The stokers and common sailors, who've been treated like dogs for years, have finally realized that nothing functions without them." On the SMS *Thüringen*, stationed in Kiel, the crew even locked up their officers. No one had any desire to risk his life for a lost cause. Navy commanders ordered the mutinous ship to be surrounded and threatened to sink it with cannon fire. Three hundred crew members were arrested. But the *Thüringen* never put out to sea for the final battle.

On November 7, after several people had already died in Kiel, individual acts of resistance in Wilhelmshaven coalesced into open rebellion. Large numbers of sailors abandoned their ships to demonstrate on land. Stumpf, too, put on his dress uniform and followed his comrades over the gangplank to join the mutiny. A large crowd gathered on the parade ground in front of the navy barracks. A makeshift speaker's platform was erected. There, encouraged by applause from the ever-growing crowd, the rebellious navy men set out demand upon demand. Stumpf had the impression that the assembly would have gone so far as to cheer if someone had called for the Kaiser to be hanged.

Together, the men went on the move. To keep a modicum of order, the official shipyard band started playing songs and marches. The music attracted more and more seamen from other ships. The sailors no longer followed any chain of command but were directed by herd instinct alone. An older captain stood at the barracks gate brandishing a revolver. He drew and pointed it at the first sailor who tried to pass, but he was quickly seized, disarmed, and stripped of his epaulets. Cries and jeers went up. Stumpf, however, silently admired the officer's devotion to duty.

There was still minimal discipline among the demonstrators, but the further they went, the more incendiary the mood became. The men wolf-whistled and harassed women. Soon the first red flag appeared, but Stumpf didn't consider it an honor to march behind that "filthy rag."

By noon, the demonstrators were starting to get hungry, when suddenly everyone went silent. They scarcely dared breathe while a speaker read out a message from Admiral Günther von Krosigk, saying that the concessions won by the sailors' council in Kiel would also apply to Wilhelmshaven. Sailors would no longer have to submit their correspondence to censorship. They would enjoy freedom of speech and would not be answerable to their superior officers while off-duty. The crowd greeted this announcement with frenetic celebration. Then a dockworker spoke up and demanded, his voice breaking, the immediate creation of a soviet republic. There was more applause, but it was quieter and quickly faded. Someone else suggested that the sailors could now return to their posts since they had gotten everything they wanted. That drew some hearty laughter.

As it happened, the sailors and dockworkers did disband— not to return to their posts but to scrounge up a meal wherever they could find one. "The revolution had triumphed without blood," Stumpf later wrote, using the word that had caused panic and terror in Germany for decades. For sure, this "revolution" was not the glorious triumph foretold by the German socialists Karl Kautsky and August Bebel, nor did the revolt in the North Sea port bear comparison to the tremendous upheaval in St. Petersburg. As far as Stumpf was concerned, what he saw was a triumph not of the proletariat but of small-mindedness, stupidity, uncertainty, and worry. Stumpf was something of an involuntary revolutionary, someone who joined the rebellion against his better judgment, carried away by the unfolding of events. "I'm now two days older, and during this period a transformation

I would have previously considered impossible has taken place within me," he wrote. "From a monarchist to a committed democrat—I no longer know my own heart."

Now on November 10, Stumpf sees just how far-reaching the consequences of what will become known as the "Kiel Mutiny" are. But the German revolution will need far more committed advocates if it wants not just to drive the Hohenzollerns from their throne, but to create—with energy and conviction—a new social order.

WITH EVERY JOLT of the wheels on the damaged tracks, stabs of pain shoot through Marina Yurlova's injured shoulder. Exhausted, she is lying in a compartment filled with wounded soldiers on a train that is skirting the Ural Mountains from Chelyabinsk to the West Siberian plain. Through the compartment window she can see evergreen forests stretching toward the horizon, so vast and monolithic it almost seems as though the train weren't moving at all. Nights are the worst, stuck in this stuffy compartment with the snores and groans of wounded men, the rattling and grinding of the rolling car, and the stench of filth and blood. Her new Czech comrades who freed her from prison have taken control of a massive locomotive pulling sixteen Trans-Siberian Railway cars. Most of the passengers are civilians. The Czech soldiers have guns, so they get to decide who can board the train, who must leave it, and whose provisions are subject to confiscation.

Even in this part of Siberia, empty of people, thousands of kilometers away from St. Petersburg and Moscow, civil war is raging between the Bolsheviks and their White enemies. When the train stops at a tiny wooden hut of a station, Marina sees an angry crowd. Men and women brandishing guns, hoes, shovels, and knives have captured two Bolshevik agitators who were travelling east. "Death to the Bolsheviks!" they bellow. One of the captives, a towering, powerfully built blond seaman, seems completely unaffected by the general hostility. He watches with his hands in his pockets as a gallows is erected at the station. When the rope is ready for the execution, he walks over calmly, carefully examines the noose, and then loops it around his own neck. The mob goes silent. "Well, why don't you pull?" he yells at the dumbfounded men who have volunteered to act as executioners. Finally several of them overcome their astonishment and pull the noose up with a jerk. The giant of a man is now hanging in the air, just a few centimeters above the ground, as his feet twitch around searching for something to stand on. He clutches at the rope around his neck until his movements slacken. The second man behaves exactly as you'd expect a Bolshevik Jew to behave, at least according to Marina's personal race theory: he throws himself on the ground before his executioners, clutches their ankles, and begs for mercy. Marina shares the prejudices of many counterrevolutionaries and anti-Semites of her day: they're convinced the revolution is actually a conspiracy of Jews, that after conquering Russia they'll turn their attention to the rest of the world, and that the revolution is evil because Jews are evil. Consequently Marina feels little pity for the man. The train remains stopped at the tiny station all day. The two bodies sway in the wind in front of the window of Marina's car.

DURING THOSE FATEFUL November days, Crown Prince Wilhelm has slept fitfully, dogged by thoughts about his own future

and the future of the Hohenzollern dynasty and the German
Reich. From early in his childhood, he's been accustomed to
other people telling him what to do. And now he's supposed to
make a decision on his own? Is the moment finally at hand? The
moment for which his education has been preparing him his
entire life but that has always seemed so far away? The moment
when he'll finally rule?

On November 7, the crown prince witnessed firsthand the
harbingers of a new age. On his way to inspect troops near
Givet, he drove past a train that had been commandeered by
soldiers. For the first time, he saw with his own eyes that symbol
of revolution, the red flag. From the broken windows of the troop
train came the battle cry of rebellion: "Lights off! Knives out!"

Wilhelm told his driver to stop. In a loud voice, he ordered
the soldiers off the train. Several hundred men in ragged uniforms
assembled in front of him. At their head was "a tall-as-a-tree
noncommissioned officer from Bavaria who stood at ease, his
hands buried deep in his pockets, the very picture of insubordi-
nation." Wilhelm puffed out his chest and addressed the man in
the drill-sergeant tone he had practiced since childhood. "Attention!" he barked. "Stand like someone fit to be a German soldier."
The old reflexes still functioned. The Bavarian stared straight
ahead, took his hands out of his pockets, and put them on the
seams of his trousers. For a moment, order was restored, and a
young fellow asked Wilhelm to excuse his comrade's behavior.
They had been on the go for three days without any rations. "We
are all devoted to you," the soldier said. "Please don't be angry."
Moved, the crown prince handed out cigarettes to the almost-
revolutionaries.

The following day Wilhelm receives an order from his father

the Kaiser to appear in Spa, and he travels in thick fog through land battered by war. On November 9, just before noon, he reaches the villa La Fraineuse outside the town gates; shortly before the war a local industrialist had constructed an estate modeled on the Petit Trianon at Versailles. Upon arrival, Wilhelm is received by his "chief of staff," Count von der Schulenburg, who looks "pale and visibly and deeply agitated." He tersely briefs the crown prince on the situation: General Wilhelm Groener, Hindenburg's new right-hand man in the German high command, is in La Fraineuse, where he has been leading discussions since that morning. Groener doesn't come from the Kaiser's inner circle of old confidants and speaks to the monarch in a tone his predecessor would never have dreamt of using. But these aren't the old times. With the armistice approaching, that predecessor, Erich Ludendorff, is on the verge of disguising himself with a fake beard and fleeing to Sweden. As Schulenburg reports, Groener offered a bleak appraisal of the military situation and the home front. Evidently the atmosphere in Berlin was so tense that "conflict could break out any minute and unleash a torrent of blood throughout the city," and there was no way a beaten army could be expected to march back to the German capital and defend it against revolution. Groener didn't state it explicitly, but his words implied only one course of action: the Kaiser had no choice but to bow to the mounting pressure from abroad and from home and abdicate. Only that would take the wind out of the revolutionary sails.

Kaiser Wilhelm II was completely appalled, Schulenburg tells the crown prince, but let Groener make his case without interruption. Then Schulenburg himself spoke up, offering a more hopeful picture of the situation. He suggested playing for time at the front so the troops could regain their strength. The flash-points of revolution could be extinguished with a minimum targeted use of force. But Groener refused to give in, and delivered a final shattering argument. Even if Wilhelm II were to order the troops to return to Berlin, Groener declared, they would not obey, because in his view the army, including the officer corps, no longer supported the monarch. Wilhelm II demanded to see evidence of this, claiming he would only stand down if the officers withdrew their loyalty in writing. But the most recent news from Berlin confirmed Groener's claims. There were bloody battles in the streets, troops had deserted, and loyalists had no means of quelling the spreading revolution.

After this briefing, Crown Prince Wilhelm steps out into the autumnal garden, where the trees have already lost their faded leaves and the flowerbeds have been dug up. The Kaiser is standing with a group of gentlemen in uniform who appear "bent, weighed down, like a picture of hopelessness . . . frozen in dull silence." The Kaiser is the only one speaking. When he notices his son, he motions him over. From up close the crown prince can see how distraught his father looks, "how his wan, yellow face twitched and quivered." Words tumble from the monarch's mouth like a waterfall. The upshot is the resigned recognition that he, the Kaiser, won't even be allowed to lead his troops in battle and die an honorable death. The danger that this could negatively influence the armistice negotiations is too great. At that moment, the crown prince comprehends that his father is no longer the master of the situation. But under no circumstances, the crown prince implores him, can the Hohenzollerns renounce the Prussian crown. His voice trembling with emotion, he invites the Kaiser to join him and Army Group German

Crown Prince. Together they can lead their troops back to the fatherland, the monarch and his successor side by side. Schulenburg supports the crown prince's idea. The majority of soldiers would keep their oath to flag, Kaiser, and country, he says, and follow their supreme commander, if necessary to the death. Groener shrugs and says: "Oath to the flag? Supreme commander? These are mere words, in the end nothing more than an idea." The moment marks the collision of two worlds: the old Reich based on loyalty and obedience and a modern society where people act more flexibly and pragmatically.

The color has now entirely drained from Wilhelm II's face. Seeking help, he turns to Hindenburg, but the field marshal just stares at the ground. Here, in the garden of a villa in Belgium, stands the German Kaiser, the master of Central Europe, the embodiment of the law, the supreme commander of the German army, the creator of the imperial German fleet, the sovereign who wanted to give Germany its place in the sun, possessor of all privileges and powers—and he slumps in defeat. He has allowed generals and advisors to tell him what to do for too long to summon any imperial will at this decisive moment. The dissolution of the German Reich and of his proud army, which once seemed forged for all eternity, has progressed too far for him to regain control. The monarch feels weak, fatigued, and bewildered by a situation that doesn't conform in the slightest to the visions of greatness and splendor that have been synonymous with imperial rule for his entire life. In a hoarse voice, Wilhelm II says that Reich Chancellor Max von Baden is to be told by telephone that he is prepared to lay down the imperial crown. Only the imperial crown, Wilhelm II hastens to add. He is still king of Prussia, and as such, he intends to lead the army back to the fatherland.

The gentlemen go back inside the villa to have a breakfast that resembles a funeral meal. After the final course, more dreadful news arrives from Berlin. Without consulting with Spa, Chancellor Max von Baden has declared that the German Kaiser has renounced both the imperial *and* the royal crown, and that the crown prince has also renounced the throne. The news has already been relayed over the Wolffs Telegraphisches Bureau. What's more, a new government has formed in Berlin. The revolution from below has been completed by a revolution from above. Wilhelm II is beside himself, but there's absolutely nothing he can do.

This is the end of the German monarchy. There is no heroic battle, no great words or gestures. Passive and resigned, the Kaiser—who can look back on centuries of dynastic rule—simply submits to his fate. He didn't require much persuading. Four years of war have exhausted the Reich and brought it to the brink of collapse. That failure has made it clear how incompetent his leadership has been. Defeat has demoralized him and stripped his regime of its gloss and the last vestiges of legitimacy. Suddenly the lord of Central Europe is nothing more than a tired old man. No one is afraid of him anymore.

On November 9, 1918, extra editions of newspapers flood the center of Berlin. One of them, from the socialist *Vorwärts*, falls into hands of Käthe Kollwitz as she is strolling in the Tiergarten. "The Kaiser Has Abdicated!" says the banner headline.

As she reads the article, Kollwitz walks along the Siegesallee to the Brandenburg Gate, where thousands of people have gathered and are moving toward the neighboring Reichstag. The crowd is so thick that Kollwitz has no choice but to follow the flow. In front of the massive entrance to the Reichstag, which is crowned with the inscription "For the German People," the crowd stops. A group of men can be seen on the balcony. "Scheidemann!" murmur those in front to those farther back. Then thousands fall silent as the Social Democrat Philipp Scheidemann, now a minister without portfolio, begins to speak: "What is old and rotten has collapsed. Militarism is over!" He then makes a historic declaration: "We must ensure that the new German republic we will establish is equal to any threats. Long live the German republic!" The cheering seems as though it will never end. When at last the masses do calm down, a soldier and a sailor speak from below the portal, followed by a young officer who tells the crowd, "Four years of war weren't as bad as the struggle against prejudice and everything outdated." The officer waves his cap and cries out: "Long live free Germany!"

Kollwitz lets herself be dragged along by the crowd to Unter den Linden, where red flags fly over the heads of demonstrators. Soldiers tear the cockades from their caps and throw them to the ground, laughing. "That's the way it truly was," Kollwitz writes in amazement. "You experience it, but you can't really believe it."

At that moment her mind is filled with the image of her youngest son, Peter. He was just eighteen when he enthusiastically marched off to war in 1914. From the front he sent letters full of heroic phrases that sounded as though they'd been copied from official military announcements. But then a few weeks later a black-rimmed envelope lay in her mailbox. It was as though a hole had opened in the ground and swallowed her. Today, on the founding day of the republic, Peter is again with her. "I think if he were alive, he would join in," she writes. "He too would tear off his cockade. But he isn't alive, and when I last saw him and he looked his best, he wore his cap with the cockade and his face was gleaming."

Elsewhere in Berlin on that same day, a completely different new state is proclaimed. This time the speaker is the socialist Karl Liebknecht, and the setting is the Hohenzollerns' Berlin Palace, "the very window where the Kaiser always spoke." In contrast to Scheidemann, Liebknecht speaks of a radical socialist republic—not a "German" one. The two rival declarations reveal the dangerous tensions within the revolutionary movement, the schism between the more moderate Social Democratic Party (SPD) and the far more leftist Independent Social Democratic Party (USPD). The situation in the city is extremely precarious. Rifle shots regularly crack in the streets, machine-gun salvos rain down over squares, and even cannon fire can be heard. Over and over, crowds disperse in a panic only to regroup again, as if drawn together by magnets. The workers' council formed by the revolution, it is said, is planning public executions to discourage looting.

Is Crown Prince Wilhelm still a crown prince at all? What matters more, the word of the Kaiser or of the chancellor? In any case, Wilhelm von Hohenzollern departs Spa soon after lunch to return to his troops. As he leaves, his father is still insisting that the Berlin declaration is illegal, that he is still the king of Prussia and that as such he intends to lead the army. But is that more than "mere words, nothing more than an idea"? And why won't his father and the other men in power even consider the possibility that the heir to the dynasty ought to take over the running of the state in this dire situation? Was it not his calling in life to stand ready if the ground beneath the throne began to tremble? For a moment it looks as though the son might go his own way for the first time. He sets out to rejoin his men.

A short while later, his father's white and gold royal train rolls through the Netherlands. The former Kaiser Wilhelm II has been forced to ask his close relative, the Dutch queen Wilhelmina, for asylum. With the fate of the tsar and his family in Russia fresh in her mind, she doesn't have the heart to turn him away at the border, even though her subjects in the Netherlands are anything but happy about their monarch's act of royal kindness. The journey of "Wilhelm the Last" takes him to Maastricht, Nijmegen, Arnhem, and, finally, Amerongen. At all the stations along the way, angry crowds give him a hostile reception, berating him for four years of war, the destruction of cities, hunger, poverty, sickness, and the death of so many people.

His son, in the meantime, reaches the headquarters of the Army Group Crown Prince in Vielsalm, Belgium. The same questions keep swirling around in his head. Should he mount the resistance his father has decided against? He is still the commander of these men and could lead them back to Berlin. While he is discussing the matter with Schulenburg, who has accompanied him, news that Field Marshal Hindenburg has pledged his loyalty to the new government arrives from Spa. The great idol of the former crown prince and so many others has decided to support the republic and the armistice—and to come out against further bloodshed and a battle that would have pitted Germans against Germans. With that, the crown prince's decision is made. He will not oppose his father's deputy, Hindenburg.

For protection, Wilhelm moves nearer to the front, where the troops remain largely disciplined. At a training camp for replacement troops, cheers break out when the former crown prince drives by. "None of these young fellows believed in the revolution. They asked me to march with them back home," he writes. "They wanted to smash all rebellion!" He presses on toward the front along potholed roads, but he's taken a wrong turn, through a "giant forest cloaked in the black of night." He stops for directions at a château that houses a school for cadet officers and is told how to reach the 3rd Army High Command. Along the way, at the railway hub of La-Roche-en-Ardenne, Wilhelm witnesses a "desolate" scene: soldiers "hooting and howling as they throw off the discipline of the front." His entourage is blocked at a railway underpass where two columns of artillery seem to have collided. Nothing is moving either forward or backward. Rain has softened the road, and Wilhelm's car sinks ever deeper into the mud. By the time the car finally reaches headquarters it is after midnight. The crown prince goes straight to bed, but once again he cannot sleep.

The following day, November 11, he succeeds in getting a telephone line to his staff back in Vielsalm. They, in turn, are in contact with Berlin. But there's no news on the question that interests him the most right now. Will he retain command of his army group under the new regime? He suspects that the silence coming from Berlin means "no." Night falls early. Wilhelm stands at the window of the country château where the high command is billeted and stares out at the bare trees. Wet snow is falling. Outside, a company is passing by in the street. The men are singing: "For my homeland I do yearn / where I long so to return . . ." Thus far, the crown prince has maintained his composure, but now, in the solitude and darkness, he weeps.

A bit later, news arrives that the new government has indeed relieved him of his command. After another sleepless night, his agitation gives way to resignation. All Wilhelm wants is to put everything behind him, avoid bloodshed, and find a little peace. In a convoy of two cars, he and his innermost circle make their way to the Dutch border. He signs his final letter to his troops "Commander Wilhelm, Crown Prince of the German Reich and Prussia." These are now definitely just "words" and "an idea." A companion holds out a common infantryman's cap, suggesting he wear it in order not to be recognized. But Wilhelm insists upon donning the tall, black hussar's hat with the death's head. For one last time, he wants to be a Prussian officer. He is driven over the badly cratered roads across the border, where the army is already disbanding. At Vroenhoven, the car stops in front of Dutch barbed wire. It costs Wilhelm his entire strength of will to take those final few steps across the border. The young Dutch officer on the other side can't believe his eyes. What should he do with this unexpected visit from on high? Wilhelm is forced to surrender his weapons, and then hours pass until he is given permission to proceed on to Maastricht. All the way, he's showered with hateful stares and insults. Notwithstanding the queen's gesture to his father, the Dutch government doesn't feel it has any duty to protect the son in the Netherlands.

GEORGE GROSZ—WHO was born Georg Gross, but changed his name in 1916 as a sign of disgust with his war-besotted homeland—is also on the move that November: namely to Nassauische Strasse, in the central Charlottenburg district of Berlin. At the beginning of the month he was still living in the Südende neighborhood, in the studio that was the center of his world.

There he worked amid furniture built from painted crates. Empty bottles lined the walls, which Grosz decorated with their labels. A large black widow spider made of wire hung from the lamp. Shards from a broken mirror, which Grosz had scattered throughout the studio, provided fragmentary reflections of the many photos on the walls, including one of millionaire carmaker Henry Ford with a fake dedication forged by the artist himself. Grosz was a huge fan of Ford and everything American: ragtime, the gold rush, dollars, skyscrapers, boxing, neon lights, bourbon, and tomahawks. He described his studio in those days as a "carnival tent." To keep it heated he had to insert ten-pfennig coins into a gas stove.

As the news of the end of hostilities on the western front reaches Berlin, it still doesn't seem to Grosz that the war has concluded. "Maybe it was never truly over?" he will write.

> "For us, peace was declared, but not everyone was drunk and happy. Basically people didn't change much, with a few exceptions: the proud German soldier was now a beaten, worn-out soldier, and the army had fallen apart like the uniforms partially made of wood pulp and the fake-leather bullet pouches. I was not disappointed that the war was lost. That people had supported and put up with it for years and that no one listened to the few voices that protested the mass slaughter—that was my real disappointment."

Grosz hadn't supported the war, and he didn't participate in it. He had spent much of the conflict lying on his back in bed. The first time he was drafted, he had been granted a deferment because of sinusitis. The second time, he either faked or suffered a nervous breakdown and was found half-conscious with his head in a latrine. Grosz was taken to the infirmary and then to a mental hospital where he was revived with "dried vegetables," "rutabaga coffee," "gray wartime bread rolls" and "grayish-green artificial honey." He never set eyes on the front and had likened his countrymen's enthusiasm for the incipient war in August 1914 to "pandemonium." But even far from the fighting, he could see the evidence of the devastation, destruction, mutilation, and death the war left behind. Grosz made sketches in his notebook of all the horrors he observed. "For me, my 'art' was a kind of release valve that relieved all the hot angry steam that had built up," he would write in his autobiography. "Whenever I had time, I would vent my rage in drawings. I sketched everything I didn't like about my surroundings in notebooks and on the backs of envelopes: the bestial faces of my comrades, the men horrifically crippled by war, the arrogant officers, lascivious nurses, etc." For Grosz, the only purpose of drawing and painting was "to record the ridiculous and grotesque world of the industrious and murderous ants around me."

Over and over he sketched the effects of the violence unleashed by war on buildings, nature, the human body, and the human soul. Over and over, with a mixture of revulsion and fascination, he depicted detonations and their catastrophic consequences in works with titles like "Assassination" or "Aerial Bomb." When he was at last definitively exempted from military service in May 1917, he created an oil painting entitled *Explosion*.

Employing harsh contrasts of fiery red and jet black, the painting depicts a city ripped apart by a huge bomb blast. The core of the explosion takes place level with the upper stories of the buildings—an accurate depiction of where bombs dropped from warplanes were designed to detonate. Lines collapse, façades waver, and a blazing red glow comes from the windows, as a cloud of oily black smoke darkens the sky. Toward the bottom of the painting, rendered in black, green and blue, an abyss seems to open up, and the viewer can just make out the figures of people trying to flee the catastrophe and the bodies of those who didn't make it, now plunged into darkness. But these figures are depicted as mere flimsy silhouettes, transparent and meaningless.

In *Explosion*, as in all his works, Grosz explores the violence and destructive potential of human existence. Behind the façades of the monarchic-bourgeois order he saw society as decayed, brutal, and perverse—and what he experienced during the war only strengthened this conviction, confirming his darkest judgments. In the spring of 1917, for example, a doctor declared him cured after he'd spent many months in a military hospital, but Grosz refused to leave his bed and furiously disputed what he considered the mistaken diagnosis. He would never forget "the glee, indeed lust, with which around seven of my sick 'comrades,' who were allowed to leave their beds, voluntarily attacked me." He added, "One of them, a baker in civilian life, kept jumping up and down with his full weight on my cramped legs, gleefully bellowing: 'We'll have to stomp him until he calms down.'" For Grosz, war was human ugliness raised to its highest power. *Explosion* captures the moment when civilization is ripped apart by the power of its own capacity for evil, falling into the abyss that it has itself excavated.

Grosz's descriptions of Berlin in November 1918 conjure images of a city where all that remains after the catastrophe depicted in *Explosion* are ruins. The former capital of the German Reich now resembles "a gray corpse of stone." Grosz writes:

"Cracks ran through the walls of the buildings, stucco had broken off, paint had peeled, and in the dirty, dead eyes of the broken windows, from which people had once kept a lookout for those who would never return, you could see the traces of fallen tears."

By the final months of the war, Grosz has come to feel that it isn't enough to try to influence society with his art. So the revolution that reaches Berlin a few days before the end of the fighting is all the more enticing. It seems to offer the only way to transform his rage and disgust with the old Germany into action. Grosz now wants to take part in the explosion; indeed he wants to *be* the explosion. He becomes a popular speaker at gatherings of the radical Spartacist League. Somewhere deep inside, he must realize that he disdains the revolutionary protagonists and their political gestures as much as he hates Imperial German society and the war. But in his deeds, he becomes an advocate of the new age whose activism and theatricality fit in well with his own personality. He particularly enjoys thundering on and on about the creation of a new educational system. Higher education shall no longer be a privilege of the wealthy! Academies and universities shall be open to all! On the last day of 1918, along with several of his artist friends, the painter joins the newly founded German Communist Party (KPD). Rosa Luxemburg herself hands him his membership card.

ON NOVEMBER 4, 1918, Walter Gropius travels from Berlin to Vienna to demand custody of his daughter Manon from his estranged wife, Alma Mahler-Gropius. In a letter, he made his case for why he wanted custody. Alma, he wrote, was apparently unwilling to put an end to her love affair with writer Franz

Werfel. Moreover, even if Manon came to live with him, Alma would still have her daughter from her first marriage and her newborn son, Martin. When Alma reads the letter, she breaks out in tears and remains disconsolate for the rest of the day.

That afternoon, both her husband and her lover turn up. In a dramatic moment, Alma declares that she's decided to leave both of them. From now on, she wants to live on her own. But her children, she insists, are staying with her. Gropius, stunned by Alma's determination, already regrets his harsh demands, made in desperation, and asks his wife to forgive him.

The Gropiuses' marriage has lasted only three years. They first met in 1910 during a restorative stay at the cosmopolitan spa town of Tobelbad, Austria, while Alma's first husband, Gustav Mahler, was still alive. Alma felt neglected by her famous composer husband, and a spark was ignited between her and Gropius. But aside from causing a marital crisis in the Mahler household, which ended when the composer promised to pay more attention to his much younger spouse, this first encounter led to nothing. When Mahler died the following year, the two initially kept their distance from each other. The young widow immediately began a liaison with the mercurial, pathologically jealous young painter Oskar Kokoschka.

Then the Great War broke out, and Gropius was called up. It was the beginning of nearly four years of continuous deployment on the western front and in Italy. A brief furlough in February 1915 was the first chance for him and Alma to see each other again. A short time earlier, the now thirty-five-year-old widow had reestablished contact, and their former passion was rekindled the moment they met face-to-face. From that point on they wrote each other nearly every day. Alma spiced up her letters with expressions of tenderness and wild erotic allusions. In August 1915, during another of Gropius's furloughs, the two eloped to Berlin. After the wedding, however, Alma's letters took on a different tone. Gone were the protestations of love and desire. She began to complain about the unbearably long separations, and Gropius's "secrecy" and "neglect." Tortured by jealousy, she suspected he was being unfaithful and visiting bordellos. Their correspondence makes little reference to the fact that Gropius was risking his life every day on the front lines or that the young architect was finding it increasingly difficult to endure being part of the "always destructive, never constructive business of war." He didn't want to burden her with such unpleasant truths in his letters, and for her part, she never took the slightest interest in the conflict.

In October 1916, Alma Mahler-Gropius gave birth to a daughter, named Manon after her paternal grandmother. She was pregnant with a second child in the final summer of the war when Gropius was sent to a Vienna hospital. Although he wasn't seriously injured, he was badly traumatized: the sole survivor of an artillery attack near the village of Soissons, he had been dragged from the rubble of a bombed-out house. As soon as he could get out of bed, he went to see Alma. It was August 25, 1918. While he was waiting for his wife, he overheard a telephone call in which she spoke in a suspiciously intimate tone with another man. Enraged, Gropius confronted her, and in the end she confessed. The previous winter, unable to bear waiting for her husband any longer, she had begun an affair with Werfel. The child in her womb was almost certainly his. The news literally knocked Gropius, already weakened by the psychological and physical effects of being buried alive, off his feet. He fell to the floor "as if hit by lightning."

The next day, Gropius regained his composure. He set out to confront his wife's lover at his apartment. Werfel was sleeping and didn't hear Gropius knocking. But the architect left behind his visiting card with the chivalrous words: "Go easy on Alma, or there could be a misfortune. All the agitation—it would be terrible if the child were to die on us." Gropius spent the next few days in his hospital bed, tortured by his thoughts, until he was called back—much too soon—to the front and the war-wasted landscape of the Argonne Forest. Barely recovered from his trauma, Gropius had to leave the crucible of jealousy and recrimination and return to the fire of battle.

In October 1918, the military doctors finally took pity on the poor lieutenant, who was utterly exhausted from four years of war, and granted him an extended furlough. Only upon returning to Berlin, where signs were accumulating that the war was almost over, did he realize how precarious his situation was. For four years, he had devoted all his energy and talent to the battle against Germany's enemies. He had been wounded three times and had been awarded the Iron Cross. And just when he no longer had the strength to go on, when he desperately needed to be loved and cared for, his marriage was in ruins. He hadn't worked as an architect in four years, nor had he maintained his previously excellent contacts. Given the dire economic circumstances, particularly in Berlin, he worried whether he would be able to survive. "If I come home and no longer draw my lieutenant's salary," he feared, "I'll have nothing—with inflation all around."

In his desperation, Gropius realizes that he'll have to do something fundamentally different. It's as though he's been struck by a beam of light, he writes. Although the first projects he had done

before the war had put him at the head of the architectural avant-
garde, he'd always been politically conservative. But now, in
November 1918, he feels the urgent need to forge a completely
new path. "After the war," he writes, "it dawned on me . . . that
the time was over for all the old stuff." Traveling to Vienna and
confronting Alma are the first steps in reorganizing his private
life. At the same time, he goes door to door in Berlin looking for
a job as an architect or for commissions to set up an architectural
practice of his own.

Gropius also sees the need for change beyond his individual
concerns. He wants to be part of the enormous transformation
setting everything around him in motion. Together with other
artists and architects, he founds the "Work Council on the Arts."
Along with fellow architect Bruno Taut, he draws up a manifesto
for a new architecture. "A building is the direct carrier of spiritual values, shaper of the sensibilities of the general public which
slumbers today but will awake tomorrow," Taut writes in his 1919
essay "An Architectural Program," which emerged directly from
the Work Council. "Only a total revolution in the realm of the
spiritual can create this building." The two men dream of *Volks-
bauten* (buildings for the people) constructed on free land outside
the densely populated urban areas: "The big city, rotted to its
core, will disappear just like the old powers. The future lies
in newly won land that will support itself." Such model settlements are conceived as having all the infrastructure of a proper
city: streets, squares, shops, hotels, restaurants, and cultural
and educational centers. The new suburbs, Gropius and his colleagues dream, will lead to a new society. Based on the Garden
City Movement, orderly, clean, equitable, and healthful, these suburbs are intended to encourage reconstruction after years of

destruction and become the architectural backdrop for a new era, whose promise continues to resonate in today's affordable state-built housing projects. Gropius and Taut are designing a world to replace the one destroyed by Grosz's explosion. They are resurrecting life from the barren landscapes of war, from the ruins of the old Reich and the old social order.

Gropius is not only a visionary; he is also an adept organizer, thanks to his wartime experience as an officer, and soon becomes president of the council. He thoroughly enjoys the coming together of creative minds and becomes convinced that the war was necessary to spark an "internal cleansing" in his own life and to tear down the old repressive barriers in Germany. He can hardly wait to start building the cities of the future he has envisioned.

WHILE LOUISE WEISS is trying to keep up with the breathtaking pace of events from her small, blue-wallpapered Paris office, Hyacinthe Philouze holds court in the ostentatious front salon rooms on the same floor, where he chats, uncorks bottles of wine, smokes, and receives an endless parade of guests. He even has the kitchen redecorated for evening revelries by an artist of no talent. Wine and champagne flow in rivers, and young women of questionable repute, the kind who don't mind a pinch on the behind, are invited to participate. When the neighbors complain about the noise, he simply bribes the concierge to ignore the ruckus.

Louise has no time for such merrymaking. There are revolutions going on everywhere she turns. The shock waves from Russia are spreading across the globe, jolting not just Europe and the Ottoman Empire but the Americas, Japan and China as well. Against the wishes of Philouze, who would prefer to publish a profitable paper and not risk trouble with the authorities, the tone of *L'Europe nouvelle* is becoming more provocative. A new world is rising on the ruins of the old, and Louise wants to know and report everything about it. She and her colleagues are convinced that it will take many revolutions throughout Europe and elsewhere, not just in Russia, to get the world back on track after the great inferno. Massive transformations are taking place in Germany, Austria-Hungary, Eastern Europe, the Balkans, the Baltics, and the Ukraine. But what about France, the mother of revolution? Is the revolutionary tide being turned back at the borders of the victorious Allies? Even though France won the war, the country—so it seems to Louise—is ripe for radical change: in her editorials she calls for new elections, for the expansion of workers' rights, and for a new policy toward the colonies. Above all, she argues, French women finally need to be given full civil rights, including first and foremost the right to vote.

Revolution is without doubt the correct term for the events in Milan Štefánik's native Czechoslovakia, which Louise follows with enthusiasm. For some time now the populace of Bohemia has been engaged in open rebellion against Habsburg domination. There are demonstrations, mass protests, and strikes. While Milan is in Siberia trying to save the remnants of an army that is supposed to form one of the pillars of a new Czechoslovakian state, his compatriot Edvard Beneš has drawn up the constitutional principles for the new nation, even if for now it only exists on paper. Beneš often spends long hours in the editorial offices of *L'Europe nouvelle* and is beginning to influence the outlook of the magazine. One day when Louise, disgusted by Philouze's

escapades, decides to quit her job, it is Beneš who convinces her
to carry on. He appreciates what he has in her and her magazine.
She is keeping the Czechoslovakian cause alive for the general
public and for many influential politicians. Thanks to Louise's
articles, the world knows that Beneš formed a provisional Czech
government in Paris in September 1918, and that on October 18
it proclaimed Czech independence. In November, with revolution breaking out in Vienna, Louise explains to her readers that
Kaiser Karl has renounced his powers, finally clearing the way
for a new Czechoslovakian state.

FOR ALMA MAHLER-Gropius—composer, Viennese society lady,
and muse—Walter Gropius's revolutionary activities offer at least
a temporary respite. Her husband has confronted her lover
Werfel both in writing and in person. He has asked her to end the
affair and join him in Berlin—and threatened consequences if she
does not. But with a sleepwalker's unerring sense of direction,
she has followed her own inner compass, which is pointing
more steadily toward the young, unusually talented, and increasingly successful poet. After the scene on November 4 and Gropius's
collapse, his opposition to the extramarital affair evaporated. In
a matter of days he is preoccupied with the revolution in Berlin.
This in turn allowed Alma and Werfel to take the first steps
toward a joint future, one in which they can be together without
having to play hide and seek. A few weeks later, she writes: "A
glorious night. Werfel was with me. We were wound together
and felt the most intimate intimacy of our souls, which are
bound to each other in love. It is a great turning point in my life."
    At the same time, though, she considers it an "inner truth"

that her love for Werfel doesn't necessarily blot out her earlier amorous relationships. "They all go on at once," she writes. "I can't deny any of them. Gustav Mahler, Oskar Kokoschka, Gropius . . . everything was and is true!" When her youthful love Gustav Klimt dies, she writes: "How close we were once! And I've never stopped loving him—albeit in greatly changed form." Every man she loved has left behind traces and memories. She neither wants to deny or forgo them, nor is she able to. Unlike in the old Vienna, the capital of the Austro-Hungarian monarchy, in which the façade of female virtue had to be maintained at all costs, by the end of the war such amorous ambivalence is no longer inevitably censured by society. "I'm skeptical about marriage, which is nothing but state-sanctioned tyranny, and to get around it, I choose voluntary ties," Alma writes, in what amounts to a miniature sexual revolution.

Alma Mahler-Gropius experiences the revolution in Vienna, which breaks out on November 12, 1918, a few days after the unrest in Berlin, in her redecorated music salon. In her eyes the "so-called 'revolution'" is "simultaneously droll and eerie." She writes: "We watched along as the proletariat marched to parliament. Ugly figures . . . red flags . . . unpleasant weather . . . rain and slush, all over gray and more gray. Then the alleged shots from the parliament building. A storm! The same pale people who had stood in orderly rows now stormed back, yelling and undignified. I had some visitors. We got out my pistols." The day before, Kaiser Karl I had given up power and fled Vienna. The demise of the German Reich has brought down the Austro-Hungarian Empire as well.

On November 13, Franz Werfel is standing outside Alma's door. He is wearing a uniform and asks for her permission to join the demonstrators. For her, this is a "false revolution," one she opposes "with all her heart." But Werfel begs her until she finally takes his head in her hands, kisses him, and then dismisses him like a young boy who just won't learn. When the poet returns in the middle of the night, "his eyes were a sea of red, his face was puffy and covered in filth, while his hands and uniform were in a terrible state," she writes. "He reeked of cheap alcohol and tobacco." Proudly, the poet describes to her how he had addressed the crowd from a bench on the Vienna Ring, calling for them to ransack the banks, and how he had formed a "Red Guard" with some artist friends. Alma chastises him sternly: "If you did anything nice, you'd look nice now." She then sends the filthy, smelly revolutionary to a friend's house to sleep off his intoxication. She's not about to let him into her home like that.

The police gets wind of Werfel's revolutionary activity, and in the end, it is none other than Gropius who sets off to warn him that he's been betrayed by an informant. The poet goes underground until the situation blows over. Not for an instant does Gropius consider exploiting the circumstances and letting the police remove his rival for him. It's not just basic decency that causes him to act this way; he's also worried for Alma. Believing that her lover is risking his reputation, and possibly more, she's on the verge of a nervous breakdown.

Unlike the men in her life, Alma has hated the revolution from its very inception. Even later she finds it impossible to reconcile herself to "red Vienna." As much as she profited from the liberties of a new era in her private life, all the more profoundly did she mourn the passing of the belle époque. Months later, she writes that she wishes the Kaiser would come back along with "the most terrible archdukes who live at the expense of the country." She adds that she only longs for the return of "splendor from above" and nothing but "silence and subservience from the slave class upon which humanity is built. The cry of the masses is music straight from hell."

NGUYEN TAT THAHN'S room in Paris is so tiny there's hardly space for a narrow iron bed, a table, and a chair. The dishwasher has moved from London to the French capital and is living in a cheap hotel in a working-class district in the east of the city. He gets up early in the morning and prepares a bowl of rice with fish; he eats half and saves the rest for supper. Winter has set in, and he makes sure to put a brick in the hotel kitchen stove when he goes to work. In the evening he removes it from the embers, wraps it in newspaper, carries it home, and places it under his bedding so he doesn't freeze at night. Nguyen lives off a variety of odd jobs, spending his free time in one of the municipal libraries to read and improve his French. He especially likes Émile Zola and Anatole France. Now and then, if he's not too tired, he attends political lectures.

Since he's been in Paris, Nguyen has gotten to know a different side of the French. In his native Indochina they appeared exclusively as a master race who violently oppressed and exploited the local inhabitants on the pretext of bringing them Western civilization. He has seen much of the world in his long time at sea and learned that his own people aren't the only ones to suffer this fate. He still trembles at the memory of a scene in Senegal at the port of Dakar. A storm had prevented the ship he'd signed on to from entering the harbor. The waves were running so high that not even a lifeboat could be lowered. To make contact with the ship, the harbor control ordered an African to swim out to it. Knowing that he could not refuse an order, the unlucky man sprang from the quay into the water. For the first few strokes, he managed to keep his head up, but as soon as he left the protection of the harbor, the waves battered him so viciously that he lost consciousness and drowned. After that a second, third, and fourth swimmer were sent out. None of them reached the ship, and none of them survived. The scene, which reminded Nguyen of things he'd experienced in his youth, etched itself deeply in his memory.

But in the motherland of the empire, he discovered that not all French were rich and powerful. As soon his ship docked in Marseilles, he noticed the prostitutes who visited the sailors on board. Why do the French not civilize their own people before they try it with us, Nguyen asked his shipmates. Later, in Paris, he discovered that whole districts of the City of Light were utterly dilapidated, and the people there lived in extreme poverty. It fascinated him that in France the disparity between rich and poor was not simply a fact of life but a political issue, and he began attending socialist meetings more often. At first he just listened, but in time he himself took to the podium, speaking in calm, measured words. He always knew how to pick up on the topic of the meeting and apply it to Indochina and other colonies. Because he was usually the only speaker who wasn't French, people listened to him. For the most part his impression was that the French were friendlier in their home country than they were in Indochina. But perhaps that was because Nguyen was becoming more like them; in any case he remained unfailingly polite and reserved. He was a guest in France and wanted to be taken seriously, and not come off like some two-bit revolutionary. That was the only way he could realize his dream of an independent Vietnam.

At the same time, it became painfully clear to him that French socialists only took a limited interest in conditions in the colonies. One of the few left-wing newspapers that even bothered to report on Indochina was *Le Peuple*. Its headquarters was in Brussels, but since the end of the war it maintained a subsidiary editorial office in France. The man in charge there was the socialist Jean Longuet, a grandson of Karl Marx, who had a seat in the National Assembly.

One day Nguyen introduces himself to Longuet and is surprised at the very cordial reception—the French politician calls him "dear comrade" and tells him he should write articles about Indochina for *Le Peuple*. Nguyen is excited even though he knows his French isn't good enough to compose even the shortest of news items. But he doesn't want to let this opportunity pass him by. He asks a compatriot whose French is much better than his own to write short articles based on his ideas. His countryman agrees but has some questions about who should sign as author of the pieces. So Nguyen proposes the pseudonym Nguyen Ai Quoc, which means "Nguyen the Patriot." Only after some time does Nguyen, who isn't always satisfied with his ghostwriter's work, dare write his own articles. At first they consist only of a few lines that require substantial editing. But by comparing the texts he hands in with the printed versions, Nguyen learns from his mistakes so that his articles get markedly better—and longer.

MARINA YURLOVA CONTINUES her journey east along the Trans-Siberian Railway. The landscape has disappeared underneath a thick blanket of snow. From the window of her car, all she can see is white, so pervasive that it seems to press in on the train. In the midst of this seemingly infinite expanse, the brakes squeal and the locomotive slows and comes to a halt in the middle of nowhere. When the officers ask a conductor why the train is making an unscheduled stop, they receive an unsettling answer. The city of Irkutsk, the next big station on their route, has fallen into the hands of the Bolsheviks, and the conductors are refusing to continue the journey. Heading back is impossible as well because the last town they passed through, Tomsk, is also said to be no longer safe. The train stays where it is, a black worm in the white vastness.

The soldiers set up camp next to the rapidly cooling locomotive. They pitch a few tents and build a large fire in the snow at which several of the aristocratic Russian ladies aboard the train warm themselves. What now? Should they wait until the Bolsheviks arrive on one of the next trains and kill them all? At the end of the day, one of the officers loses patience. He's going to disguise himself as a peasant, he says, and try to pass through Irkutsk unnoticed. Manchuria, to the east of the city, is said to be unoccupied. Many of those present support the plan, but the crucial question is how to make it to Irkutsk on foot in the middle of the Siberian winter. The city is still hundreds of kilometers away.

Soldiers sent out to reconnoiter the area stumble across a Mongolian village. After some tense negotiations with the inhabitants, they explain their plan and agree on a price for some warm clothes and guides to lead them along a horse path to Irkutsk. Almost a hundred people are willing to go along with this and use their travel funds to pay the Mongols. A short time later, the Czech soldiers and Russian travelers are tramping in a long line across the snow-covered plain. Mongol men ride ahead of them on horses so small the riders' feet practically scrape the ground.

Their weather-worn faces give no indication of what they think about the intruders who have strayed onto their land. They themselves could find their way in their sleep, although the path is buried in many places under the snow. They also know where there are small settlements in which the group can rest.

To Marina it seems like the march through the monotonous, icy landscape will never end. After several days, the expedition reaches a Russian village, empty save for two or three dead White Russians. Farther along on their trek, the trail is littered with two hundred bodies frozen black in the snow. The image will haunt Marina in her dreams.

Days later, the Mongol guides suddenly disappear, as though they've been swallowed by the earth. The group sends out scouts. Several hours later the quiet is pierced by a locomotive whistle not far off, and the scouts return with good news. Irkutsk is only forty-eight away, and there's a Russian village just an hour's walk from where they are. But the best news is that Czechoslovakian units have retaken the town. Soon, Marina can see Irkutsk's towers rising in the distance. When they arrive in the city, it feels as though they've been saved, even though it's merely one more station on their journey, and their limbs ache unbearably as they begin to thaw out after days of freezing cold.

IN HER WELL-heated house in Richmond, Virginia Woolf has been working with immense concentration on her novel *Night and Day*. Leonard has limited the amount of time she's allowed to work, but she does have time to read the newspapers that bring the world to this London suburb. On November 9, as reports arrive about the unrest in German port cities, it is still unclear if the German Reich is coming to an end. Woolf notes in her diary that the Kaiser "still wears a phantom kind of crown." She adds: "Otherwise there is revolution, & a kind of partial awakening, one fancies, on the part of the people to the unreality of the whole affair. Suppose we wake up, too?"

The writer finds it not unlikely that a victorious England might soon face difficult times. With seismographic precision, she registers the small changes that the transition from war to peace has brought to Richmond and her immediate environs. For instance, an incident she witnessed on Shaftsbury Avenue in which a common soldier threatened, for all to hear, to put a bullet through the head of an officer. Woolf is positive that scenes like this signal that change is afoot. The drunken soldiers and surging crowds on the street are also signs of a world in motion. But where is it headed? "Peace," she writes,

> "is rapidly dissolving into the light of common day." For the people of Richmond, priorities are shifting faster than anyone expected. "Instead of feeling all day & going home through dark streets that the whole people, willing or not, were concentrated on a single point, one feels now that the whole bunch has burst asunder & flown off with the utmost vigour in different directions. We are once more a nation of individuals. Some people care for football; others for racing; others for dancing; others for—oh, well, they're all running about very gaily, getting out of their uniforms & taking up their private affairs again."

Will the end of the war and the lack of a common enemy exacerbate the tensions within English society? Woolf finds it difficult to answer this question clearly: peace, she writes "dropped like a great stone into my pool, & and the eddies are still rippling out to the further bank."

Night and Day, which is published at the beginning of 1919, explores the questions that the war has stirred up in Virginia Woolf. Centering on five characters with complex relationships, the novel depicts the constraints of prewar English society and shows how women in particular are trapped within a net of conventions, rules, and marital subjugation. Might not such unbearable social claustrophobia have helped cause the war, she asks. Which "freedom" did Britain defend in the conflict? Was this society really worth the deaths of so many people who perished protecting it?

In conversation, Woolf hears the most diverse opinions about what the end of the war will mean for British politics. Several of her friends, including the painter Roger Fry, are convinced that England is on the brink of revolution. "The Lower classes are bitter, impatient, powerful, & of course lacking in reason," she writes. "The impenetrable wall of the middle class conservative was never more stolid; dynamite may smash it to powder; but—it is impervious to reason."

TERENCE MACSWINEY SPENDS the heady days of November 1918 with other arrested Sinn Féin fighters in the filthy cargo hold of a ship. The vessel has set sail from Dublin headed for the English mainland. As soon as it leaves the harbor, high seas make themselves felt. Most of the men get seasick right away and lie about miserably in their berths. MacSwiney finds a small porthole that can be opened, breathes in the fresh ocean air and lets the spray from the waves splash across his face. He doesn't care if he gets wet. Who knows when he'll be able to breathe fresh air again?

The Irishman is already acquainted with his destination—the imposing redbrick walls of Lincoln Prison, in the east of England, which looks a bit like a medieval castle—from past stretches inside. Over the years he's gotten to know a number of Irish and English jails. Just before the start of the Great War, he joined a clandestine army, the Irish Volunteers, in his home town of Cork. Their goal was Irish independence. MacSwiney believed that a small avant-garde of fighters prepared to sacrifice their lives could inspire the entire Irish nation to rise up. He had previously argued his case in newspaper articles, poems and books, but now he worked underground, recruiting men, procuring uniforms and weapons, and raising money for the day when the decisive rebellion would come.

The British police have been on MacSwiney's trail for quite a while. Although never convicted of any major crimes, he still keeps landing in the courts and in prison. And despite the fact that Cork remained calm during the 1916 Easter Uprising—something MacSwiney will always consider a personal failure—they continue to pursue him. His wife, Muriel, who hails from a wealthy Cork family, rarely sees him, as it has been too dangerous for him to stay in one place for any length of time. At least when he's in jail Muriel knows where he is, and the two are able to write each other tender love letters. In June 1918, when Muriel gave birth to their daughter, Máire, she had to take the baby to the visiting room of a prison so her father could hold her in his arms. In their letters, the couple reassure each other that the Irish cause was more important than their personal happiness. Let no man be afraid, MacSwiney writes, "that those he loves may be tried in the fire, but let him, to the best of his strength, show them how to stand the ordeal, and then trust to the greatness of Truth and the virtue of a loyal nature to bring each one forth in triumph."

At Lincoln Prison, MacSwiney quickly falls back into the all-too-familiar, monotonous jail routine. The rare bits of news from his homeland are the only things that bring the excitement of the Irish revolution to his cell. Before Christmas, MacSwiney learns that—despite, or perhaps because of, his imprisonment—his countrymen have elected him as an Irish representative to the House of Commons. The pro-independence Sinn Féin, for which MacSwiney had stood, has won a landslide victory on December 14, 1918, against the moderate Irish Parliamentary Party and Sinn Féin's mortal enemies, the Unionists. But instead of taking their seats, the Sinn Féin deputies decide to pursue a far more radical course of action, unilaterally declaring an independent Ireland and establishing a separate Irish parliament, the Dáil Éireann. MacSwiney only hears about it secondhand when the Dáil convenes for the first time on January 21, 1919, and ratifies an Irish constitution. What he wouldn't have given to be able to take up his appointed place among the deputies!

On that very day—as MacSwiney will hear in prison and later read in the newspapers—his comrades Séan Treacy and Dan Breen are lurking with seven other independence fighters behind an embankment on the road to the Soloheadbeg quarry near Tipperary. A transport of gelignite is on its way there under police guard, and the Irishmen intend to intercept it. Their real purpose is less to get their hands on the explosives than to start a war. The attack is intended as a signal to resume armed resistance to British domination. The men wait several torturous days before a scout finally spots the vehicle approaching in the distance.

Everyone takes his post and tries to keep his nerves under control. The horse-drawn cart, which comes ever closer, is escorted by policemen specially trained for this sort of situation, while the Irish fighters have hardly ever used their weapons. They've had no chance to practice firing their guns—ammunition was too scarce, and they were afraid that the loud reports of their revolvers would give them away.

When the cart reaches the point of ambush, the Irishmen yell at the police to surrender, but the officers are having none of that. They duck behind the cart, cock their rifles, and direct them menacingly at the hidden attackers. For a moment, everything stands still, tensely silent, with the two sides pointing their guns at each other. Then nine revolvers fire from behind the cover of the embankment, and two policemen fall dead to the ground. The noise alarms people who live in the area. Within a few minutes, a crowd gathers at the scene of the violence, and soon hundreds of police arrive. The attackers rush to jump aboard the cart, lashing the old horse to get all the speed out of him. The explosives bounce up and down. The Irishmen have heard that if shaken too much, they could detonate. Finally they arrive at a location with a pre-dug hole to hide what they've captured. Then they disappear, aided by a heavy snowfall.

AROUND THIS TIME, Mohandas Karamchand Gandhi is in the mountain town of Matheran recovering from a near-lethal bout of the Spanish flu. His physician, Dr. Dalal, promises a full recovery, but only if he's prepared to revoke his pledge to do without milk. Gandhi is still so weak that the mere thought of food fills him with fear, and it hurts terribly whenever he tries to relieve himself. Nonetheless, the decision to violate his principles weighs on his conscience. Only after he has pondered the situation for a long time do his survival instinct and his will to complete India's independence win out. Cow and buffalo milk are out of the question for the Mahatma, but he does allow some goat milk to be brought to him.

While his strength is returning, Gandhi receives an alarming bit of political news. The end of the war has rendered obsolete certain emergency laws that the British colonial authorities had used to curb the growing Indian independence movement. To compensate, a new commission under Judge Sidney Rowlatt has devised a fresh package of laws that give the British rulers free rein to quell any public unrest. Gandhi begins to organize resistance to this legislation as soon as he hears of it. "The idea came to me last night in a dream that we should call upon the country to observe a general hartal [hunger strike]," he writes. "Let all the people of India suspend their business on that day and observe the day as one of fasting and prayer." If Indians follow him, he thinks, it will be an impressive victory for his strategy of passive resistance and might even prevent or at least soften the legislation. With such high hopes, Gandhi contacts fellow independence activists throughout the country.

AFTER THE SAILORS' rebellion and the cease-fire, the ships' crews in Wilhelmshaven resume their bustling activity on the docks. Their dutiful industriousness reminds Richard Stumpf of 1914, except that now the cranes aren't loading munitions but rather unloading them, to be stored away in the clammy coal dust of the warehouses. The shells are the same type that only a short time ago German seamen were inscribing with sarcastic greetings addressed to their English targets. Now the seamen are preparing to turn over the German war fleet to the English, in accordance with the armistice agreement.

Getting rid of these machines of destruction could be seen as a good day for Germany, but to Stumpf it seems that he and his comrades are preparing for a funeral. In his eyes, Germany's surrender of its warships is not the beginning of a general disarmament that might bring peace to the world but an act of betrayal. And that is how he regards the entire armistice. He is convinced the disgrace will burden Germany for centuries. One day, these German warships that are being handed over to the English may even direct their fire against Germany itself.

Life on board ship has changed fundamentally. Discipline is lax, and the new soldiers' council hasn't succeeded in establishing calm and order. Theft and fistfights have become everyday reality. But at least the crews have enough to eat as well as a ration of rum punch three times a week. All this fine food and drink comes from the officers' mess. There is even sufficient whiskey to go on a respectable bender, which is how the delegates to the soldiers' council celebrate their victory. Singing and braying loudly, they stagger around on deck. What was it that one of speakers said on the second day of the revolution? "We rebelled because they treated us like children." That's right, Stumpf thinks, and now they're acting like children.

For some time Stumpf has been eagerly waiting to be discharged. But now that it's about to happen, he feels nothing. There will be no music, no flowers, and no honor guard. On the contrary, the massive war effort for which he risked his life will end in the shame of defeat, the catastrophe of a lost fleet, the disgrace of an unjust armistice, the weakness of a new regime, and, worst of all, the nagging thought of being complicit in the rebellion that helped bring all this about.

On November 18, 1918, Stumpf watches the warship *Friedrich der Grosse* leave Wilhelmshaven for its final journey under German command. It is accompanied by the SMS *König Albert* and will soon be followed by the rest of the ships, and after that, the submarines. The crews stand on the pier, holding their kit bags, and watch the floating fortresses disappear over the horizon.

IT'S GOOD THAT Wilhelm, the former crown prince of Prussia, doesn't have to watch as the disarmed imperial fleet, once the pride of his father and the entire Reich, sails toward England— of all countries! In Maastricht, Wilhelm and his entourage are put up in the prefecture hall. An angry, shouting crowd gathers on the square in front of the building. Hours pass. The hands on the clock over the fireplace seem to stop. One of Wilhelm's companions is rolling from side to side on a red velvet sofa, groaning with stomach pains. Wilhelm's thoughts swirl around the recent days and hours, memories of the war, his wife, Duchess Cecilie, and his children, who are back at the New Palace in Potsdam. Not far from the tumult of the German capital.

It takes almost two weeks for the crown prince's fate to be decided. The new German government has requested his extradition; the other side demands he be interned. After a complicated set of negotiations, international diplomats agree that the man upon whom all those wishing for a restoration of the monarchy can project their hopes will be exiled to an island in the Dutch bay of Zuiderzee. When he arrives in the port of Enkhuizen, Wilhelm is greeted by reporters, flashing cameras, and shouts and curses. The Dutch make no bones about showing the former crown prince what they think he deserves, drawing their hands across their throat in s slitting motion.

Wilhelm is ferried across the foggy waters to Wieringen Island, where he is now meant to pass his days. There he is driven in a creaky carriage that smells of old, mildewed leather to the village of Oosterland. His destination is a group of small cottages under a gloomy winter sky. The carriage stops in front of the pastor's house, where the former crown prince sees the two cold, sparse furnished rooms where he will spend his exile.

IN BERLIN RUMORS are going around that the former Kaiser Wilhelm has been murdered. Käthe Kollwitz hears them on November 12, 1918, as she is accompanying her friend Constance Harding-Krayl in her search for a job. At the post-revolutionary police directorate on Alexanderplatz, the two of them become acquainted with the bureaucratic labyrinth of the new regime, where no one knows anything, no one is accountable, and where everyone gets sent from one office to another without getting what they want. When Kollwitz and her friend give up in frustration, a guard at the main entrance refuses to let them leave through the main entrance because they don't have identity papers. They have to exit the building through a back door. Their description of the government offices evokes Heinrich Mann's novel *Man of Straw*, which will appear for the first time in German in a couple of days. A Russian translation had been published as early as 1915.

The streetcar is completely packed as Kollwitz makes her way to her studio—these days the train stations are jammed full of soldiers returning home. She has heard that in the troop trains coming from the front, men have regularly been crushed to death. In the middle of the pushing and shoving on the streetcar there's an old woman with a crate containing a cat that meows softly. "The cat was spooked by gunshots and fled into my house," the woman says. Now she, too, has had all she can take of gunshots and is fleeing to the countryside with the cat. The people around her laugh, amused.

Ever since the collapse of the old regime, Kollwitz has hoped that socialism would win the day, but now she is unable to ignore the realities of the situation. She thoroughly rejects how the communist Spartacus brigades are behaving and decides to keep her distance from them, in part because she realizes how resistant the general populace is to such a radically different social order. Employing violence in order to erect a socialist state against the will of the majority of Germans seems to her a contradiction in terms. She tells herself to be patient, have faith in the democratic path of a constitutional convention, and hope that Germans will "gradually grow into socialism . . . although it's somewhat disappointing when you think you can feel something and you're told you'll have to wait." But will those "who can only stand to benefit if socialism is implemented" be prepared to wait? Or will they now try everything in their power to strike while the iron is hot?

THE DEFEAT OF the army, the ignominious abdication of the Kaiser, and the end of the Reich have left a vacuum. In Germany and elsewhere, the forces of order that had previously held together governments and whole societies have weakened or collapsed completely. Revolutionary movements of various stripes are exploiting the new opportunities. Suddenly it's possible to call thousands of people to the streets or stand on a balcony and declare a new regime. In Germany and elsewhere, many people wonder how it is possible to restore the stability of the old world while giving it a new foundation. The German Reich and several of the former member states of the Austro-Hungarian and Ottoman Empires are on the verge of chaos. The great challenge in this situation is how to create a new, broadly recognized central authority and place in its charge the bureaucratic workings of the state, as well as the police and the military.

Matthias Erzberger is extremely irritated upon his return to Berlin on November 13. Although no one asked his permission, his official car is now flying the red flag of socialism. He asks for it to be replaced by the black-red-and-gold flag of the German democracy and national unification movements of the nineteenth century, which will become the official banner of the Weimar Republic. The extraordinarily tense atmosphere on the streets immediately attracts his notice. Violence can break out again at any second. A further revolution to replace the new popular representatives and the new Social Democratic chancellor, Friedrich Ebert, with a Communist leadership seems entirely possible. The new government's minister of war, Heinrich Scheuch, who calls on him that evening in civilian clothing, tells him that it is no longer possible to guarantee military protection from the revolutionary forces.

Erzberger had traveled to Compiègne as the envoy of the Kaiser. He is received back in Berlin on November 13 by the five "people's deputies" who are part of Ebert's new government. Erzberger briefs the new men in power about the negotiations and the first steps taken toward fulfilling the conditions of the armistice. To his great relief, the deputies tell him the new government recognizes that the delegation he led worked "for the welfare of the people in a most difficult time." The recently created armistice commission will henceforth monitor the fulfillment of Germany's agreement with the Allies. With that, Erzberger's initiative has the blessing of the new regime, which, like its predecessor, has no choice but to recognize the inevitable. The meeting also clarifies his own future role, and he departs with the certainty that he will serve the new government as he did the old one. This is a useful compromise for both sides. Since Erzberger is a member of the Catholic Center Party, his continued activity signals that the new social-democratic government is open to working with moderate bourgeois politicians. At the same time, the move rescues Erzberger's professional career, helps ensure the survival of his party in the new government, and hopefully will prevent Germany from lurching further to the left. This is not a step Erzberger takes out of a deep personal conviction, however. For him, the revolution remains a fundamental mistake, the consequence of the old regime's failings and ultimate collapse. On one occasion, Erzberger complains to the art collector and pacifist Count Harry Kessler that the military commanders who ordered their troops not to use their weapons against the revolutionaries in Berlin should themselves be put before a firing squad.

Erzberger nevertheless devotes himself to his new task, which consists first and foremost of ensuring compliance with conditions of the armistice. In addition, he tries to find several thousand reliable soldiers to guard the most important government buildings in Berlin. That proves impossible, but the initiative still earns him the hatred of all those who want to expand their revolution. He's convinced, like Chancellor Ebert, that the German people must elect a national assembly to draw up a constitution as soon as possible. In his opinion, that is the only way that the new regime—the product of revolutionary unrest, spontaneously formed councils of workers and soldiers, and a couplike remaking of the government—can achieve true legitimacy.

ON NOVEMBER 20, along with thousands of other Berliners, Käthe Kollwitz squeezes herself into the main hall of the Potsdam station. The train she and her husband, Karl, are so anxiously awaiting is late. When it finally arrives and the homecoming soldiers pour out of the carriage doors, the platform is cordoned off. Kollwitz climbs on a fence and scans the gray faces of the returnees with a hammering heart. At last she spots Hans in the crowd. He sees her, too, and waves. Mother and son soon fall into each other's arms.

Back at home, Hans's seat at the table is decorated with flowers, and there's wine with the meal. They drink to his return, to "Germany's life and future," and raise a glass as well to the memory of his brother, Peter, whose seat will remain forever empty. It's strange how little pain there is now in remembering Peter, Kollwitz thinks. She used to believe the wounds would never heal. But that's no longer true.

Should they unfurl the German flag from their window to greet the homecoming soldiers? And if so, which one? Kollwitz discusses the matter intensely with her husband. Ultimately they decide on the red-white-and-black banner of the German Reich, the "dear German flag." But they add a red streamer symbolizing the republic and a pine bough wreath for all "the ones who will never return." Kollwitz is not alone in these sentiments. Many of her friends have also lost children.

AT THIS POINT, according to his autobiography, Rudolf Höss is still on his way back home from the front. Under no circumstances did he want to be taken prisoner by the British in Palestine, so he, as his unit's junior officer, asked the men under his command if they were willing to join him and fight their way back to Germany. Army command had explicitly warned troops against going off on their own, but all of the soldiers, including those older than Höss, agreed to follow his leadership. What came next was an adventurous trek into Anatolia, across the Black Sea and up through the Balkans to Austria. "We travelled without maps, trusting the geography we had learned in school, requisitioning food for horse and man," Höss will write. "No one expected us to return." It was a journey through a world in upheaval, a world of falling empires, socialist revolutions, struggles for national independence, and anti-colonial battles—to say nothing of hunger, disease, and misery.

YOU CAN FEEL the "terrible divisions today," Kollwitz notes in her diary. There are daily mass protests, demonstrations, and violence in Berlin. Even those crippled in the war are putting their wounds on public display and taking their demands to the streets, chanting, "We don't want pity—we want justice!" The Left is split, and the Allies have refused to enter into peace negotiations or even deliver food to Germany until a democratically elected government is in place. In her heart, Kollwitz supports the Communist groups without whom the war would not have ended or the Kaiser been driven from power. Like the radical leftists, she hopes the revolution will continue rather than settle for the status quo. But her head knows that Germany is on the verge of breaking apart. "They will have to put down [the Spartacists] to get themselves out of this chaos, and to an extent they're right to do that," Kollwitz writes. It hurts her to think like this and to oppose those who risked being mowed down by machine guns to fight against war and hunger.

Christmas Eve brings tear gas and machine-gun fire to central Berlin. People are killed and wounded in both the army and the "people's navy division," which has holed up in the stables of the Berlin Palace and taken a prominent Social Democrat named Otto Wels hostage. In the final days of the year, the Communists quit the Council of People's Deputies, thus deepening the divisions within the Left. On December 29, the streets around Unter den Linden are packed as the Spartacists and the moderate socialists stage simultaneous demonstrations. Kollwitz loses sight of Hans in the crowd. It's all she can do to extract herself from the aggressive pushing and shoving of the crowds.

On New Year's Eve, Kollwitz takes stock. At least her family is reunited, and all of her loved ones who were spared by the war are in good health. "But peace is still not at hand," she frets. "The peace will no doubt be very bad. Yes—there's no more war. But you could say that, in its stead, we now have civil war."

In early January 1919, the artist watches with growing concern as the conflict between the various revolutionary factions escalates. "Here in Berlin, there are strikes wherever you look," Kollwitz notes in her diary. "The electric lighting is gone. It's said that the water supply will be cut off because workers at the water company are on strike. We've filled our bathtub to the brim." As the city infrastructure breaks down and people can no longer obtain basic necessities, far-leftist groups go on the offensive. They are determined at any cost to prevent the formation of a social democratic republic and wish instead to impose a socialist republic of soviet-style councils.

On January 5, an agitated Hans returns from a demonstration, at the end of which, he reports breathlessly, the editorial offices of the mainstream socialist magazine *Vorwärts* were occupied. Material intended to influence opinion at the national convention was taken into the street and set on fire. The editorial offices of other social democratic and centrist publications have evidently also fallen into the hands of the revolutionaries. "There are no newspapers left except *Freiheit* and *Rote Fahne*," he says, naming two radical leftist publications. The Social Democratic government has to use special flyers to communicate with the populace and call upon Berliners to stage counterdemonstrations. On January 6, Käthe and Karl Kollwitz join masses of people who take to the streets in defense of the infant republic. They lose track of each other in the crowd. When an exhausted Karl finally returns home he brings a shocking bit of news: "The government has no weapons." They've all been confiscated, he adds. Yet that night, they can hear cannon fire. Who is shooting, if the government has no weapons, Kollwitz asks herself. And where is Hans?

Her remaining son comes back home late at night, excited, tired but unharmed. Thinking out loud, he wonders whether he should join the government's troops. Kollwitz asks him if he means "with a weapon," and he answers, "Yes." That night, Karl ventures out into the city once more and sees people battling for control of the police directorate. On January 11, news goes round that the offices of *Vorwärts* have been liberated. Kollwitz assumes that this is the work of government troops, but it soon becomes clear that other forces are at play. The government has freed *Vorwärts* with the help of the "Freikorps Potsdam," an illegal militia of former frontline soldiers who are using weapons they kept from the war—flame throwers, mortars, and machine guns— against the revolutionaries. That night, the police directorate is retaken. Kollwitz is growing more tense: "I'm very downcast, even though I agreed that the Spartacists had to be put down. I have the uneasy feeling that it's no coincidence these troops are being deployed and that the reactionaries are on the march. What's more, the use of raw violence and the shooting of people who should be comrades are horrific." In the days that follow, counterrevolutionary movements become increasingly visible. At an event at Zirkus Busch, the red-white-and-black Reich flag is unfurled, but without Kollwitz's red streamer and pine boughs. Men sing "Hail to Thee in the Victory Wreath" and "Deutschland, Deutschland über alles." Some 150 people will ultimately lose their lives in the Spartacus uprising.

On January 16, just as the waves of violence seem spent, there is further shocking news. The leaders of the newly founded German Communist Party, Rosa Luxemburg and Karl Liebknecht, have been murdered. For Kollwitz this is a "dastardly, outrageous" act. Could the government be behind it, she asks herself?

It is scant consolation that the elections for the national assembly, against which the Spartacus uprising was aimed, do indeed take place a few days later. Kollwitz is among those who cast their ballots on January 19. It's the first time in her life she's been allowed to vote—the republic has instituted universal women's suffrage.

"I was so looking forward to this day, and now that it's here, I feel a new indecision and halfheartedness," Kollwitz writes. "I voted for the majority socialists . . . In my heart I'm further to the left."

Liebknecht and thirty-one others are buried on January 25. Kollwitz has been asked by his family to make sketches of the hero of the German Left and proceeds to the morgue early that morning. "He was lying in state amidst the other coffins," Kollwitz writes. "Red flowers were laid around his forehead with its gunshot wound, his face was proud and his mouth was open slightly and twisted in pain. His expression was somewhat surprised." Meanwhile, people have gathered for a massive funeral procession in the city, beginning in the working-class district of Friedrichshain. Masses of people, too many to count, walk behind the coffin. Kollwitz stays at home working on her sketches, but Karl and various friends tell her about the great number of people who turned out, the pushing and shoving even at the open grave, and Liebknecht's widow, who got so upset she fainted. They also relate how Freikorps militias kept a tight watch over the march all along the route. "How small-minded and wrong all these measures are," she writes. "Berlin, or at least a major part of it, wants to bury its dead. That's not a revolutionary matter. Even between battles there are hours of calm, in which the dead are laid to rest. It is ignoble and outrageous to have soldiers and paramilitaries harass Liebknecht's followers all the way to his grave. It is also a sign of the government's weakness that it has to condone such harassment." Still, Kollwitz must have known that the moderate republic she, too, favored would have been toppled had the Freikorps not intervened. In this sense, she, too, is a cosignatory to the pact that the new German republic has concluded with the devil.

— Four —

Dreamland

The war is destroying the old world with its contents: individual domination in every state. The new art has brought forward what the new consciousness of time contains: a balance between the universal and the individual. The new consciousness is prepared to realize the internal life as well as the external life. Traditions, dogmas, and the domination of the individual are opposed to this realization.

Piet Mondrian, Manifesto I, The Style, 1919

Marcel Duchamp, *L.H.O.O.Q.*, 1919

FROM A DISTANCE, with its angular contours softened by smog, New York City looks a bit like his misty mountain home. On May 22, 1919, Alvin C. York is standing on the deck of the SS *Ohioan,* his heart filled with homesickness. The farther the ship steams into the Hudson River, the clearer the Manhattan skyscrapers emerge, towering against the sky, which suddenly seems blue. York has been away for over a year. He has survived hunger, bombs, and the ghastly ocean crossing on this swaying barge of a boat. Now, with the harbor in sight, he vows that he will never again leave the US mainland. He's not the only one. "When we passed the Statue of Liberty I sorter looked her in the eyes," York will write. "And I kinder understood what the dough-boy meant when he said: 'Take a look at me, Old Girl. Take a good look at me, because whenever you want to see me again you will have to turn around.'"

A delegation from the Tennessee Society greets him at the pier, and a "right-smart heap" of press photographers jostles to get a shot of the famous sergeant smiling or making a victori-ous gesture. "So you see I was under fire again," he writes. He had gotten used to the intrusiveness of the press in France when Marshal Foch had personally awarded him the Croix de Guerre. After that, York was granted a special furlough in Paris, where he took in the sights like a dutiful tourist. "I liked Paris all right," he wrote, even though the endlessly long boulevards in the French capital all looked so much alike that he constantly lost his sense of direction.

Once in New York, the country bumpkin from Tennessee is bundled into a big black open limousine and driven through the canyon-like streets. People flock to catch a glimpse of the war hero, slowing the car's progress to a snail's pace and often stopping it altogether. Wherever York appears, people start cheering. Everyone on the street seems to know who he is. Admirers blow kisses and toss flowers. Does every returning soldier get such a welcome, York wonders? He doesn't grasp how much America longs for a story like his, the tale of a soldier who personally— with his own two hands, as it were—performed a heroic deed amid all the mass, mechanized, anonymous killing.

The limousine stops in front of the imposing entrance to the Waldorf Astoria. A concierge holds the door for him, and York is ushered through the luxurious foyer, motioned into an elevator, and escorted to a massive suite. He should get a bit of rest, he's told. In one room he discovers an enormous double bed.

That evening he's picked up for a banquet replete with speeches by military generals and statesmen whose names he doesn't catch. When the food is served, York eats slowly so he can figure out by watching his neighbors in which order he should address the bewildering assortment of glasses, china, and silverware. The fuss being made over him leaves him somewhat dizzy, "tired inside of my head." He wants nothing more than to go outside and take a walk. "I thought to myself, if this is fame," he writes, "then fame ain't the sorter thing I used to think it was."

The next morning, York wakes up early and slips out of the

hotel to go marching around for a bit. Old habits die hard, and the fresh air and exercise will do him good. But at breakfast he is once again besieged. The gentlemen of the Tennessee Society ask him what he would like to do most. He can come up with anything he likes—his wish is their command. York considers for a moment while the others look on expectantly. After a while he says he'd like to call his mother. A hotel clerk immediately hurries off to make the connection, but unfortunately no one in Pall Mall, Tennessee, answers. That wasn't a real wish, the gentlemen insist. All of New York is at his feet—anything he can imagine, even his craziest dream, will become reality. York racks his brains. He's getting a bit dizzy again, when an inspiration comes to his rescue. He remembers that a few years ago they completed one of the first underground train systems in the world in New York City. He's long been fascinated with the idea of climbing inside such a modern vehicle, speeding through tunnels underneath a bustling city, and then surfacing again wherever you wanted. The gentlemen laugh out loud, but if that's what he wants . . . A special train is hastily arranged, and York spends the rest of the day riding the subway below the Manhattan asphalt.

The next days are full of excitement. In Washington he's received at the White House and Congress. Back in New York, he's shown the New York Stock Exchange on Wall Street, although he can't quite figure out how people can work amid such commotion. Men in expensive suits who smoke fat cigars offer to make his story into a movie. They put so much money on the table it leaves York breathless. "I would have been interested in helping to make the pictures if I didn't have to be in it myself and if they would do it, not to make a heap of money for themselves or for me but jes to show what the boys done over there, and also to show what faith will do for you if you believe in it right," he writes. "But I knowed they weren't interested in that. They jes wanted me to show how I done killed the Germans in the Argonne." York doesn't want to write newspaper articles or go on a speaking tour on theater stages through North America. "I thought to myself, wouldn't I look funny in tights, ho, ho." In the end he loses patience. If these gentlemen want to do him a favor, they should just send him back home as soon as possible.

DURING THAT FIRST spring after the war, among those who expressed their thoughts about it, York is one of the few with no clear vision for the future. The diaries, letters, and memoirs that document the time between February and June 1919 are suffused with an unusual energy—as though the return to warmth and light at the end of winter has illuminated people's thoughts and private lives—and especially art—with the comet-like glow Paul Klee captured in his painting. For many soldiers this is a time of demobilization and homecoming. Like many civilians, they hope life will once again proceed in an orderly fashion and without the privations of war. Despite all the suffering, upheaval, and uncertainty, many people in that first postwar spring countenance bold dreams of alternatives to the social order and conceive of new visions for a better future. After all the darkness, after the experience of a thousand failures, they now are tempted by optimistic illusions of success. And what's true for ordinary people also holds for the great powers: in January 1919, on the grand political stage in Paris, negotiations begin over a final peace treaty. Statesmen from the world's major nations try to hammer out nothing less than a new world order. Everyone involved suspects the talks will last months, perhaps even years. The end result is open. Will Europe be renewed? And at the end of the negotiations, will a different world emerge?

BACK IN NEW YORK, the stream of homecoming soldiers has not let up since the armistice was signed. Throughout the winter, Moina Michael has watched countless ships dock in Hoboken and discharge boatload after boatload of pale, exhausted men. On Christmas Day 1918, she proudly stood among the crowds waving from the shore as the victorious American fleet sailed in formation up the Hudson.

The teacher from Georgia is still working for the YMCA on the campus of Columbia University, now training young men and women to be sent to Europe to help with the logistics of the US troop withdrawal. But the greater the number of soldiers in New York, be they in transit on their way home, in demobilization camps, or in hospitals, the more help is needed on the American side of the Atlantic. The war that previously unfolded faraway has now arrived at Moina Michael's doorstep.

Shortly before that Christmas, she began helping maimed soldiers from her home state of Georgia. The Georgia Society, a ladies' social club of which she is a member, put together Christmas baskets for the wounded who had to spend the holidays away from their families. Moina made forty-five deliveries to nine hospitals. Her first patient was Tom Lott, a black soldier from Mayswill, Georgia. One of his legs had been amputated directly below his hip, but he was able to hobble to the door of his hospital room on crutches. Moina presented him with the basket and some flowers and said how proud her state was of him. The man beamed, pinned a flower to his lapel, and showed her around the hospital ward. It was a happy moment. But as Moina worked through her list of patients, she realized that the maimed and traumatized former soldiers, most of whom would never be able to work again, would probably need support for a long time, perhaps for the rest of their lives. She was determined not to allow Americans so eager to return to normal life simply forget about those who had risked their lives and sacrificed their health for their country.

Experiences like these strengthened her commitment to the cause of the remembrance poppies, which had taken up more and more of her working hours. On the day the armistice was announced she met with Talcott Williams, the head of Columbia's Pulitzer School of Journalism. As the jubilant masses thronged outside his office windows, she told him about her idea, and the gray-haired professor was immediately enthusiastic. Right then he contacted influential colleagues and began writing to newspapers suggesting they interview Moina. For her part, she knew there was no more important instrument than the press for realizing her dream that people all over the country would remember the fallen and meet the needs of those permanently injured by the war.

Meanwhile, she was writing to friends throughout America asking them to lend a hand in popularizing the remembrance poppy as a symbol. An acquaintance helped ensure that a letter describing her cause reached the Department of War. At every step she received encouraging responses, and several people promised to use the poppy as a symbol for events related to the war. But for the initiative to succeed, Moina also had to master the logistical and material side of her project. If the American public was to get behind the symbol, a nationwide awareness campaign was not enough. Thousands, maybe even millions of artificial red flowers had to be produced. And if she really wanted to help the invalids, she would have to figure out a way to make money with her "Flanders Field Memorial Poppies."

Moina had no business experience, so she looked around for a partner, eventually settling on professional designer Lee Keedick. In December 1918, the two signed a contract in which Keedick promised to create a logo to adorn pins, buttons, flags, and banners and have them produced and distributed across the country. Keedick also intended to copyright his designs in various countries. Moina paid him an advance of one hundred dollars, which she borrowed from friends. By April 1919, the contract stipulated, the campaign was to be fully under way. The press was to be contacted and thousands of letters sent out to clubs, women's associations, patriotic organizations, churches, universities, and political leaders across the spectrum.

It's now February 14, 1919, and everything is in place. Keedick's design, a poppy intertwined with a torch of liberty, is unveiled in New York. That same day the Canadian flying ace Billy Bishop from Owen Sound, Ontario, is giving a lecture on aerial warfare over Flanders Fields at the Aviation Society of New York. The stage and the hall are decorated with red poppies, and at the end of Bishop's lecture, a large banner with the new poppy and torch logo is unfurled across the back wall. The Canadian poet James A. Heron explains the symbol and recites his countryman John McCrae's "In Flanders Fields," which inspired Moina, as well as her response, "We Shall Keep the Faith." The event is widely acclaimed in the press. It's Moina's first success, but she herself has been back in Georgia for two weeks, having resumed her old job as a house mother at a women's college. She has also returned to teach at the University of Georgia, and that summer she begins offering seminars for war veterans, hundreds of whom are undergoing rehabilitation at the college hospital. Her dream of the flowers atop the graves has finally begun to take shape.

THE HARLEM HELLFIGHTERS returned home the previous week. Many of the soldiers' families had boarded boats and ventured into New York Harbor to witness the arrival of the ship carrying the regiment. But the Hellfighters were not allowed to rejoin their loved ones straightaway. Instead, they were sent to Camp Upton on Long Island, where they were made to wait several maddeningly long days for their official discharge. Ever since they marched back from the Rhine to the French port of Brest, from where they set sail for America, all the men have been able to talk about is the upcoming victory parade. The soldiers from Harlem dream of crowning the heroic story of black people serving their country by marching through the streets of New York. That triumphant moment will make up for all the effort, suffering, and humiliation they experienced during the war, a final atonement for the insult of having been excluded from the 1917 parade when they shipped out. It will be the start of a new life they've earned by fighting in the war.

Arthur Little's officers are quick to understand the disciplinary power possessed by the idea of the parade. Whenever one of their subordinates gets out of line, they threaten to prohibit him from taking part—a threat that proves uncommonly effective.

But will America allow these black soldiers their turn in the spotlight?

Little began to have his doubts even as he prepared to leave France. The US military police's treatment of his men suggested that perhaps not all of America would look favorably upon the Hellfighters' achievements and the accolades bestowed upon them by the French Republic. In Brest a military police officer had beaten a black soldier to the point of splitting his head open when the soldier had asked him for directions. Little confronted the MP, who explained that the soldier had refused to wait until the officer had finished talking to one of his peers. When pressed on the matter, the MP admitted he was acting under orders. Little would recall: "He let slip a line to the effect that they had been warned that our 'Niggers' were feeling their oats a bit and that instructions had been given to 'take it out of them quickly, just as soon as they arrived, so as not to have any trouble later on.'" And that was by no means the end of the friction. A short time later, two MPs approached Little, complaining that they had been insulted by black soldiers: "There's a lot of your niggers yelling at us as we pass, 'Who won the war?'" Little dismissed the MPs' complaints. Since their days on the Rhine, that line had indeed become a favorite of the Hellfighters, though the victorious soldiers weren't just celebrating themselves but all those who had helped achieve the victory. "We've travelled all the way down from the front lines—hundreds of miles," Little told the MPs. "At every stop, wherever troops of other branches have been at the railway stations, our men have called out 'Who won the war' and then, in good nature, they've answered with their own call say-ing: 'The Bakers,' or 'The Q.M.'s,' or 'The Stevedores,' or 'The Red Cross' or 'The R.T.O.'s,' or 'The M.P.'s.'"

On February 17, 1919, Little's doubts are resolved. Units of the Harlem Hellfighters assemble on Madison Avenue north of Twenty-third Street. At 11 a.m. word comes that the city dignitaries have taken their seats. The companies take up a wide rectangular formation, a phalanx, as they've learned from the French. The officers stand a few steps in front of the unit. The parade is led by Jim Reese Europe's military band. When the marching order is given, the musicians strike up a song. But not even the band, whose numbers have swelled to ninety, is able to make itself heard above the din of the cheers that greet the marchers in the streets of Manhattan. New Yorkers are indeed giving the Hellfighters a triumphant welcome home. People have even arranged a special lunch for the soldiers. That day, Little writes, "New York City knew no color line."

But the most moving part of the parade comes when the Hellfighters reach their home, Harlem. Colonel Hayward has the men march in smaller rows instead of one grand phalanx, so that every individual soldier can be clearly seen and cheered on by his family, friends, and neighbors. Reese Europe's band launches into the ragtime "Here Comes My Daddy Now," and for the final kilometer, the marching dissolves into singing, waving, laughing, and dancing. Military discipline gives way to overwhelming joy, as mothers see their sons, wives their husbands, and all rush into the ranks of soldiers to embrace them. The parade ends in a cheering confusion of heads, hands, flowers, and kisses. "About every fourth soldier" has a girl on his arm.

Henry Johnson, the only officially decorated African American hero of the Great War, rides in an open-topped car. He is still very weak from the many injuries he incurred during his one-man battle against the German unit. The bones in his legs and feet have been so badly damaged that doctors don't know whether he will ever be able to walk without crutches. But Johnson repeatedly jumps up and waves to the crowd affectionately, as if the parade were being held in his honor alone. His face is beaming, and he seems about to call out to the countless people cheering him: Who won the war? Henry Johnson won the war!

It isn't until April 1919 that Harry S. Truman reaches the shelter of New York Harbor, having crossed the Atlantic on a former German ship, the SMS *Zeppelin*. The mayor of the city comes out to greet the returning troops on a boat that also carries a band playing "Home Sweet Home." Even the most hardbitten soldiers have tears in their eyes as the strains of the familiar song drift over the water. When the soldiers disembark, charity organizations compete with one another to give them gifts. "The Jews gave us handkerchiefs; the Y.M.C.A., chocolate; The Knights of Columbus, cigarettes; the Red Cross, real homemade cake; and the Salvation Army, God bless 'em, sent telegrams free and gave us Easter eggs made of chocolate," Truman writes. A banquet has been prepared for the soldiers directly on the pier, and Truman, who was seasick for most of the Atlantic crossing, eats enough for three. The festivities continue at Camp Mills, where Truman and his men are next ferried. There the soldiers are able to shower and are given fresh clothing. In the canteen, they consume scoop after scoop of fruit-flavored ice cream, which is carted in in huge tubs.

The end of the war has not been good for his waistline, Truman wrote Bess from France. The long periods of idly waiting to ship out and the short furloughs in Paris, Nice, and Monte

Carlo have left their mark around his hips, which had been positively bony during the hostilities. Now, he's positively fat, Truman
admits. Forty additional pounds mean that his uniform is now
skin tight. Will Bess still love him when she sees his new round
cheeks and double chin?

His thoughts repeatedly turned to Bess during those excru-
ciating months of waiting. She was the only one at whose side
he could imagine the future he sketches out over and over in
his letters. Truman doesn't want to be too rich or too poor—
moderate wealth makes people happiest. He repeatedly assures
her that he possesses the finest girl in the world, someone with
whom he can share all his troubles and joys. He intends to buy a
Ford, drive around the United States, and maybe even France,
engage in a bit of politics, and go to a dinner party or two. He
also plans to purchase one of the guns he used to fire at the
"Huns" from the army. He'll put it out in his front yard where it
can rust in peace. He never wants to fire another shot in his
life—that's his own private dream of peace.

Again and again Truman imagined himself with Bess at the
altar—only to wake up in a muddy foxhole somewhere near
Verdun. He wrote to her every time his duties left him a free
minute. He wooed and flattered her, begging for letters and complaining when she didn't write back often enough. She was something to cling to in a precarious situation. He kept a picture of
her in his left shirt pocket.

Sometimes he worried that Bess might lose patience on the
home stretch of this long journey. Or even worse—that something might happen to her, just after he had managed to survive
a hundred potential deadly situations. Truman had heard about
the devastating effects of the Spanish flu epidemic. Many of his

brothers-in-arms had lost loved ones to the virus. "It seems that war and pestilence go hand in hand," Truman wrote. "If it isn't the Black Death it is something equally as fatal. We hear that the poor Russians are dying by the hundreds and the damnable Hun is murdering himself for pleasure. I suppose it will be some time before we have a golden age of health, peace, and prosperity such as the ten years before 1914 were."

Once, during a particularly long interval between letters from Bess, he felt an acute anxiety about the woman at the center of all his dreams for the future. Had she not written that the flu was beginning to go round her family? Further letters confirmed that Bess was in bed with a fever, and even when he later learned that she had recovered, he could never completely relax. He realized how delicate and vulnerable his dreams of ordinary happiness were.

Now that he's back in New York, though, those dreams seem within reach. Truman is convinced that the American economy will flourish after the war, since money will be spent not on armaments but on consumer goods. He begins making plans based on this optimistic prognosis. How should he know that American prosperity is built on a foundation of sand?

In February 1919, after an odyssey lasting months, Rudolf Höss arrives back in his home town of Mannheim. As he was doing his military service his father died, and then a short time later his mother. She left behind a letter reminding her son that his father had decreed Rudolf was to become a man of the cloth. As soon as he returns home, an uncle who has been named his guardian, along with all his other relatives, tell him that he must immediately enter a seminary and start studying for the priest-hood. Höss's relatives have already divided up his parents' belongings and packed his sisters off to convent schools. "Only now did I feel the true loss of my mother," Höss will write. "I no longer had any home! I stood there abandoned, with just myself to rely on."

The uncle insists that Höss's father's will be carried out and refuses to release the son's inheritance to finance any other career. But Höss had already begun to doubt his calling to the priesthood during the war and has no intention of submitting to his relatives' dictates. He forgoes his inheritance, passing it on to his sisters. He even has his decision certified by a notary, resolving, as he later writes, to "make my own way in the world."

A bit later, Höss travels to the east of the German Reich, where First Lieutenant Gerhard Rossbach has set up a small "volunteer machine-gun company." At the start of 1919, this paramilitary group was incorporated into the "preliminary Reichswehr"— the rump military force left over after the armistice—and was assigned to help guard Germany's eastern border. In general, the paramilitaries blamed Germany's defeat on betrayal from within and only tolerated the new government as an interim phenom-enon. They retained their weapons, waiting for the moment of revenge to come.

Joining Rossbach's company instantly seems to solve all Höss's problems. He now has a job, a salary, a father figure, a political belief system that is almost as firm as a religion, and "a home, a feeling of security in the fraternity of brothers-in-arms." Höss writes: "Strangely enough, I—a loner, who had to cope alone with all my inner experiences and turmoil—always felt attracted to fraternities in which you could rely on others in times of emergency and danger."

FOR VIRGINIA WOOLF, 1919 begins with a thudding pain in her jaw and a throbbing ache in her head. The writer has just had a tooth pulled and feels so fatigued that she spends two weeks in bed—an experience she describes as "a long dreary affair, that receded & advanced much like a mist on a January day." By the end of January she's up and about again, but Leonard refuses to allow her to write for more than a single hour a day. During that brief time she has difficulty operating her typewriter because the muscles in her right hand cramp up "as I imagine a servants [sic] hand to feel." She notes with resignation, "Curiously enough I have the same stiffness in manipulating sentences."

Leonard doesn't include writing diary entries in the hour Virginia is allowed to work, and besides he isn't always home, so Woolf doesn't abide strictly by his regimen. In contrast to her literary texts and reviews, which she types out, Woolf uses a fountain pen for her diary entries. With that she doesn't experience any stiffness or writer's block. Sentences race out at a "rapid haphazard gallop." Even if the swift flow of words produces many clumsy formulations that "jerk . . . almost intolerably over the cobbles," one advantage of diary writing is that thoughts that would never have passed the scrutiny of her critical mind, if she had a chance to think them over, still get recorded on paper. Woolf seems to recognize that such uncensored observations have a value as inestimable as it is unrecognized. She describes them as "the diamonds of the dustheap."

There's not much to write about in the winter of 1918–19, other than encounters with friends and acquaintances, the difficult search for good help and the consequences of a seemingly endless series of labor strikes that, in Woolf's eyes, put greater strain on English life than the war had done. "If I were a painter, I should only need a brush dipped in a dun colour to give the tone of those eleven days," she writes. "I should draw it evenly across the entire canvas. But painters lack subtlety; there were points of light, shades beneath the surface, now, I suppose undiscoverable."

Indeed, there is some movement below the surface of the monotonous, gray-brown winter. During the months after the end of the war, Woolf sets out on a path that would lead in directions she could only vaguely suspect. Her reflections on this departure are contained in her essay "Modern Novels," which she publishes that April in the literary supplement to *The Times*. In it, she sharply criticizes the British writers of her day for being "materialists" who cling to the external attributes of their characters and to inherited narrative conventions. "The mind, exposed to the ordinary course of life, receives upon its surface a myriad impressions—trivial, fantastic, evanescent, or engraved with the sharpness of steel," Woolf writes. "From all sides they come, an incessant shower of innumerable atoms, composing in their sum what we might venture to call life itself; and to figure further as the semi-transparent envelope, or luminous halo, surrounding us from the beginning of consciousness to the end. Is it not perhaps the chief task of the novelist to convey this incessantly varying spirit with whatever stress or sudden deviation it may display, and as little admixture of the alien and external as possible?" The novelist, Woolf argues, ought to follow the consciousness of her characters along every bizarre detour and must not be afraid of getting lost in the details. James Joyce, whose manuscript she has recently rejected, seems to her to be the only valid example in English-language literature of a writer who has captured the stream of human consciousness.

Woolf's short stories "The Mark on the Wall" and "Kew Gardens," which she self-publishes in May, are the first forays in this new literary direction. But will anyone be interested in her epiphany? What difference will it make if she succeeds in capturing life as it really is? Will the reading public pay any attention to a novel told by a taciturn, note-taking psychiatrist, in which the main characters lie on a couch and let their thoughts run freely?

For the time being, Woolf has no choice but to earn her living writing reviews. This is a task she dispatches with maximal efficiency as long as she is feeling well. A friend puts her in contact with the editorial board of the respected journal *Athenaeum*. During her initial visit, she has tea with the literary editor, Mary Agnes Hamilton, who insists on Woolf's calling her Molly. Woolf feels at a distance from this energetic woman, "with her ability to think like a man, & her strong serviceable mind, & her independent, self-respecting life." At the same time, her conversation with Hamilton—whose desk is piled high with manuscripts, whose office vibrates with gossip from the literary world, and who asks the reviewer about her own literary projects—makes Woolf feel "a trace more professional."

In March she made a few "niggling, bothersome corrections" to the manuscript of *Night and Day*, the novel she had been laboring over since 1916, before sending it to Gerald Duckworth's publishing company. And now, she realizes, it is spring: "I must notice that though the sky is as black as water one has washed one's hands in, a bird is singing romantically & profusely at the window," Woolf writes. "On our walk today, we passed almond trees in full flower. The daffodils are on the point of bursting." The months until the publication of this book—which focuses on two couples caught in inarticulate, ossified prewar English society—bring inner turmoil. As Leonard reads the manuscript over the course of two afternoons and evenings, she tiptoes nervously about, fearfully watching for signs of approval or displeasure. When he finishes reading and praises her work, a weight lifts from her heart. Only now does she allow herself to hope the book might possess certain qualities that will make it a success and allow it to stand out from the literary mediocrity of the day. At the same time, she feels the need to curtail her own optimism: "I certainly don't expect a second printing."

In conversation with Leonard, she defends herself against his remark that the book is quite melancholy. "If one is to deal with people on a large scale & say what one thinks, how can one avoid melancholy?" she asks. "I don't admit to being hopeless though— only the spectacle is a profoundly strange one; & as the current answers don't do, one has to grope for a new one; & the process of discarding the old, when one is by no means certain what to put in their place, is a sad one."

Woolf considers the biggest burden of writing to be the writer's dependence on praise. "Unpraised, I find it difficult to start writing in the morning." How intensely she longs to liberate herself from the ups and downs of approval, the skeptical weighing of compliments, the worthiness of her champions and their possible hidden agendas, and from racking her brains over someone's silence. If only she could concentrate on the "main thing," the "fact of the pleasure I myself take from art."

Returning from a springtime trip to Asham on Whitsuntide 1919, Virginia and Leonard are surprised to discover a large pile of letters on the table in their hall, which they begin to open. Most of them are orders for Virginia's story "Kew Gardens." There are so many orders that they cover the sofa and the couple have to take frequent breaks as they work their way through them. A glowing review in the literary supplement to *The Times* has unleashed this wave of public interest. The Woolfs' evening begins with happy excitement and ends with a quarrel as "opposite tides of excitement coursed in us." It almost seems as though Leonard is a bit jealous, while Virginia, who was bracing herself for "complete failure" ten days earlier, is unwilling to let anything dilute the success she has craved for so long. But it's difficult to spend time quarreling when ninety copies of "Kew Gardens" have to be produced. "Covers have to be cut, tables printed, backs glued, and the stories sent off," Woolf writes. Nonetheless, the author exclaims, "How success showered [me] during those days!" If only this magnificent feeling would last, she thinks. If only it would come more frequently, more regularly, more evenly dispensed in "little sips." "I think the nerve of pleasure easily becomes numb," Woolf decides. "I fancy one's friends take the bloom off." Will she be able to take the next sip from the sparkling beverage of success when her novel appears, or will she be forced to drink from the bitter cup of disregard?

IN MARCH 1919, Terence MacSwiney is released from prison in England. He hasn't served out his sentence, but the authorities show pity because his wife, Muriel, has contracted the flu and is in critical condition. So the insurgent returns to his hometown of Cork. In his absence his name has been celebrated—at least in Irish separatist circles and among the members of the newly elected Irish parliament, the Dáil Éireann.

On April 1, shortly after his homecoming, MacSwiney travels to Dublin to take part as a representative in the first session of the Dáil. It takes place under the tightest security. The British government is still refusing to recognize the Irish parliament. Nonetheless, the Irish separatists feel closer to their goal of an independent state than ever before.

MacSwiney enthusiastically participates in the first parliamentary debates, but he pours his greatest energy into the financial affairs of the still nonexistent Republic of Ireland. The Irish "finance minister" is Michael Collins, and together they draw up plans for an immense campaign for donations, so-called Dáil loans, to fill the coffers of the future Irish state. The initiative is not confined to Ireland but will extend to North America, where many Irish have emigrated since the nineteenth century. MacSwiney organizes the collection of donations in Cork efficiently and clandestinely. He and his closest associates are the only ones who know the identities of the heads of five main "sub-executives" in the mid-Cork region—even those men have no contact with one another—in order to prevent the police from being able to wipe out the whole network in one blow. In Dublin, a brochure is printed explaining to potential donors what charitable purposes the money is to be used for: the establishment of state institutions, the allocation of land and creation of jobs so as to end mass emigration, the replanting of Ireland's forests, the stimulation of industry and fishing—in short everything that can bolster Ireland's material welfare and morale. Only when the argumentative groundwork is set do separatist representatives go door to door collecting money and valuables.

The police are hot on the trail of the conspirators, and MacSwiney and his associates have a number of close calls. Several times he is stopped and searched by the authorities, but he always takes care not to carry any incriminating material on his person. When the MacSwineys move in the fall of 1919, their happiness in their new home is short-lived. "The attention of old 'friends' became so overpowering we had to evacuate again before Xmas," he wrote to a close acquaintance. "The 'friends' were so pressing quite a number of them followed me to the old house with another invitation to go on another 'holiday' presumably over the water. Having spent really too much time on holidays these last five years, I had to deny myself this time."

Despite these difficulties, by the end of 1920 MacSwiney is able to collect more than five thousand pounds in banknotes and gold, which he passes on to Dublin. On the whole, the fundraising campaign is so successful that "Finance Minister" Collins begins to consider imposing a secret Irish income-tax system. The contours of a new Irish social-welfare system are coming into view—but so too are the fronts in a bitter battle that will soon reach its bloody climax.

THE *HARTAL*, OR general strike, that Gandhi has called begins on March 30, 1919. The first metropolis the movement brings to a standstill is Delhi, where Hindus and Muslims alike refuse to go to work and assemble for a huge march in the city center. "All this was more than the authorities could bear," Gandhi will write in his autobiography. "The police checked the *hartal* procession as it was proceeding to the railway station, and opened fire, causing a number of casualties, and the reign of repression commenced in Delhi." Similar scenes take place several days later in Lahore, and far worse violence occurs in the Bengal city of Amritsar. There the colonial British authorities are convinced that they must set an example to combat the increasing mobilization of the Indian populace. On April 13, a great mass gathers for a demonstration on Jallianwala Bagh square. At the first sign of unrest, British commander Reginald Dyer orders his troops to fire into the crowd. The square is walled in, so there's no way for the demonstrators to escape. Four hundred protestors die in the hail of bullets.

Several days before, on April 6, in Bombay, Gandhi realized how the situation was deteriorating. A large crowd congregated at Chowpatty Beach to bathe in the sea before marching to the city's central Madhav Bagh square. Gandhi gave a speech in a nearby mosque. In an act of civil disobedience, copies of two of his books, which had been banned by the colonial government, were printed and openly put on sale. That night, Gandhi himself walked through the streets of Bombay, selling these illicit publications. Many of the people he encountered paid more than what he asked for the books, and all of them momentarily forgot their fear of ending up in prison. The authorities took no action, but the following evening Gandhi learned of plans to arrest him. He was on his way to Delhi and Amritsar when he received written notification that he was prohibited from entering Punjab province. At the Palwal station the authorities detained him and took him back to Bombay via a roundabout route. Upon his arrival he saw that a huge crowd had gathered in the southern part of the city center. When the people recognized him, they cheered with joy. A procession began to form but was halted by mounted police. The riders galloped into the crowd, and Gandhi only narrowly escaped being beaten as the multitudes scattered in panic. "Some got trampled underfoot, others were badly mauled and crushed," Gandhi would write. But the police continued to plow a path through the masses of people. For a moment it had seemed as though Gandhi's dreams of a peaceful movement to end British colonial rule might come true, but now those dreams were turning into a nightmare—was a revolution without violence and bloodshed even possible?

FOR AN AVANT-GARDE artist, George Grosz's idea of an evening of fun seems to stem from a rather conventional male fantasy—you could almost say, from a wet dream. His friend the photographer Erwin Blumenfeld has pilfered sixty bottles of wine from his parents' cellar, and Grosz creates a poster reading: "Well-built young society ladies with filmic talent are invited to a party at the studio of the painter Grosz. 8 PM. Proper evening attire! Olivaerplatz 4." Grosz and Blumenfeld then parade up and down the Kurfürstendamm wearing the poster on a sandwich board. The stunt is a huge success. In addition to eleven male friends from the art world, more than fifty excited young ladies turn up at Grosz's studio that evening in hopes of being discovered by the film industry. So many people want to get in that the hosts eventually have to bolt the studio doors. To get the party going, Grosz orders everyone to take off their clothes. The male artists all retreat to the kitchen, but instead of disrobing, they decide to keep their suits on. When they reopen the kitchen door, the would-be movie stars are all naked, and the "orgy" begins. "Everyone got drunk, and empty bottles flew through pane of the studio window into the street," Blumenfeld will later remember. "There were shards of glass, cries and noise. While everyone rhythmically cheered them on, Grosz contracted a dose of the clap from Mascha Beethoven on a chaise lounge in the middle of the studio." Two days later, Blumenfeld wakes up in Grosz's bathtub, freezing cold and missing his blue suit, which someone must have stolen.

"They were wild years" is how Grosz will sum up the postwar era in Berlin, when all restrictions seemed to be lifted. A wave of vice, pornography, and prostitution rolled though the city. "'Je m'en fous,' is what everyone said. 'I want to have fun again for a change.'" In reality, though, the times are "tired and not fun." Berlin's nightlife and the art scene are merely a cheerful bit of froth on the surface, with hunger, destruction, and violence roiling the depths below.

The ever-sensitive Grosz carefully notes the frank aggression of his contemporaries. While saxophones and banjos begin appearing in Berlin nightclubs and patrons start to master the erotic twitching of dances like the shimmy, the tension between increasingly radical political antipodes is growing. "Outside a group of men in white shirts marched by, chanting in unison 'Germany awaken! Death to Jews!'" Grosz writes. "They were followed by another group also marching in military four-man columns and rhythmically chanting 'Hail to Moscow! Hail to Moscow!' Afterwards there were always men lying on the streets with fractured skulls, smashed shins and occasional gunshot wounds to the stomach."

Aggression and violence have always been subjects in Grosz's art, and the times offer him no shortage of material to support his belief that in this regard the infant Weimar Republic has changed nothing. Confronted with defeat, collapse, dissatisfaction, and a bubbling discontent throughout society, Grosz stages "meetings" with his art-world friends in bars and small theaters. People pay a couple of marks to get in and "be told the truth" by the performers. Usually the "truth" consists of ugly tirades of insults hurled at the audience. "You old piece of shit, up front, there—yes, you with the umbrella, you stupid ass," the performers say, or "Stop laughing, you ignorant ox." The audience can't stop laughing at such violations of taboos, and the people on stage don't treat one another with kid gloves either. And if some of the performers are drunk, there's an even greater ruckus. "We were complete, pure nihilists," Grosz will recall. "Our symbol was nothingness, the vacuum, the empty hole . . . We mocked anything and everything. Nothing was sacred. We spit on everything. That was Dada."

The format of Dada performances is infinitely variable. A "race between 6 typewriters and 6 sewing machines combined with a cursing contest," for example, ends in a brawl. Members of the movement passionately debate what "Dada" really means. The high functionaries of this new artistic school are given funny-sounding titles like "OberDada," "PropaganDada" and "Dada Diplomat" and devote enormous time to one fundamental question. Is Dada "the art (or philosophy) of the dustbin," as suggested by the collages Kurt Schwitters creates from garbage and advertising? Even the "Dadacon," the Bible of the movement, which is made of pasted-together newspaper clippings, cannot provide a definitive answer. A short time after the Spartacus uprising, a magazine conceived as the central organ of Dada was published. It was called *Everyman His Own Football*. The very first issue contained Walter Mehring's poem "Coitus im Dreimädler-haus," which ends with a parody of the lyrics to the German nationalist song "Watch on the Rhine." Mehring's verses read: "The cry resounds like thunder's peel / like crashing waves and clang of steel / a German broad and German booze / come man and rip my bodice loose!" The poet was summoned to appear in court to explain himself, and the newly founded magazine was banned after its first issue.

MARCEL DUCHAMP, WHO moves from New York back to Paris in 1919, enriches the international Dada movement with his so-called readymades, which anoint found objects as sculptures: a bottle-drying rack, the fork of a bicycle frame, and, most famously, a pissoir. In Paris he marks the four-hundredth anniversary of Leonardo da Vinci's death by drawing a moustache and a goatee on a reproduction of one of the most famous artworks ever, the *Mona Lisa*. In the style of someone vandalizing a painting, Duchamp not only mocks the fine art canon and its sacred figures but messes around with femininity and masculinity in irritatingly opaque fashion. He adopts the nom de plume Rose Sélavy—a play on *"L'éros c'est la vie"* (Eros is life)—and has himself photographed in drag. The title of his bearded Mona Lisa is *L.H.O.O.Q.*, possibly a phonetic reference to the phrase *"elle a chaud au cul"* (her ass is on fire). In an interview, Duchamp himself loosely translates the title as "there is a fire down below." But Dada is about more than mocking tradition and dogma and violating the rules of polite society, its mores and morality. The Dadaists also parody the revolutionary movements of their time, even though the initial impetus for their insouciance comes from a similar drive toward freedom. The Dadaists know only too well what they want to free themselves from. But it is far less clear to what end they would like to be free. Do they stand for freedom of artistic expression? Freedom to live out the urges, the anarchic side of human nature? There is probably no way of establishing a new society on those sorts of pillars. Nevertheless the Dadaists believe it is a worthwhile enough aim simply to recover the autonomy of the individual and unfetter desire after years of being subjugated to the all-dominant demands of war.

FEBRUARY 6, 1919, would have seen Käthe Kollwitz's son Peter turn twenty-three. That date and the memories she associates with it appeared in her dreams the night before. Now, on the day itself, Kollwitz takes out some sketches she made during the war for lithographic prints. In one, the artist depicts herself as a mother protecting her children, Hans and Peter, by embracing them in her arms. It's a simple, almost spare image, very serious, with no trace of Dada-esque mocking. As Kollwitz works away, the violence continues in the city, and more fathers and sons die.

AFTER BEING DISCHARGED from the navy in Wilhelmshaven, Richard Stumpf returns to his home town of Nuremberg. But in the difficult economic times after the war, he can't find a job either in his previous profession as a plumber or as anything else. So after six years of military service, Stumpf becomes one of the growing army of unemployed in Germany. In April 1919, when a soviet republic is declared in Munich, he considers it his duty to resist. He has extremely ambivalent feelings about the German revolution, which denied him his due glory as a soldier, and the new regime has very little to offer someone like him who sacrificed so much for the fatherland.

So Stumpf joins a Freikorps group marching off to do battle with the Bavarian Soviet Republic, and in the first days of May, the national army and paramilitaries from all parts of Germany overwhelm the defenders of that new republic. In the aftermath of the fighting, Stumpf witnesses how brutally the victorious counterrevolutionaries treat real and imagined Spartacists. On May 6, a counterrevolutionary patrol storms a Catholic working men's club whose members have been denounced as Spartacists, in Munich's central Maxvorstadt district. The members are lined up on the street. They loudly protest their innocence, but a certain Captain von Alt-Stutterheim accuses them of violating a ban on demonstrations. Seven of the men are summarily executed in a building courtyard. The others are taken to a cellar, where drunken soldiers physically abuse them so badly that fourteen more die. Their bodies are plundered and stripped bare. Two of the soldiers perform an inebriated dance of victory next to the mutilated corpses. After that day Stumpf quits the Freikorps.

IN THE SECOND week of May 1919, Alma Mahler travels with her daughter Manon to Berlin to visit her husband, Walter Gropius. The visit is one of farewell even if the couple doesn't realize it yet. The trip, which takes Alma through newly independent Czechoslovakia, is an adventure in itself, and no sooner do mother and daughter arrive in Berlin than they receive terrible news. Martin, Alma's nine-month-old son from her affair with Franz Werfel, has died in a Vienna hospital. He was born with hydrocephaly, known as "water on the brain," for which he has been hospitalized since February. Even though his death was expected, none of the three parents was at the child's bedside when he died. Gropius breaks the grim news to Alma, saying that he would have willingly died in Martin's stead. Nonetheless, the adults hardly seem overwhelmed with sadness and sympathy for the sick child, although Werfel does blame himself for precipitating Martin's premature birth with an overly passionate sex act.

The Gropiuses are expected in Weimar, where Walter has just been named director of the Bauhaus, the newly founded state art academy. The couple has social duties, and they perform them. These joint appearances, however, amid the endless social gatherings, only show them how far they've grown apart. Alma takes no interest in the Bauhaus with its shabbily dressed, politically and artistically radical students. She considers her husband's dreams of a new world to be created through Bauhaus architecture deeply suspect—like everything else claiming to be revolutionary.

The heat generated by their early encounters has cooled off, leaving only distance. "Why didn't my marriage to Walter Gropius work?" she will ask in her memoirs. "He's a lovely person in every sense, a highly gifted artist of my type and my blood . . . He pleased me so much . . . I was in love with him . . . I loved him very much." Is it, as Alma surmises, his lack of understanding of music, or her scant appreciation of architecture that has driven them apart? Or did the war and their long separation prevent them from coming back together?

In a letter he includes in the paperwork for their later divorce,

Gropius puts forward a different explanation. With Werfel in mind, he writes: "Your magnificent essence has been corroded by the Jewish spirit. At some point, you will return to your Aryan origin, and then you will understand me and look for me in your memories. Today I am alien to you, because you have been pulled away by another of the world's poles." He knows that these thoughts will hurt Alma since she herself mocked Werfel as a "crooked-legged Jew" before commencing her affair.

Even after these experiences and the hurtful exchange of letters, Alma is reluctant to divorce Gropius and looks for some form of compromise. She has grown depressed, is tortured by indecision, and even tries to convince Gropius to let her live half the year with Werfel in Vienna and the other half with him in Weimar. Gropius will have none of that. "The malady of our marriage requires surgery," he writes.

The couple's marital state remains undecided for months while Gropius lays the foundations for the Bauhaus. It was only in April that he received the state approval he had so anxiously awaited, which allowed him to transform the former Grand-Ducal Saxon Academy for the Visual Arts into a new model of teaching institution. Now he urgently needs to attract top professors as quickly as possible to welcome the first incoming students. The courses of study are based on the principle that "the individual 'arts' are to be released from their lonely isolation and brought back into intimate contact under the aegis of one great art of construction." In line with this idea, students are expected to spend three years learning a trade in the Bauhaus workshops before deciding on a degree course like architecture. Gropius is completely in his element. He believes that theory and practice, the education of young people and visions of a better society, have to be harmonized. But there are a lot of political details to be taken care of in order to establish the Bauhaus as part of society in Weimar Germany.

As always, Alma is torn between the men in her life. Werfel, who is pushing his mistress to get a divorce, continues to occupy his position as her favorite lover. As with all the others, she serves as his muse, and tries to create ideal conditions for him to practice his art. That includes doing everything she can to prevent Werfel from masturbating. She believes that this wastes his energy not only as a man but as an artist, also that it endangers his health. By contrast she isn't put off by the fact that in the aftermath of the war Werfel finds himself turned on by physical injuries. "The more important a man, the sicker his sexuality," Alma has decided. Apparently Werfel's preferences are contagious enough that one day after an intense erotic dream, she considers hiring a "one-legged person" so that she and her lover can live out their fantasies. The effects of the war even reach into Alma and Werfel's sex life.

At the same time, Alma doesn't want to let go of Gropius completely, and old lovers also reenter the scene, first and foremost the painter Oskar Kokoschka, with whom she had had a stormy affair. He lets it be known via an intermediary that he wishes for nothing more than to return to her. She pretends to be outraged, but inside she's in turmoil. "Since I heard from OK, I'm full of desire for him and wish that all the obstacles, which ultimately are only in me, were removed so that I could live my life to its end with him." Of course she knows that a rekindling of their mutual passion would quickly burn out. Moreover rumors are multiplying that Kokoschka is losing his mind. His worship of Alma and his desire for her maternal, sensual, and inspiring affection is so great that he orders a life-size doll made in her likeness. He's disappointed with the results, but even so he keeps his ersatz Alma on his sofa for a while. He dresses her up in Parisian lingerie and expensive outfits and talks to her for hours. After a while, desperate because the doll can never replace his real-life beloved, he tries to free himself from his passion. During the drunken apotheosis of a wine-soaked garden party, he chops the doll's head off. The next morning the police ring his doorbell, and Kokoschka has to explain what was going on with the "body" in his backyard. In the end, the trash collectors dispose of the doll's remnants.

Composer Arnold Schönberg has been friends with Alma Mahler for a long time and often calls on her. Once he brought along his wife and daughter and some of his students, who performed on Alma's piano. Schönberg's obvious poverty makes Mahler feel a bit ashamed of her own wealth. She gives Schönberg's daughter a platinum bracelet studded with diamonds and intends, the composer believes, "to give her more, much more."

In January 1917, Schönberg returned from his military service to his apartment on Gloriettegasse 43 in a state of profound confusion. When the Great War broke out in August 1914 he considered it something "magnificent and grand." Watching Austrian society become mobilized, he was seized by a desire to "join the ranks and do battle together with thousands of others," and immediately volunteered for the Royal and Imperial Army of Austria-Hungary. Upon being summoned for duty, the composer was only too happy to put the "public's insults"—the catcalls at live performances, the hurtful critical reviews and derisive remarks about his art—behind him. A malicious colleague once rather bizarrely called Schönberg's groundbreaking experiments in painting as "green-eyed, watery bread rolls that look to the stars."

The enthusiasm with which the composer traded the sounds of the orchestra for the din of war didn't last long. His application to be granted an officer's rank because of his artistic achievements was rejected. The eyes of the newly minted soldier welled up with tears of anger when he was given his uniform and discovered that his cap was stained with the blood of its previous owner. His asthma, not helped by his copious consumption of tobacco and alcohol, and his advanced age precluded his winning glory on the front. Instead of performing heroic deeds for the fatherland, he was assigned to the tedium of training in a reserve officers' academy in the small town of Bruck an der Leitha. "At the age of 42," he would write, "I became an apprentice in the military and let myself be ordered around by idiots." This was not how he had envisioned a soldier's life. Although he considered himself an "artist above the people," the composer found himself at the bottom of the chain of command. In an attempt to do him a favor, his superiors charged him with scoring marches for the army band.

No sooner had he returned to Gloriettegasse than he recovered his usual restless productivity in all areas of art and life. His wife, Mathilde, looked on as he disappeared behind his desk to write an essay about nothing less than his idea for "eternal peace." Three years of war had convinced him that while human beings were "terribly evil," a small group of "people of our sort," that is men of education and good judgment, could achieve within one week the armistice that the world's governments and diplomats had been unable to bring about despite Woodrow Wilson's highly publicized peace proposal. Schönberg was convinced that the "energetic will of the majority of the people" was "to avoid war in future." Straying far beyond his area of expertise, Schönberg proposed the creation of an international court of arbitration whose decisions would be enforced by a multinational "army of guardians." Schönberg's vision anticipated the League of Nations, but no one at the time paid it any mind.

Conditions in his reeling homeland further strained the composer's already jangled nerves. Despite constant financial worries, before and after 1918 he worked on a piece of music that would reflect the perceptions and desires of the late war and postwar years as few others did. His *Jakobsleiter* (Jacob's Ladder) oratorio begins with an insistent, ostinato bass figure. The strings march dynamically, even violently ahead, undaunted by the painful dissonance of the brass and woodwinds. The clear tenor of the Archangel Gabriel then offers salvation from the tension of the opening measures. "Whether right or left, forward or backward, uphill or downhill," the tenor sings, "you must go on without asking what lies before or behind you." Here was the reality of military service, persistence in dark times. But then the libretto switches into the past tense, suggesting that the inexorable march forward is over. As in the Bible, Schönberg's angel is a mediator between heaven and earth. He draws attention to the higher sphere, a better world above to which the rungs of the ladder lead. This is an image of hope, of promise, indeed salvation. A longing for the dissolution of earthly suffering in divine grace. Back in 1912, Schönberg had written, "I want . . . to write an oratorio whose subject matter is: how modern man, who went through materialism, socialism and anarchy and who was an atheist, nonetheless retained a bit of his old faith (in the form of superstition). About how this modern man quarrels with God . . .

and ultimately succeeds in finding God and becoming religious. About how he learns to pray!"

In his Viennese apartment, rented with money from patrons, Schönberg finds his way to the faith that is the only help against "the overthrow of everything we used to believe in." The oratorio is the musical representation both of the collapse of the old edifices of meaning and of the hope that they will be restored. It contains Schönberg's first tentative steps toward an entirely new, mathematical, abstract understanding of music: the twelve-tone technique. At its core, it points not toward the promises of salvation contained within the great ideologies, but toward God himself.

MAY 1919. ALVIN C. York drops to his knees when he sees the small shack in Pall Mall at the foot of the mountains. Slightly off to one side from all the fuss made by his family and neighbors, out of view, he thanks God for getting him home safely, for holding a protective hand over him in the war, preventing all harm. York doesn't have to say anything to his Creator to express his gratitude. All he has to do is feel it.

When he runs to the shack he calls home, his hunting dogs dash up to greet him, jumping around in circles, barking and wagging their tails wildly. They're so excited to see him again they almost knock him over. York kneels down to pat their flanks and stroke their heads, while they lick his hands. Soon he'll be tracking game with them through the woods of Tennessee, which haven't changed at all in his absence. There the razorbacks still hunt for acorns in the ground, cowbells sound, and the dogwood trees bloom as they do every spring. York, however, now sees these things with different eyes. While here everything stayed the same, he has become someone else. He has seen the world and fought for his life. His former existence lies so far behind him it seems like part of another age. He feels restless, agitated by dreams and shadowy memories. What he experienced in the past months has to have some sort of deeper meaning, he believes. It can't have been in vain. York sits down on the mountainside and ponders what he, who survived the Great War, should do with the rest of his life.

AFTER THE HARLEM Hellfighters' parade, Arthur Little can scarcely stand to put on his uniform. Why does it take so much longer to be discharged from the army than to be called up? There are so many medical examinations and interviews. A report has to be filed for each individual soldier, his discharge papers need to be signed, and the whole process is accompanied by an endless series of speeches and ceremonies.

Three days after the parade, Henry Johnson finally returns to Camp Upton. Following his triumphant trip through Manhattan, he had to tell his story again and again to excited reporters, and when the regiment was ordered back to Long Island that evening, there was no trace of Johnson. Now he's come back, and it's Little's duty to punish him for going AWOL. Pressed to explain his absence, Johnson reports that a group of fine gentlemen invited him on an excursion, generously wining and dining him in the clubs and restaurants of Fifth Avenue. The food and drink were heavenly, and the gentlemen gave him money. After the festivities he was tired and needed to sleep it all off in a soft hotel bed. How could he have turned down such a wonderful offer? Would that not have violated the regiment's insistence on being polite? To prove the truth of what he's saying, he shows Little a bundle of bills, more than six hundred dollars in total. Little decides to look the other way and sends the deserter back to his unit.

Several days later, as Little is sitting at his desk processing the seemingly infinite paperwork, a knock comes at his door. It's Johnson. This time he's holding his letter of discharge. Little recounted the exchange as he heard it:

"Suh, Major Suh," the man Little describes as a "little homicidal king" says. "Ah've been discharged from the U.S. Army. Ah'm er goin' home. Ah'm er goin' back ter mah reg'lar job, and Ah've cum ter say good-bye."

Little knows that the rest of the troops are already on a train to New York. Johnson must have stolen away from his comrades and run back the kilometers between the train station and Little's office on his crippled feet. When Little looks him in the eye, he chokes up and stares out his window at the empty camp lying abandoned in the sun. This porter from the Albany train station is giving him a lesson in comradeship. Little gets up and walks over to Johnson, who is still standing at attention. With teary eyes and a trembling voice, he addresses Johnson by his Christian name.

"Good-bye, Henry, don't forget me."

"Furgit you, Suh Major Suh?" Johnson responds. "Why Suh Major Suh, yer made a man of me!"

ONCE AGAIN IN Kansas, Harry S. Truman rejoins his beloved Bess, although his first glimpse of her is from a distance. The 129th Field Artillery Regiment has to take part in one last parade.

Three days later, on May 6, 1919, the members of the regiment are officially discharged.

When the couple at last is reunited, the first and only fight Harry and Bess will ever have breaks out over whether they should move in with Bess's mother, who considers Harry a bad match, after their wedding. Harry is against the idea, but in the end Bess wins out, and a few weeks later the moment they both have waited for so long finally arrives. On June 28, the same day the Versailles Peace Treaty is signed, the Kansas weather is so hot that the flowers in the church wilt, as Harry Truman and Bess Wallace stand before the altar. The serious face Truman makes on the wedding photos can't conceal his tremendous joy.

After the wedding, Truman has to relearn life as a civilian. Together with a war buddy named Edward Jacobson he comes up with a plan, sells the livestock on his farm, and takes out a loan. The two intend to open a men's haberdashery in downtown Kansas City. Their logic is simple. There are so many men returning from the war, and they all need things to wear. Their aim is to open "Truman & Jacobson" on the ground floor of the Glennon Hotel, an excellent location. The newly minted entrepreneurs intend to offer their customers fine menswear: shirts, socks, ties, belts, undergarments, and hats for the discerning gentleman. The shop opens that very year. The company name is painted in bright letters over the entrance, the tile floor is polished to a shine, and large electric fans spin overhead above the merchandise. Truman & Jacobson opens for business at eight in the morning and doesn't close until nine at night. The two owners take turns manning the till. Right from the start, former comrades stop by the shop. It almost seems as though they miss the war—or at least being led by their commanding officer, to whom they present a cup with his name engraved on it as a keep-sake. Battery D will not cease to be part of Truman's life just because the war is over. A former brother-in-arms even cuts his hair, as he once did under a tree near St. Mihiel.

NOT EVERYONE'S DREAMS in the spring of 1919 are so easily translated into reality. Many people suffer from terrible night-mares instead of having images of a better, more peaceful future. Soghomon Tehlirian is one of them. As he will later explain to a court of law, he cannot forget the horrible memories of long columns of refugees from his hometown of Erzincan in East Anatolia, of Turkish soldiers who stole their valuables and took away his sister, of shots and screams, of his mother falling to the ground, of the ax that split his brother's head open, of the blow to his own head that knocked him unconscious, and of waking up under the corpse of his own brother. Every time the images haunt his mind, his body is racked by cramps, and he passes out. It's February 1919, and Tehlirian has come from Tbilisi to Constantinople in hopes of finding some of his family. In the capital of the Ottoman Empire, which has been ripped apart by the war, he takes out classified ads in the newspapers in an attempt to locate friends and relatives. Tehlirian is an Armenian, hundreds of thousands of whom have been massacred by Turkish soldiers and civilians. He is one of the survivors, but his ads all remain unanswered. Can it really be true that everyone he held dear perished in the 1915 genocide?

Five

A Deceptive Peace

The dreamland of the armistice period, where everyone . . .
could conjure up his own fantastic, pessimistic or heroic vision
of the future, is now closed.

—Ernst Troeltsch, *Spectator-Briefe*, June 26, 1919

Curt Herrmann, *Flamingo*, 1917

In April 1919, Milan Štefánik returns to Paris. It's the moment Louise Weiss has been longing for. "Paler than a corpse," the man she loves walks into her office and sinks into a chair, as stories of all he's been through these last few months tumble from his lips. He was able to save himself and most of his men in Siberia. In temperatures of minus 35 degrees Celsius, the French commander of the Czechoslovakian Legion, General Maurice Janin, awarded him the cross of the Légion d'Honneur for his heroism. Afterward, Milan began making his way back to Europe via the Pacific. In Kobe, Japan, he learned that an armistice had been reached, and in Tokyo, he heard that he had been named the first minister of war of the new Czechoslovakian Republic. The news only intensified his desire to get back to Europe as quickly as possible, as he saw his new posting as an opportunity to play a major role in the international peace negotiations, which were scheduled to address the issue of international recognition of Czechoslovakian independence. But by the time Milan finally arrived in Paris, the conference was already well under way, and other leaders—most notably the new Czechoslovakian premier, Karel Kramář, and the new foreign minister, Edvard Beneš—had taken their seats at the negotiating table with the world's most powerful men. Milan cannot even persuade General Foch to launch a rescue mission for his comrades-in-arms still trapped in Siberia. After all the hardship and danger of the preceding years, this is not how Milan envisioned his return to Europe. He simply feels useless in Paris and hardly has he arrived than he plans to dash off again to Prague, where he can at least expect a welcome befitting a war hero. His fondest dream would be to fly to the Czech capital, descending directly from the heavens to his homeland.

Louise is captivated by every detail of Milan's stories and thoughts. Her passion for the Czechoslovakian cause and for the man whom she sees as its embodiment has not diminished in the slightest. Perhaps she can now fight at his side and help bring about Czechoslovakian independence? While visiting Milan at his apartment on rue Leclerc, Louise cautiously steers the conversation toward what she hopes will be their joint political and personal future, but his expression darkens. He looks her straight in the eye, and Louise senses that he has something to confess. After some hesitation, he breaks the devastating news that in April 1918, at the Congress of Oppressed Nationalities in Rome, he met a young Italian noblewoman, Marchesa Giuliana Benzoni, and fell in love with her. A second meeting followed a short time later and now the couple is engaged.

Louise can't believe her ears. "And what about me?" she asks the man whom she considered the love of her life. "You?" he answers, using the informal *tu* in French for the first time. "I would like you to tell me that I am free. I owe you so much. Too much. And besides I could never be your master." Louise is numbed by pain, as Milan's cold-hearted arguments rain down on her like blows. "You are not innocent like this pearl which I intend to give to my beloved." He opens a little box and shows

her a piece of mauve-pearl Oriental jewelry. Milan sees Louise's
tears but can't find the words to console her. "Your grasp of political matters is instinctive, simply amazing," he says, making
another attempt. "You act like an elder statesmen . . . You're
always thinking. But I want to give my people a virgin, with a
virgin body and above all a virgin soul. A soul. You see what I
mean." Louise is dumbstruck. She senses that, despite all her
talent, she possesses nothing that would allow her to compete
with her rival. She doesn't even try. She knows that the beautiful young marchesa has won Milan's heart and will do more
to enhance his legend than Louise ever could—something as
important to Louise as it is to Milan. Then he delivers one final
crushing blow. "I told her that you're my best friend," he says. "I
told her that she can turn to you in times of difficulty and that
you'll help her. Promise me you will." Louise is weeping. "I can't
manage without you," Milan says. Suddenly, Louise feels rage
boil up within her. "You will never marry Giuliana," she shoots
back. "Not her, not me, nobody. For you there's no one but you."

"Perhaps, *ma chérie*," Milan murmurs and bids her goodbye.
Louise's visit is over. A short time later, Milan leaves Paris for Italy.

SPRING 1919 IS a time of broken dreams as well as ones fulfilled.
That's particularly true for the myriad imaginings tied to the
negotiations in Versailles: the victorious nations' fantasies of
omnipotence, the quiet hopes of the defeated that the price of
peace would be less steep than they feared, the colonized peoples'
dreams of national liberation and independence, and the general
belief that a just, peaceful world order could be created. But as
the summer progresses and the negotiations approach their

conclusion, these profuse desires for a better future are quickly diminished. The more the spectrum of possibilities shrinks, the more people have to face reality. Wherever the results of the negotiations are perceived as a betrayal of hope, disappointment quickly turns into rage. The very treaties meant to settle the global conflict often become the object of new quarrels.

In 1917, Berlin artist Curt Herrmann painted a picture of a flamingo with shimmering light-pink feathers. This splendid bird isn't prancing around on long, elegant legs; it's lying dead with its neck twisted beside an empty food bowl, its beak marked with a dark red splotch of blood. Painted in the third year of the Great War, at first glance the image seems to symbolize the lost hopes for a glorious victory—and more generally the downfall of the Belle Epoque and the end of the old world and its elites. Beyond this specific historic context, however, the death of a beautiful creature can also be seen as an emblem for the defeat of something marvelously graceful that was too delicate to survive a harsh reality. This was precisely the fate of many dreams in the spring and summer of 1919.

So MANY SACRIFICES and so many promises were made during the world war that the expectations were correspondingly great when peace negotiations officially commenced on January 18, 1919, in the Clock Hall of the French Foreign Ministry on the Quai d'Orsay. Representatives from thirty-two nations took part in the first phase of talks, even though only the Western enemies of Germany consulted with one another. The "council of four"— Great Britain, France, Italy, and the United States—set the tone. To underscore America's new role in the world, President Woodrow Wilson had arrived in Paris some weeks earlier; an American delegation of more than a thousand would ultimately follow him to the French capital. Almost a year earlier, in his Fourteen Points of January 1918, the US president had set new standards for international policy, and they remained Wilson's guiding principles. The right of national self-determination was to serve as a basis for global politics and would also apply to colonial empires. The countries of the world were to join together in a League of Nations that would peacefully resolve international disputes. Only if such consequences were drawn from the Great War would it truly become the "war to end all wars." These ideas and a massive publicity campaign throughout the world made Wilson the focus of global hopes and indeed a nearly messianic figure. On December 14, 1918, Louise Weiss had the chance to meet the president and the first lady, but the American savior left behind a mixed impression. The journalist described him in her journal as a "Protestant pope" and a "Savonarola without a past." Louise wrote: "He cut through the human magma according to standards that only existed in his philosophy, while the poor Europeans, including the English, constrained by their traditions, interests, protégées and vassals, were proposing more or less viable solutions." The French view of Wilson's policies, by no means restricted to Weiss, remained sober as the negotiations progressed. For the French people, exhausted by war, the question of reparations was more important than any lofty ideals. And Wilson's Fourteen Points raised the hopes of peoples on the edges of the French empire—something that concerned and irritated the motherland of the *empire républicain*.

NGUYEN AI QUOC is in Paris during the negotiations, now trying
to earn a living as a photographer. In an issue of the magazine
Vie Ouvrière, he had taken out an ad reading: "If you want a vivid
keepsake for your parents, let Nguyen Ai Quoc brush up your
photographs. A nice portrait and a nice frame for 45 francs." But
there's not much demand for Nguyen's services, and he's still
living hand to mouth.

The near-daily reports on the progress of the conference puts
Nguyen and many other immigrants from French and British
colonies in a feisty mood. Like most opponents of the colonial
system, Nguyen has paid close attention to Wilson's program-
matic writings. The men in Versailles and Paris are deciding
the fate of the world, and if, as Wilson proclaimed, the hour of
national self-determination is truly at hand, Nguyen's homeland,
French Indochina, must be included. Spring 1919 offers him a historic chance that cannot be allowed to pass.

Together with a group of fellow activists, he draws up a peti-
tion in the name of "a group of Vietnamese patriots." Emulating
Wilson's Fourteen Points, it lists eight demands. There's no talk
of self-determination, to say nothing of independence. The list
is aimed solely at giving Vietnamese more rights: the right to
a fair trial, freedom of the press and education, freedom to assemble, and better representation for Vietnam in the French National
Assembly. In addition, political prisoners are to be freed, arbitrary
decrees are to be replaced by the rule of law, and the Vietnamese are to be allowed to travel abroad. These are all demands that
should be self-evident to France, the motherland of human rights,
although since its own great revolution France has withheld the
achievements upon which its national pride and identity are
based from the people it rules throughout the world. But now

the world is being shaken by seismic tremors capable of causing empires to collapse. The global earthquake creates new independent nations and calls forth unrest in countries as far-flung as Egypt, Japan, India, Korea, and Mexico. In a time like this, France's global empire may also be shaken or even destroyed.

Nguyen doesn't merely put his name to the demands made on behalf of his homeland; he also ensures that they reach the intended addressees. He is spotted up and down the hallways of Versailles, personally delivering the demands to each of the delegations. He even tries to get a meeting with Wilson and borrows a nice suit for the occasion, although in the end he can't get past the president's receptionist. Nonetheless, written responses from various delegations show that the negotiators have taken notice of the demands for a liberalization of colonial rule in Indochina. On June 18, Nguyen succeeds in getting the Vietnamese demands published in the newspaper *L'Humanité*, raising awareness of his cause among the general public as well.

It's at this time that the French police first register the existence of this immigrant, who is living underground in their midst. Security forces expel Nguyen from the Palace of Versailles, and from then on the French secret police begin trailing him. A spy is smuggled into Vietnamese resistance circles, and Nguyen's apartment is placed under surveillance. The level of police scrutiny is incommensurate with the actual effectiveness of the Vietnamese cell: the fate of Indochina plays no role in the negotiations at Versailles. Wilson's high-minded, if not completely selfless ideas do not deter victorious France from pressing for its archenemy Germany to be severely punished, or from pursuing the reinforcement and expansion of its own global power. As for Wilson, the colonial issue is by no means his central concern. If anything, he's afraid that the activity of independence fighters could torpedo the emerging world order. In his first draft of the covenant for the League of Nations that he presented to the conference on February 14, 1919, he had expunged the word "self-determination."

"EVERYBODY SEEMS TO be here," writes T. E. Lawrence to his mother in January 1919. By "here," Lawrence means Paris, where the delegates are arriving for the massive conference. Even Prince Faisal, son of Hussein I, the king of the Hejaz and Lawrence's brother-in-arms, has come to the French capital. Lawrence takes him out rowing on the Seine to escape the swarms of reporters pointing their cameras at the Hashemite prince in his flowing white robes. The two men who together braved the many perils of the war in the Middle East are up by 6 a.m. and are driven from the Hotel Continental on the rue de Rivoli to the boathouse at the Bois de Boulogne on the edge of Paris.

It is Lawrence who forced the English to allow Faisal to participate in the negotiations as a representative of the Arab peoples. The English officer has taken up the Arab cause both publicly and privately. On November 17, 1918, he wrote: "The Arabs came into the war without making a previous treaty with us, and have constantly refused to listen to the temptations of other powers. They have never had a press agent, or tried to make themselves out a case, but fought as hard as they could (I'll swear to that) and suffered hardships in their three campaigns and losses that would break up seasoned troops." The Arabs' only motivation, Lawrence added, was a free Arabia.

The British show a certain amount of understanding for

Lawrence's perspectives, but the French are deeply skeptical, to the point of questioning whether Faisal should even be at the negotiations. The Arab prince is quoted as telling a French negotiator: "I have not come here to make bargains, but to impress on the world that we have not escaped from Turkey to enter a new servitude, or to be divided up. I beg to inform you that I revolted to be free and sovereign, and we will die for this principle. I am not ready to hand over any part of my country to England." But France insists that the so-called Sykes-Picot Agreement between Great Britain and France be honored without taking any account of the Arab war of independence from the Ottoman Empire. That 1916 pact stipulates that predominance over Asia Minor be divided between France and England. Nonetheless, Lawrence and Faisal hope the Americans will support their cause, apply the principle of national self-determination to the Arab peoples, and promote the creation of an independent Syria.

In fact, much to France's dismay, Wilson suggests sending a commission to Syria to determine the wishes of the Arab population. France does everything in its power to prevent this from happening. Lawrence organizes a meeting between French premier Georges Clemenceau and Faisal to work out their disagreements. Lawrence is so committed to this idea that he refuses to leave Paris even when a telegram arrives with the news that his father has died. Only after he knows that the meeting is indeed going ahead does he take a week to go see and console his mother.

Faisal and Clemenceau meet in mid-April, but the occasion is not worth the effort the prince and Lawrence have put into it. Clemenceau purports to give in and grant Syria independence, but only on the condition that Faisal agrees to place the Syrian nation under a French mandate. A bald contradiction, of course—so with that Faisal's hopes are dashed. He leaves Paris on a French air force plane, not neglecting to first draw up his last will and testament.

A short time later, in May, Lawrence boards a British airplane en route to Cairo, perhaps to consult documents at the Arab Bureau, where he worked during the war, or perhaps to lead a covert military operation against Saudi leader Abd al-Aziz ibn Saud. In any case, he is frustrated, writing in his memoirs: "Youth could win, but had not learned to keep; and was pitiably weak against age. We stammered that we had worked for a new heaven and a new earth, and they thanked us kindly and made their peace."

At a refueling stop in Rome, the pilot of Lawrence's plane fails to put on the brakes in time. He has no choice but to accelerate, but as the plane begins to climb again, it gets tangled in a tree and crashes to the ground. The pilot dies instantly, while the copilot succumbs a few days later to a skull fracture. Lawrence is pulled from the smoking wreck. Miraculously, he suffers only a broken collarbone and some pulled muscles. A few days later he continues his journey to Cairo. In July, he sends a letter and a check for ten pounds to the mechanic who saved his life, Frederick J. Daw. It reads: "Will you buy yourself some trifle to remind you of our rather rough landing together at Rome? I was not at all comfortable hanging up in the wreck, and felt very grateful to you for digging me out."

By this time the situation in the Middle East is anything but calm. Ordinary Arabs are increasingly aware that the nego-tiators in Paris are not acting in their interests, and attacks increase not just on British troops stationed in the region but also on Jewish settlers in Palestine. Although Faisal has made his own attitudes known toward the Zionists in Paris, even signing an agreement in January with Zionist leader Chaim Weizmann, promising that a Jewish state will be established in Palestine, the agreement has no support among the Arab population and never takes effect. Faisal's agreement was coupled to international recognition for Arab independence.

While Faisal and Lawrence are away, French, British, and American negotiators begin to close the gaps in their positions, coming up with a provisional solution that looks like at least a partial success for Arab nationalists. Britain agrees to withdraw to Palestine, France wins control over Beirut and the Syrian coast, and the Arabs are given authority over the interior of Syria. Damascus, which has been liberated in the war, is put forward as the possible capital of a new Arabian state. When the initial news of the agreement arrives, Lawrence can hardly believe it and drafts a letter of thanks to British prime minister David Lloyd George, in which he expresses his astonishment:

> "I must confess to you that in my heart I always believed that in the end you would let the Arabs down—so that now I find it quite difficult to know how to thank you. It concerns me personally, because I assured them during the campaigns that our promises held their face value, and backed them with my word, for what it was worth. Now in your agreement over Syria you have kept all our promises to them, and given them more than perhaps they ever deserved, and my relief at getting out of the affair with clean hands is very great."

For a brief historical moment, Arab independence seems to be at hand.

GANDHI IS TORTURED by the thought that he has made a "Himalayan miscalculation" by calling for a campaign of civil disobedience against the colonial regime and its emergency laws. All that it has brought are uproar, police deployments, and violence. He feels some sense of responsibility for those who have been killed and for the suffering of their loved ones and admits as much in public—to the astonishment and displeasure of his listeners in a number of Indian cities. How is it possible that his followers threw stones, blocked trains, and even injured people after he had called upon them to protest nonviolently? In the wake of the riots, he decides that his people must themselves become more mature before resistance can be mounted. Only when they have learned to follow instructions and maintain self-discipline, only when they are prepared to uphold the general rule of law and act with a moral conscience will they be able to carry out collective acts of civil disobedience against specific, carefully chosen targets. This is the only way, Gandhi now believes, of preventing protests from getting out of hand, thereby giving the other side a pretext to use violence. His critique of the colonial authorities remains strict, but he also knows that he can only change the regime if he makes his own political movement more effective, and more adroit at mobilizing people. One step toward this goal is the creation of a core group of experienced activists to help him educate the masses in the ways of *satyagraha,* or nonviolent resistance. Like other revolutionaries, he opts for the mass medium of the printed word and begins publishing a newspaper called *Young India.*

Gandhi isn't the only one who blames himself for the outbreaks of violence in 1919. His adversaries blame him as well. Testifying to a committee of inquiry, chaired by Lord Hunter, about the Jallianwala Bagh massacre in Amritsar, Brigadier General Reginald Dyer characterizes Gandhi as the main culprit in the unrest, even though he was hundreds of kilometers away from the violence. The man who ordered British soldiers to shoot shows no remorse for his own actions or for making his subordinates fire until the crowd completely dispersed or for failing to offer medical help to the wounded. It wasn't his job to treat the injured, Dyer says. There were hospitals for that. In the end, Dyer is found guilty of exceeding his orders and is removed from duty. But the work of the committee fails to placate the Indian independence movement. None of the victims were invited to testify. Gandhi helps see to it that an alternative account of the massacre is published.

Several months later, in a speech to Muslims in Delhi, Gandhi uses the word "noncooperation" for the first time. He senses his listeners' anger and fear and knows that they are frustrated not just about conditions in India but also about the course of the peace negotiations in Versailles, which give no reason to hope things will improve. The concept of noncooperation is an attempt to mobilize this frustration. It pops into Gandhi's head as he is speaking, although he doesn't have a clear notion what it might mean. But the word seems to inspire his audience. As soon as he says it, the audience breaks out into applause. Only later in the speech, and in the weeks that follow, does the concept begin to take shape and enable the type of precise, disciplined civil disobedience that Gandhi has envisioned. Some central aspects of noncooperation include the refusal of Indian employees to work for the colonial administration and a boycott of British products in favor of Indian ones. Additionally, Gandhi wants to distribute simple spinning wheels for producing Indian cloth, or *khadi,* so that people at the bottom of Indian society have a way of earning a living. It's the beginning of Gandhi's *"khadi* program."

Viewed from Delhi, Paris seems both tantalizingly close and very far away. In January 1919, at least according to a resolution by the Indian National Congress in December 1918, Gandhi and other representatives of the Indian national movement were to have attended the start of the peace conference. Instead, it was the British colonial government that sent a delegation to Paris to represent the interests of the empire and push for Indian membership in the League of Nations. The delegation was led by the British secretary of state for India, Edwin Samuel Montagu, and included a representative from the National Congress. Although he was a moderate, the representative still emphasized that 1.2 million Indians had fought for the empire in the Great War and now expected some sort of reward.

Perhaps Gandhi chose not to travel to Europe because he knew he could do far less good there than at home. Unlike other Indian freedom fighters, he did not adopt Wilson's rhetoric of national self-determination. Instead he tried to formulate concepts of his own that would allow him to jettison Western ideologies entirely. Aside from tactical considerations, Gandhi may also have stayed home because one of his long-time allies, Bal Gangadhar Tilak, had been in London since October 1918 and was trying to influence Paris from there. The sixty-two-year-old Tilak was an experienced politician who had worked for decades to achieve Indian autonomy.

In January 1919, Tilak turns to the Allied leaders—Lloyd George, Clemenceau, and especially Wilson, whose promises have met with a broad and positive response in India. He writes to Wilson, saying "the world's hope for peace and justice is centered in you as the author of the great principle of self-determination." He includes a copy of his pamphlet "Self-Determination for India" with the letter. It contains an illustration of a giant ocean liner with people from all continents on board, ready to set sail from "autocracy to freedom." The first officer has Lloyd George's features. India, depicted as a woman in a sari, wants to get on board, but the officer doesn't have a ticket for her.

The only answer Tilak gets is a letter from Wilson's private secretary thanking him and offering a few lukewarm assurances. The Indian politician stays in the United Kingdom until November 1919 but cannot even get the British government to issue him a passport allowing him to travel from London to Paris. Nonetheless, the official Indian delegation does achieve its goal of assuring India a place in the League of Nations. It's a paradoxical situation. Indian representatives will be able to vote on the independence of other peoples without being independent themselves.

DELEGATES FROM THE negotiations are constantly wandering in and out of Louise Weiss's office. It's not the most powerful international figures who are dropping in to see her, but armies of advisors, functionaries, and experts drawn by her newspaper's reputation and their own hopes of getting the latest news, and of using her pages to influence public opinion. They show her maps, unveil bold plans, and invite her for dinners in discreet restaurants. There's no doubt anymore. Louise has become a person who carries a certain weight in political Paris, one of the few women who have a say in how things are run. Only her mother seems to have a problem with her daughter's rise. "If she supported my initiatives, it was only out of obligation, never fondness," Louise writes. "She wanted me to be confined in some hierarchy my entire life and probably found it hard to bear that my name, which was also hers, began to shine." It's the continuation of a lifelong mother-daughter rivalry that is suddenly overshadowed by a much bigger drama. Louise learns the terrible news from the papers.

On May 4, Milan Štefánik boarded a plane in Italy bound for Czechoslovakia. Attempting to land in Bratislava, the pilot lost control, the aircraft crashed, and Milan died in the wreckage. Despite their painful past, Louise's world collapses. For whom is she now supposed to work endlessly, spending her nights at the printers and her Sundays at political receptions? How can she go on without the idea of her friend, no matter how badly he disappointed her? As she weeps for Milan, Louise weeps for herself as well. She has devoted her life to serving him, to serving his cause. What will now give meaning to her existence? Her first impulse is to retreat completely into private life like so many women of her day. All the ambition that has driven her for so many years is simply gone. For the first time, she takes no interest in politics. She feels completely deflated. But is she really going to seal herself away in her own sorrow and either "consume myself or consume the planet"? She'd have to be a completely different person. Or should she keep pressing forward? But for what or whom? Louise pulls herself together and decides to carry on in Milan's memory. "Determined and unhappy," she writes, "I committed myself to this inner justification."

That same evening, unable to sleep, she receives a visit from a stranger. An elegant woman with shining black eyes enters her salon. She throws herself into Louise's arms and whispers in broken French: "I'm Giuliana. Milan told me I should come to you in times of difficulty. That's why I've travelled here from Rome. Oh, I loved him so." Louise' first thought is just to turn her away. But the sight of the grieving young woman tugs at her heartstrings. Louise offers her a place to stay and a shoulder to cry on. Giuliana shows Louise gifts that Milan brought her back from Japan. Never, she says, will she get over him.

ON HER JOURNEY east on the Trans-Siberian Railway, Marina Yurlova made the acquaintance of three young Russian ladies in elegant low-cut dresses who claimed to be students at the Smolny Institute for Noble Maidens in St. Petersburg. On the train, they were quite forthright about being kept by a wealthy Russian. Now in the Russian-Chinese city of Harbin, they take an immediate interest in the local menfolk.

"It's already nine," says Katya one evening, and all three of them spring to their feet and begin to get dressed. Marina has never seen such fine undergarments in her entire life. While the three women transform themselves into seductive, luxurious ladies, they curse in a fashion that's not fine at all. "Come on with us, Marina," says Nadia. "We are invited to a Chinese dinner. Lots of fun." Marina has no desire to spend the entire evening alone in the shabby quarters she and her new acquaintances have moved into. So she gets up from her bed and starts to dress, although she has nothing else to wear but her Cossack uniform.

The four women walk through the dark streets of nighttime Harbin to a respectable-looking restaurant. The doorman shows them into an elegant dining room, where one of the tables is already richly set and decorated with flowers. A curtain draws back to one side, and five elegantly dressed Chinese men enter the room. Marina feels uncomfortable in her heavy army coat. A waiter serves some fiery alcohol, the party converses in French, and finally dinner is served. It consists of an endless series of small bowls containing Chinese and European delicacies. Marina doesn't speak a word of French, the cigarette smoke chokes her, and the alcohol makes her dizzy. Slowly, her tired head drops down to the surface of the table between two teacups.

When, after a while, Marina opens her eyes and woozily gets back on her feet, the scene has completely changed. Nadia is playing a tango on the piano, the men are sitting on cushions with their backs against the wall, and Katya is disrobing in time to the music. She moves lasciviously in her pink chemise, one of her silk stockings has already slid to the floor and her undone hair plays around her face, flushed from dancing, while the men throw money to encourage her.

When Sonia notices Marina, she approaches with the studious concentration of the extremely inebriated. She takes Marina by the hand, leads her to one of the men, a fat fellow, and presses her down on his lap. The man begins to grope her, from her shoulders to her knees, while the piano strikes up a march. A second man comes over and begins to fumble with the middle button of her uniform. Marina has posed as a man for so long that she's completely unused to a man perceiving her as a woman. Forced to transform back into her true sex, she sobers up immediately.

"I don't want you!" she screams, then dropping to a whisper. "Oh please let me go."

"Little bitch, you don't know what's good for you," Sonja exclaims, but she shoves her toward an exit, where she can hail a rickshaw.

All Marina wants to do is get away from here. She takes the next train to Vladivostok.

AFTER BEING DISCHARGED from military service, James Reese Europe becomes a whirlwind of activity, knowing that he has to take advantage of his moment of fame in the first months of demobilization. The Harlem Hellfighters are still idolized by both black and white Americans, and their music is still considered the fanfare of triumph. In March 1919, a few weeks after the great victory parade in New York City, the former band of the 369th Infantry Regiment commences a ten-week tour of the East Coast and the Midwest. The opening concert takes place in the distinguished Hammerstein Ballroom of the Manhattan Opera House. The popular singer Noble Sissle performs a number of solos. The concert is a huge success. The audience erupts, demanding one encore after another, and the newspapers bubble over with enthusiasm for this "echo of camp life." From New York, the band heads to Philadelphia, then Boston, where they are received with similar enthusiasm. After that the group travels in two buses westward, stopping to perform in places such as Chicago, Buffalo, Cleveland, and St. Louis. Wherever they go in the heartland of jazz, their big-band sound, their tricky compositions, the squawk of the muted horns, and their sheer virtuosity and joy in playing completely wows their audiences. Their repertoire is broad: from French marches to American folk songs to Europe's own wartime hit "On Patrol in No

Man's Land," which reproduces with light and sound effects the booming of bombs and the crackle of machine-gun fire. The band even offers up syncopated versions of classical compositions like Grieg's Peer Gynt Suite. The *Chicago Defender* newspaper raves: "The work of the 'Hellfighters' would not suffer by comparison with the best of them. In many ways it surpasses them all: for it is safe to say that no other organization in the world could complete with this one in the rendition of 'Blues,' 'Jazz' and Negro folk numbers." But at a concert in Terre Haute, the first wrong notes intrude upon this triumphant tour. The director of the local opera house insists that, in accordance with the venue's rules, white and black audience members must sit in separate sections. The crowd doesn't take kindly to this rule, which contradicts the message of black emancipation conveyed by the upbeat music of this regimental band. On the evening of the concert, angry women assemble in front of the opera house and hand out flyers condemning racial segregation. Ultimately, James Reese Europe and his band will play for two hundred white and two black listeners, the latter condemned as "traitors" in the press. But the final concert of the tour is scheduled for Harlem on May 10, 1919, and it promises to be a huge success. At the age of thirty-nine, the composer and band leader is at the height of his fame—James Reese Europe's mercurial rise during the war has continued in peacetime. But his triumph is that of the black entertainer, not the black soldier and least of all the black citizen.

HENRY JOHNSON, TOO, gets the red-carpet treatment after his return and the victory parade in New York. America wants to get a look at "Black Death," the warrior who helped the US Army achieve victory on the battlefields of France. An agent offers him ten thousand dollars for a speaking tour through the country, but Johnson turns him down. He doesn't trust white agents.

Still, he likes being famous. In March 1919 he accompanies his former commander, Colonel Hayward, to an event in Albany aimed at selling Liberty Bonds. A short time later, he accepts an offer to appear in St. Louis for fifteen hundred dollars. That event is intended to celebrate the contribution of black soldiers to the US victory in front of a large audience. Johnson first makes sure to pocket his appearance fee as a preacher warms up the crowd, celebrating the heroic deeds of black soldiers as a new beginning for America not just in war but in peace as well. He paints a picture in which black and white Americans live in harmony and recognition of each other's service to the nation.

Johnson is greeted with frenetic applause when he limps on stage, his chest covered in medals. At this moment, he seems to be the very embodiment of the new America. He steps up to the microphone. But after just his first few sentences, the audience realizes that Johnson has no intention of joining in the harmonious chorus. He wants to tell people the truth about the war. He begins to recount his experiences, from being drafted to his deficient training, his shoddy equipment, and the contempt of white soldiers who refused to take their positions next to black ones in the trenches. Even on the front lines, he tells listeners, there was no solidarity between black and white. The soldiers from Harlem were treated as inferior, barely good enough to perform menial labor and serve as cannon fodder. They were only sent into battle when things got too dangerous for white soldiers. "Send the niggers to the front and there won't be so many around

New York," he quotes a white officer as saying. His entire pent-up rage, the humiliations and trauma he suffered on the battle-field burst out of him: "Yes, I saw dead people. In fact, I have seen so many dead bodies piled up that when I saw a live one I didn't think it was natural."

He considers himself a hero, but he doesn't want to play one just to please white people, and he doubts that America will honor his sacrifice as it should. "If I was a white man," Johnson says, "I would be the next governor of New York." The longer he speaks, the greater the unrest in the crowd grows. There are groans, then interjections and whistles. When Johnson is done, the audience vents its displeasure. The local civic leaders and the preachers try to calm people down, apologizing for the angry speaker and trying to mediate.

Only when the event is over can black voices be heard that were previously hardly audible in the hall. At the exit, Johnson is received with thunderous applause and cheers. Hands reach out to touch him, and he is hoisted onto a crowd of shoulders and carried like a trophy throughout the city. Women shower him with flowers and kisses. In the speaking hall, he was a traitor, but on the streets of St. Louis, he's a hero. The following day, the press will accuse Johnson of inciting racial unrest.

It's Henry Johnson's last major public appearance. After the uproar in St. Louis, no promoter is willing to put him on stage. He lives from part-time jobs and begins to numb the pain in his wounded body and traumatized soul with alcohol. In 1923, his wife leaves him. From then on, Henry Johnson, the Black Death, lives alone with his memories and injuries.

THE PENULTIMATE CONCERT on James Reese Europe's tour across North America is to take place on May 9 in Boston. Cold and rain have settled in over the East Coast, and since the Boston Opera House is booked, the band has to settle for drafty old Mechanics Hall on Huntington Avenue. Europe has felt the symptoms of the flu coming on for days, but he's determined to make it through the final dates of the tour. The matinee is a success, and Europe is able to summon enough energy to take the stage in the evening.

What happens then is preserved in a typewritten manuscript by Noble Sissle. The concert proceeds without a hitch until the intermission. Then as the musicians leave the stage, two drummers, the twins Steve and Herbert Wright, head straight for Europe's dressing room. They're angry, and Europe tries to find the words to calm them down. There is a moment of silence, then Herbert blurts out: "Lieutenant Europe, you don't treat me right. I work hard for you. Look at my hands, they're all swollen where I have been drumming, trying to hold the time and yet, Steve, he makes all kinds of mistakes and you never say anything to him." Herbert allows himself to be pacified with compliments and leaves, but a short time later, he returns completely enraged. He throws a drum into the corner of Europe's dressing room and screams: "I'll kill anybody that takes advantage of me! Jim Europe, I'll kill you!" Everyone watches in horror, frozen by shock, as Herbert takes out a pocketknife. Europe keeps his cool, grabbing a chair for defense and telling his drummer in a decisive voice: "Herbert, get out of here." At that moment, Wright throws himself at Europe and stabs him in the neck.

Europe's uniform turns bloodred, and someone ties a towel around the wound and summons an ambulance. The band leader orders the concert to go ahead under the direction of his assistant. Sissle is to ensure that all the necessary preparations are made for the final date of the tour in Harlem. By the time the curtain goes up tomorrow, Europe promises, he'll be on his feet again.

After the concert, when Sissle arrives at Boston City Hospital, the members of the band are all being asked to donate blood. But after a few minutes it's clear that any help will arrive too late. The doctors have failed to staunch the bleeding. James Reese Europe is dead.

AT HIS WEDDING Alvin York realizes that he has become something of a hero in his small hometown in the mountains. More than a thousand people attend the celebration, taking their places at the longest banquet tables Pall Mall has ever seen. And people from all over the region see to it that those tables bend under the weight of roast goats, pigs and turkeys, eggs, cornbread, milk, marmalade, and cakes.

When the guests have left and the fanfare has passed, York gets to work. He's thought about it long enough and now knows what he wants to do with his life. He has realized that it's not by accident that he was called to war and went out into the great wide world. Nor was it by accident that he survived. The former pacifist now believes there was a deeper meaning to the war, albeit not the same one that politicians and generals were always trying to promote. The significance of the war for York is deeply personal. God put him in danger and then saved him in order to give him a mission. He was to stare death in the face so that he could understand how precious life is. He was to travel the great wide world so as to comprehend the limits and isolation of the world he comes from. He was to understand how little he understood and to draw consequences from that knowledge.

His first act is to visit the Tennessee Highway Department and convince the people in charge to build a road to Pall Mall. Previously, he thought the mountains protected the valley dwellers from the dangers of the world. Now he sees those mountains as a barrier, cutting people off from many important influences. The road that is soon to be constructed will be the beginning of new connections.

What especially weighs on York is the memory of how lost he felt when he left the narrow confines of his village. In the war, he had been forced to recognize how much he didn't know and how poor his education had been. He wants the children of his hometown to be better prepared and begins to collect money to build a new school and hire new teachers. And indeed, several months later the town has a new school, new teachers, and new textbooks. York invites children from the region, many of whom can neither read nor write, to attend the school. In the future he plans to found a vocational center, build a playground, establish a library, and ensure that people get proper medical care. The town children should gain knowledge and learn how to provide for themselves by doing skilled work. Someday, those children will change life in the mountains, bringing paved roads, modern houses, sanitary facilities, and electricity. They will have it better than he did, he who felt so small and stupid next to the enormity of the war, the diversity of the people he met, and the big cities like Boston, Paris, and New York. This is how York intends to transform the sign God gave him into deeds.

AT THE STADTSCHLOSS in Weimar, the seat of the new German republic, Matthias Erzberger succeeds in making himself even more unpopular than he was after he signed the armistice agreement in Compiègne. Although he was elected in his southern German district as a representative to the National Assembly in January 1919 and then appointed a minister in the cabinet of Chancellor Philipp Scheidemann, his realistic stance toward the peace negotiations in Paris outrages many German politicians as well as much of the German public. Ever since meeting General Foch, Erzberger knows that Germany cannot expect to be treated gently at the peace negotiations. What his American sources tell him confirms his worst fears. Germany, as Erzberger will write in his memoirs, will be forced to perform "eternal slave labor" for the victors.

In May 1919, the German delegation in Paris is presented with the conditions for peace. The delegates then take this document, which ascribes sole blame for the war to Germany, back to Weimar. "When the enemies' conditions for peace . . . became known, the first response was paralysis," Erzberger writes. "Then a cry of outrage went up at the violation of the solemn assurances that a just peace would be instituted according to Wilsonian principles." The question of how Germany should respond to these conditions divides the Weimar government. One group, which includes Chancellor Scheidemann, wants to reject the conditions as "unacceptable." Speaking in the National Assembly, he is even less diplomatic: "Which hand would not wither, having placed itself and us in such shackles?"

Erzberger, on the other hand, wants Germany to criticize the terms as "impossible to bear or fulfill." He fears that the word "unacceptable," no matter how "popular for a day" it might prove among the German public, will carry a heavy price, when Germany, having no other option, is forced to sign the peace treaty anyway.

The minister throws his entire political weight behind his approach, threatening to resign if Germany doesn't sign the peace agreement. In a memorandum, he spells out the reasons why he is in favor of signing. Germany, he argues, is not at all capable of resuming hostilities. Moreover, signing would lead to an improvement in the economic situation, and food shortages would ease. Finally, if Germany took a conciliatory approach in Paris, it would gain future room to maneuver on issues such as reparations and its role in the world—for instance, in the League of Nations. During days of heated debate at the uppermost levels of government, Erzberger repeatedly emphasizes that Germany has no other alternative. He argues, "If my hands and feet are bound, and someone puts a gun to my chest and demands that I sign a piece of paper in which I pledge to climb to the moon within 48 hours, every thinking person would sign that paper to save his life while pointing out that he cannot fulfill its demands."

Pressure is being heaped on the decisions makers of the Weimar Republic—and not just from the right-wing press. The night before the Paris delegation is due to arrive back in Weimar, inmates break out of a local prison and try to force their way into the Stadtschloss. The gate is secured only at the last minute, whereupon the fugitives begin to shoot out the windows. Bullets fly into the bedrooms of two government ministers who reside directly underneath Erzberger's apartment. All the government's ministers should be taken and hanged, the attackers yell out.

On June 19, unwilling to sign the Treaty of Versailles, Scheidemann dissolves his fractious cabinet, and a new government is formed under former labor minister Gustav Bauer, with Erzberger as the minister of finance. Erzberger knows that he has been promoted to probably the least desirable office in the entire country. In his new role he will be required to raise money from the German people to pay for war reparations. Even now, Erzberger hopes the peace treaty will at least contain some small concessions of the sort he was able to extract at the last minute in Compiègne. But two pieces of disastrous news cause the already incendiary situation to explode.

The first one comes from Scapa Flow in the Orkney Islands in Scotland, where the German war fleet was put under the supervision of the victorious powers in November 1918. On June 21, 1919, German rear admiral Ludwig von Reuter, who is still in command, orders his officers to sink the ships. The sea vents are blown and the bulkheads jammed open. As the ships slowly sink to the bottom in the shallow bay, their crews row lifeboats to the nearby shore. By taking it upon himself to issue these defiant orders, Reuter wants to protest the peace treaty that is about to be signed. The idea is that if war erupts again, the British won't be able to use the German fleet. But from a tactical point of view, Reuter couldn't have chosen a worse moment for his act of rebellion.

The second catastrophic piece of news from Erzberger's perspective comes from Berlin and spreads around the world with lightning quickness. In response to reports coming out of Versailles, French flags captured in the 1870–71 Franco-Prussian War are being publicly burned in the former Reich capital. In the face of such hostility, the victorious Allies declare that Germany's period of consideration is over. Germany will either have to accept the peace treaty or hostilities will resume immediately.

The imminent threat of an enemy invasion sparks feverish activity in the Weimar government. The Allies' first targets are sure to be Berlin and Weimar. At the same time, Erzberger receives signals from the officer corps that the army is unwilling to defend the government if it signs the treaty. A decision must be made within twenty-four hours. On June 22, the National Assembly passes a resolution accepting the terms of peace as dictated. A short time before, someone lobbed a hand grenade through a window of what is mistakenly thought to be Erzberger's bedroom. For his own safety, the newly appointed finance minister is whisked out of the boiling cauldron that is Weimar.

AFTER MILAN'S DEATH, Louise Weiss copes with her loss in her own particular way—by throwing herself into her work. She prepares the issue of L'Europe nouvelle about the peace treaty with special fastidiousness. She wants the contents to be just as Milan would have had them. After all, he was one of the promoters of a new Europe that does in fact seem to be arising. "My work will be a secret eulogy for him, the most beautiful of them all," Louise writes. "Maybe one day it will help my wounds to heal?" But Louise isn't naïve. Even as she devotes all her energy to the European project, she knows full well that the men who are writing the treaties are no saints. They are fighting for the interests of their own countries and governments; their chief concern is their own prosperity, and they are eminently willing to ignore the ideal of a better world for all. In her newspaper, she lays bare the internal tensions that have overshadowed the peace negotiations from the start.

Come what may, Louise wants to be on hand when the treaty

with the German Reich is signed in the Hall of Mirrors in Versailles, the place where fifty years ago Wilhelm I—in a deliberate act of humiliation—had himself proclaimed emperor after Germany's victory in the Franco-Prussian War. On June 28, Weiss takes the train from Paris along the Seine to Versailles. The weather is unsettled. White clouds, isolated rays of sunshine, and rain drops pass over Louis XIV's palace, where—in a gesture of respect to the vanquished—no flags are flown.

Marshal Foch doesn't attend the ceremony. He disagrees with several of the central points of the peace treaty. For instance, he finds it inexcusable that the Rhine River is not set as the border between Germany and France. The endless series of honors showered upon him since the end of the war has done nothing to change his attitude toward France's neighbor, and in protest, although the peace treaty is anything but kind to his archenemy, the architect of the Allied victory refuses to make an appearance at Versailles. Article 231 of the treaty stipulates that Germany alone bears responsibility for the war, and further provisions require the Reich to hand back Alsace-Lorraine to France and to cede most of Western Prussia and Posen to the newly re-created state of Poland. The Saar region with its valuable deposits of coal is to be put under the administration of the League of Nations, and Allied troops will occupy the Rhineland. Germany's standing army is capped at 100,000 men, and Germany will be forced to pay reparations to its former enemies, the total sum of which is still to be determined.

To Louise, the peace treaty seems less like a step toward reconciliation than a continuation of the war by other means. How new is this new world order everyone keeps talking about? Aren't the same old policies of national interest and the tug-of-war for influence and colonies around the world still in effect? And don't most of the same old global powers still control the levers of power within the League of Nations? Will this cumbersome institution, which lacks any executive organs, ever be capable of preventing new wars?

"The mirrors did as they were designed to and multiplied to infinity one single moment, in this case the gestures of an ephemeral world government," Louise writes. She feels sorry for the representatives of the German Reich, who are forced to be the first to sign this document. All these "idiots" had to do was to wait for Germany's economic might to keep growing, and the leading role in Europe would have fallen into their laps without a war. She also feels sympathy for Clemenceau, who has chaired the peace conference. For all his triumph, he will never become president. She even feels a bit bad for Wilson. During the war, people listened to him because they needed US soldiers, but now England and France simply ignore the president and his lofty plans.

Louise's conflicting feelings of sympathy reflect the conflicts within the peace treaty itself: the barely concealed national interests of the victors; the shock of realization among the vanquished who, if they haven't realized it before, now know that their defeat will have deadly consequences; and the disappointed hopes of all the peoples of the world who believed in Wilson's promise of a "right to self-determination." Perhaps even the victors in this war—the countries that are to receive reparations and that have succeeded in expanding their global power—are in some sense also losers. After all, they're the ones who are squandering the chance to institute a new constructive spirit of reconciliation. The dream of a more just and peaceful world order has been sacrificed on the altar of raison d'état. The Treaty of Versailles contains no vigorous mechanisms for keeping the peace—indeed it's full of contradictions that are bound to ignite a new war at some point in the future.

VIRGINIA WOOLF WATCHES with fascination as the products that vanished from stores late in the war return in the months after the armistice: sugar cakes, currant buns, and mountains of sweets. But the selection is still somewhat restricted compared to prewar days. Will the conclusion of the peace treaty signal a final return to normalcy? Woolf only mentions the Treaty of Versailles belatedly in her diaries, and then in passing. Nor do the peace celebrations particularly inspire her; she doubts they are worth "taking a new nib." Woolf watches the peace parade in Richmond, which plods ahead in the pouring rain, from her window, feeling "desolate, dusty, & disillusioned." Only after dinner does she pull herself together sufficiently to poke her nose outside. It has stopped raining, and drunken couples are waltzing in the corner pub. From atop a hill, Virginia and Leonard watch what can be seen of the fireworks in the mist. "Red & green & yellow & blue balls rose slowly into the air, burst, flowered into an oval of light, which dropped in minute grains & expired . . . Rising over the Thames, among trees, these rockets were beautiful."

Virginia stays away from the celebrations in London, noting only "the rim of refuse on the outskirts" that remains afterward. Otherwise, it's up to her servants to tell her about what they witnessed at Vauxhall Bridge, where "generals & soldiers & tanks & nurses & bands took 2 hours in passing." She writes: "It was they said the most splendid sight of their lives." On her own feelings about this "servants festival; some thing got up to pacify & placate 'the people,'" she notes: "There's something calculated & politic & insincere about these peace rejoicings. Moreover they are carried out with no beauty, & not much spontaneity. Flags are intermittent . . . Yesterday in London the usual sticky stodgy conglomerations of people, sleepy & torpid as a cluster of drenched bees, were crawling over Trafalgar Square, & rocking about the pavements in the neighbourhood." She feels bad about being such a spoilsport on this momentous occasion. But why should she pretend to be enjoying herself as though she were at a children's birthday party?

MEANWHILE THE FORMER crown prince of the German Reich is passing his days, each one much like the next, in his Dutch exile, occasionally doing the work of a smithy. The village blacksmith, Jan Luijt, who is teaching him the craft, was one of Wilhelm's first acquaintances on the island of Wieringen, where he has spent the past six months, but he also has cordial relations with the pastor's family, in whose house he's residing. The former crown prince reads a little, does some writing, goes swimming in the sea, and now and then entertains visitors. The initial brusque rejection by the island's inhabitants gradually mellows. The former crown prince fits in well, even donning *klompjes*, or wooden shoes, which he knows enough to remove before entering someone's house. Wilhelm's worst enemy is boredom, interrupted only by concern that the Allies could succeed in forcing his extradition.

But the former heir to the German throne is no ordinary vacationer—as shown by the fact that souvenir hunters are eager to purchase the products of Wilhelm's blacksmith training.

The first customer, an American, offers Luijt twenty-five pounds for a horseshoe made by the former crown prince and bearing the letter *W*. The blacksmith quickly recognizes a new business opportunity and before long has to secretly forge Wilhelm horseshoes at night to keep up with demand. Wilhelm himself can only shake his head: "People remain prepared to encourage delusions of grandeur in our kind, even when we're sitting on a small island covered by sea grass far removed from the whole circus. They used to collect my discarded cigarette butts, and now some class snob is offering me a sum of money with which a poor man could be lifted out of his misery back home . . . I'm not surprised that many a man has become the way he inevitably had to be with this cult of personality!" The trade in souvenirs inspires critics to ask whether this pampered son of the Hohenzollerns, who had built his whole splendid life on the backs of his subjects, should be allowed to enrich himself even after his fall from power. Only later does the general public learn that half of the proceeds from the sale of horseshoes has gone to the blacksmith and the other half to needy families in Wieringen.

The news of the peace treaty crashes down upon the summer calm of the North Sea island like a thunderstorm. Wilhelm is beside himself at the "dictates of Versailles," which a "blind lust for revenge has thrust upon us." He lashes out at the "outrageous demands that cannot be fulfilled even with the best of will [and] the brutal threats to choke the life out of us every time our strength fails—and in addition an unprecedented piece of stupidity, a document that enshrines war and hatred and bitterness for all time." The only ray of hope is that the Treaty of Versailles might serve as a basis for allowing exiled Wilhelm to return home. The former crown prince may have gone to the Netherlands of his own accord, but the decision about whether he will ever be allowed to go back to Germany depends on the good will of the Dutch and the new German government. How long will he remain trapped on this island? And what awaits him in his homeland? Realistically, the new order will only tolerate him in its midst if he forgoes any public role.

KÄTHE KOLLWITZ IS happy for the harbingers of spring in May 1919, but she's dismayed by the harbingers of peace. "The swallows are back again!" she writes.

> "Returning from an art academy meeting, I walked down Unter den Linden . . . Everything was wonderful. The sky was full of light, the foliage was still delicate, and everything looked as if transfigured. I felt again that Berlin was my home, the city I love . . . And now we're threatened with such a terrible peace. The palace still hasn't been repaired. The balcony from which the Kaiser always spoke is shot half to smithereens, and the entrance badly damaged. A symbol of crushed majesty."

The news from Versailles brings fresh unrest to Berlin, just as the city is beginning to settle back into its everyday routine. In May, masses of people are once again on the move on the streets of the city center. Public opinion is anything but unanimous. There are demonstrations for and against accepting the Allies' terms of peace, and in a situation this divided and emotionally charged, confrontations are inevitable.

Kollwitz doesn't take part in any of the public demonstrations. She's too busy trying to capture the experience of the time in her art: loss, death, sadness, and starvation are her subjects. But she finds it incredibly difficult to work. She used to be able to concentrate for hours, becoming engrossed in her creations. Now she feels nervous and worried, and her works seem inadequate even before she has finished them.

On June 29, 1919, the newspapers announce that the new government has signed the peace treaty. How Kollwitz once longed for this day, and how bitter it now appears. "I thought about this day so often," she writes. "Flags hanging from all the windows. I considered long and hard what kind of flag I would put out and concluded that it should be a white flag with big red letters spelling out: peace. Garlands and flowers were to dangle from its shaft and tip. I thought that it would be a peace of reconciliation, and that the day on which it was proclaimed would be a day of 'sobbing recognition' among people crying tears of joy that *peace* had arrived." Kollwitz does in fact feel like crying, but not from joy.

Still, what option does she have other than to carry on? Her husband has to care for increasing numbers of patients, many of whom suffer more from general privation than from any specific illness. Kollwitz herself has commissions. Life must continue. She begins to clear out her dead son's room, so that her mother, who's suffering from dementia, can move in. "This is such sorrowful work," she sighs. In a red cabinet, she finds Peter's painting kit, his sketchbooks, and examples of his keen mind, liveliness, and talent. "His room was sacred," Kollwitz writes. Now it will become profane.

BY THE TIME the peace treaty gets signed, Matthias Erzberger has become, in the words of a contemporary, the theologian and philosopher Ernst Troeltsch, "the most hated of all German politicians." Art collector Count Harry Kessler tells of how on a train journey an elderly gentleman loudly cursed the German finance minister, threatening to "put a few hand grenades under his car." The most vitriolic attacks, however, come from an ultraconservative nationalist parliamentary deputy named Karl Helfferich, who writes a series of articles in the reactionary *Kreuzzeitung*. In them, the author not only takes Erzberger to task for the political decisions he helped make in the past years, but also accuses him of having enriched himself personally from the lofty offices he occupied. Erzberger, who in his function as finance minister has had to concentrate all his energy on bringing about the largest financial reform in German history, does what he can to defend himself against Helfferich's slanderous portrayals of him as the man mainly responsible for the "peace of shame," as the embodiment of all the evil in the new republic, as the "scourge of the Reich" and a "cancer." In August 1919, Helfferich's tirades are collected in a pamphlet with the title "Erzberger Must Go!"

SHORTLY AFTER THE signing of the Treaty of Versailles, a letter reaches Arnold Schönberg in his apartment in the Viennese district of Mödling. A certain Monsieur Fromaigeat from Winterthur, Switzerland, invites him to become part of a movement that has just started in Paris. Its goal is the restoration of what at the time was sporadically called the "Internationale of the Mind," the left-wing consensus across national borders among cultural leaders, which has been destroyed by the mobilization of artists and intellectuals for the war. Schönberg's answer is extensive and brimming with the cutting cynicism the composer always uses when something rubs him the wrong way—that is, quite often. With seeming cordiality, Schönberg expresses his happiness that the reconciliation movement has started in Paris, since "it was precisely there, from the beginning of the war to the end of the war, and indeed even subsequently, that there originated the most aggressive campaigns to destroy this Internationale insofar as Germany was concerned." Restoration, Schönberg continues, will not be easy. There can be no pretending that nothing has happened. "Something did happen!" Schönberg exclaims. "It happened . . . that Saint-Saens and Lalo spoke of German music in outrageous terms and that even after the armistice a man like Claudel goes on talking about 'Boches.'" Schönberg admits that "there were sins on our side too." But "never and nowhere did anyone go to anything like the lengths they did in Paris." He adds that he is only willing to join an initiative of intellectuals who are willing to clearly distance themselves from the mistakes of the recent past. Everyone else will have to be excluded "from a community in which there can be only one kind of war: a war against all that is low and beastly, and . . . only one mode of warfare: holding aloof from such things." Schönberg never hears back from Monsieur Fromaigeat.

AFTER THE TREATY has been signed, Louise Weiss looks around the empty Hall of Mirrors and the jumble of abandoned chairs. It becomes clear to her that something has passed, not just for the world, but also for her personally. After this disappointing end to a spring of hope, she can no longer imagine spending the rest of her days in the close confines of an editorial office. She wants to leave Paris and see the European continent, about which she has written so much, with her own eyes. She wants to understand the world and work toward the peace in which she still believes, just as Milan did.

Louise has hardly any savings, but that doesn't stop her from traveling. She has become a respected journalist and has good connections. The newspaper *Le Petit Parisien* sells over a million copies a day, and its support for politicians can decide elections. With the help of the new Czechoslovakian foreign minister, Edvard Beneš, Louise sets up a meeting with the editor-in-chief, Élie Joseph Bois, who barely looks up from the papers strewn across his desk.

"How can I be of service?" he asks.

Louise knows she must get straight to the point.

"Make me your correspondent in Prague and the *Petit Parisien* will be the number one newspaper there, as it is here."

Bois gets up from his chair and paces around his office before grabbing her by the shoulders.

"That is out of the question."

There was no way he was sending a reporter in a petticoat to a place where there was still fighting between Czechs, Germans, and Hungarians.

"But I have talent," Louise insists.

That is true, Bois has to admit. So she should go, but she's on her own.

"I can't promise you anything," he cautions. "Send me some articles. If the boss likes them, I'll publish them."

The great victory parade on July 14, 1919, is one of the final impressions of the French capital that Louise will take with her on her journey. Allied divisions march from the Arc de Triomphe

down the Champs-Élysées toward the Louvre. It is the apotheosis of the careers of Marshals Joffre and Foch. But Louise is
ashamed when she sees the black soldiers from the colonies and
the troops from India who had been summoned to Europe to kill
and be killed for a cause that was not their own. Louise doesn't
know how, but she knows that everything must change. "To
impose rules on war, to limit it, to tend to the wounded, to celebrate the dead—in short to 'humanize' the war—what a farce!"
she writes. "War is unacceptable. It must be eradicated."

On a warm evening in August, Weiss boards a train at the
Gare de l'Est bound for Prague. Some of the train cars are still
armored, whereas she herself is armed only with "fifteen hundred francs in savings, twenty-six years of age and faith." No one
accompanies her to the station. Not even her parents show up to
bid her farewell.

ON OCTOBER 21, 1919, Virginia Woolf receives six author copies
of *Night and Day* in the mail. "Am I nervous?" she asks in her
journal. "Oddly little; more excited & pleased than nervous. In
the first place, there it is, out & done with; then I read a bit &
liked it; then I have a kind of confidence, that the people whose
judgment I value will probably think well of it, which is much
reinforced by the knowledge that even if they dont, I shall pick
up & start another story on my own."

The first reactions that Woolf receives in letters are encouraging. "No doubt a work of the highest genius," writes her
brother-in-law Clive Bell. Woolf notes: "Well, he might not have
liked it; he was critical of *The Voyage Out*. I own I'm pleased; yet
not convinced that it is as he says. However, this is a token that

I'm right to have no fears." Woolf also notices that her star is on the rise in the inner circle of literati—she is inundated with requests for reviews of novels, and sometimes dispatches one a day. She is constantly typing, and her hands ache as through from rheumatism. The first reviews of her novel arrive. There are rhapsodies of praise, but also some pans in which she's accused of not writing up to her own literary standards. Will she ever be able to quit writing reviews for money?

While Leonard is recovering from a relapse of malaria, which he contracted while in Ceylon, and Virginia once again realizes "how entirely my weight rests upon his prop," she keeps a step-by-step record, laced with irony and self-doubt, of her own literary rise. A short time later she will make her first appearance as a minor celebrity, "a small Lioness," at a function hosted by Lord and Lady Cecil. In attendance, along with the hosts' son, are Prince Antoine Bibesco and his wife, Elizabeth, the daughter of former British prime minister Herbert Henry Asquith. They all want to meet the writer they have read so much about, and despite her pedigree, Elizabeth is nervous when she retreats to a bay window to chat with Woolf alone. She doesn't try to say anything clever, although she is clearly very intelligent and doesn't even contradict Woolf as she criticizes an actress who happens to be her aunt, so unwilling is she to start a dispute with an "intellectual." Woolf can't but enjoy the sensation of superiority. This must be what success feels like.

THAT SAME FALL, Rudolf Höss travels with some thousand Freikorps Rossbach paramilitaries to the Baltics. In October, the German government explicitly prohibited additional armed

German units from joining the fighting south of the Baltic Sea. Defense Minister Gustav Noske even threatened to have anyone who crossed the border shot. But the paramilitary units simply ignore such proscriptions. When they reach Germany's eastern edge, they turn their machine guns on border guards, who salute and allow the paramilitaries to pass. Rogue missions like these will ultimately lead the Freikorps Rossbach to be disbanded, although the group will continue to operate underground.

Once in the Baltics, the paramilitaries join the "West Russian Liberation Army," which consists of Russian, Baltic German, and German units fighting against the newly founded Republic of Latvia and intending to do battle with Russian revolutionaries as well. Until the end of his days, Höss will remember the fighting in the Baltics for the brutality shown toward civilians, which he ascribes exclusively to the other side. That violence, he writes, had a "wildness and doggedness that I knew neither from the world war nor from paramilitary fighting." He continued: "There was no real front. The enemy was everywhere. And wherever there was a confrontation, there was butchery until one side had been completely annihilated." Höss sees houses set on fire and their inhabitants burned alive. The images of burned-out huts and charred corpses will stay with Höss until the end of his life. "Back then I was still able to pray," he writes, "and I did so."

Six

The End of the Beginning

We had fallen ill with Germany. We experienced the process of transformation as a physical pain . . . We always stood in the flickering light of the explosion, always stood near where the act of burning was happening . . . And so positioned between two orders, the old one we destroyed and the new one we helped to create . . . we became agitated and homeless, accursed bearers of terrible powers, made strong by our will to incur guilt.

—Ernst von Salomon, *The Outlaws*, 1930

Walter Gropius, *Monument to the March Dead*, 1922

AT 2:30 P.M. on January 26, 1920, Matthias Erzberger leaves the district court in the Moabit neighborhood of Berlin, where a judge is hearing a spectacular libel suit the German finance minister is bringing against Karl Helfferich. Erzberger has just settled into the back of his car when a young man jumps up onto the running board and fires two shots at point-blank range. One of the bullets hits Erzberger in the shoulder and the other ricochets off his watch chain. Everyone present freezes in shock, and then the would-be assassin is thrown to the ground and restrained. Erzberger, bleeding profusely, is taken to the hospital. He survives the attack, but he will never fully recover from the trauma, from the awareness of how vulnerable he is.

On March 12, the court renders its verdict in the libel case, fining Helfferich three hundred marks. But the real loser of the trial is Erzberger, as the court finds that most of the accusations leveled against him have a basis in fact. Erzberger now has the reputation of a corrupt politician who has exploited his office to benefit himself and the companies with which he is associated. Erzberger decides to go on leave until another court is able to render a verdict on those accusations. The right-wing press makes a meal of his provisional resignation. Even Käthe Kollwitz believes that "Erzberger seems to have revealed himself as a crook."

WHEN WE STEP from the summer of 1919 to the beginning of 1920, we leave what Ernst Troeltsch called the "dreamland of the armistice." After the Treaty of Versailles is signed, the mood expressed in people's diaries, correspondence, and memoirs changes. Little by little something akin to everyday life resumes. But especially in those countries where the end of the war caused profound upheavals, it is an everyday life fraught with uncertainty, even danger. It seems as though the hard times will never end.

Dark visions of destruction and hatred, accompanied by growing calls for violence, become increasingly prominent. The totalitarian ideologies that threaten one another with annihilation are hardening into deadly fronts. The age of extremes is on the horizon.

"UPHEAVAL—CASUALTIES . . . NOISE and fear." In March 1920, Alma Mahler-Gropius travels to Weimar to see her husband. She stays at the Hotel Elephant, where on the thirteenth of the month she witnesses disturbing scenes. "In front of me was the market square in twilight," she writes. "Eerie agitation. The young men with the pointed helmets from the Kapp Party are spit upon by workers. But they don't move a muscle. The crowd roars." Alma is witnessing an attempted putsch against the young German republic. Freikorps paramilitaries have seized control of the government both in Weimar, the seat of the German National Assembly, and in Berlin. The Erhardt Naval

Brigade has marched into the former German capital, and many of the soldiers have painted white swastikas on their helmets. The German government under Ebert, then Reich president, and Chancellor Bauer decides to flee and simultaneously calls for a general strike. One of the leaders of the putsch, the civil servant Wolfgang Kapp, is declared Germany's new chancellor.

From her window in the Elephant, Alma observes the fruitless efforts of a government emissary to mediate between the right-wing putschists and the left-wing counterdemonstrators. Night falls. "Not a light is burning. In the darkness, the masses are even more eerie than during the day. Here and there a match is struck to light a cigarette . . . Everyone is afraid of looting. We hardly dare to speak a word out loud."

It's not just the people who have taken to the streets who declare their true colors. Alma is insulted by exiled Russian artist Vasily Kandinsky, who is about to be appointed a Bauhaus teacher, for her "Jew love" for Franz Werfel. Kandinsky and his wife, she writes, "called me a Jew slave and other things like that." It's ironic that this happens to her. Like Walter Gropius, she makes few bones about the resentment she feels toward Jews. On the other hand, she is not only friends with a number of them, but she has already been married to Gustav Mahler and will yet marry Werfel.

Over the next few days the general strike, the largest in German history, begins to have an effect. "The sewers aren't being emptied, and a horrible stench pervades the streets," Alma writes.

> Water has to be brought from far away. But the worst thing is that the workers have prevented the burial of the dead. Students

who tried to sneak up to the cemetery wall where bodies were simply dumped were driven away by the greater numbers of workers who stood guard there. As a result, dead bodies have lain outside, unburied, for days. Today, the bodies of workers who fell in battle were buried. The funeral procession went right by my window. There was an endless series of placards reading: Long live Rosa Luxemburg! Long live Liebknecht! The Bauhaus was fully represented, and Walter Gropius, who saw several ministers in the procession, regretted the fact that I had dissuaded him from joining in. I just wanted him to stay away from politics. The officers who had been killed were simply put in the ground like mangy dogs. Paid slaves—that's all they were. Yes, the world is now full of "justice."

Kapp flees to Sweden, and five days after it began the putsch collapses. It lacked sufficient support both from the public at large and especially from state bureaucrats and other employees. But the March unrest has shown that left-wingers weren't the only ones dreaming of revolution. Revolutionary energy, the ability to sweep people along, the power of a strictly organized movement, the mobilization of the masses, and the will to overthrow the status quo—all could be found on both extremes of the political spectrum, together with the conviction that unfettered violence was an acceptable means to eliminate the enemy. For the moment, the Weimar Republic has survived intact, but the Kapp Putsch will not be the last potentially deadly test it faces.

KÄTHE KOLLWITZ WITNESSES the putsch in Berlin. "The counterrevolution has now commenced," she writes. "Today royalist troops with black-white-and-red banners moved in from Döberitz. The government has fled, public buildings have been occupied, [the left-wing newspapers] *Vorwärts* and *Freiheit* have been banned. People stand in packs on the streets. Everyone seems thunderstruck. What will happen? It's again March, the unruly month!" The artist lives in fear that fresh "fighting among brothers-in-arms" will break out. "It was like a lead weight on my chest, when I heard about it," she laments. "Terribly heavy."

Several days later she speaks with a young friend named Helene. Rarely has she been able to discuss the breakdowns in their mutual world so frankly with someone that age. Helene was not one of the young people instantly swept up with enthusiasm when the old Reich collapsed amid war and revolution. She regrets not having a husband and children in such uneasy times. She has a fatalistic outlook on life and simply wants to drift, or perhaps travel, letting herself become the plaything of day-to-day events. "Rarely has a girl from that generation moved me as she has," Kollwitz notes. "We are all in our own way trying to get through life, complicated and convoluted as it is right now." It's not so different for an older woman like herself, she thinks, but at least she has memories of better days. War made her into a pacifist, and the outbreak of revolution gave her a flicker of hope for a socialist, democratic, humane, and more just Germany. But now that's all gone, and all that remains is a longing for the past.

THE NEWS OF the Kapp Putsch deflates all of former crown prince Wilhelm's hopes for a quick return home. At the start of 1920, things seemed to have calmed down enough politically in

Germany that his old adversaries might have allowed him to live as a private citizen somewhere in the Reich. But the putsch has destroyed this dream. Wilhelm can't help but be deeply disappointed, although he should have known better. For right-wing Germans, he is still a symbolic figure. How else to explain why those behind the putsch had tried long and hard to establish contact with him before they launched their attempted coup d'état? They had sent out feelers as to whether he would consider serving as the leader of a restored German monarchy if the putsch were successful. Like the putschists, Wilhelm was convinced that a republic was the wrong form of government for Germany and that the country needed a stable force that stood above the quarrels of political parties—namely a king or an emperor. He also considered himself more able than his father to lend the monarchist state a new appearance and new legitimacy. But his experiences of both war and revolution had taught him that the monarchy could not be revived against the will of the people. Consequently he had clearly rejected the putschists' overtures. He probably also doubted if their plans would ever be put into action.

Neither the Allies nor Wilhelm's Dutch hosts underestimate the potential political risk posed by the prince. His return to Germany is seen as a concrete danger, and rumors swirl that he is plotting to escape by ship, submarine, or airplane. When the news of the Kapp Putsch breaks throughout Europe, the Netherlands deploys a torpedo boat off the coast of Wieringen, and it shoots down an approaching airplane—Dutch, it turns out. Wilhelm describes the dashing of all his hopes for a speedy return to Germany as "the sternest test of my life."

In the wake of the Kapp Putsch, the former heir to the throne begins to look upon the small front garden of his home in exile with different eyes. Thus far, he hasn't taken any interest in this little square of land, simply letting everything grow wild, so that the first rays of spring sunshine fall upon scrub brush and weed-ridden flowerbeds. Now that he knows that he may well spend years in this place, Wilhelm feels the need to cultivate the garden. He grabs a spade and digs in the soil until his back begins to ache.

ON MARCH 20, 1920, Terence MacSwiney learns that one of his closest comrades, and his longtime friend, Tomás MacCurtain has been executed by a group of police officers. Early in the morning, men with blackened faces forced their way into his house and restrained his wife as they opened fire on her husband. It was MacCurtain's thirty-sixth birthday. Riddled with bullets, the Lord Mayor of Cork tumbled down his front stairs and died.

   MacSwiney inherits his office. He knows that his new position makes him a more prominent target than ever before and that he will have to take part in the revenge the Irish independence movement is sure to exact for MacCurtain's death. It's the start of a vicious cycle, a murderous tit-for-tat in which Irish independence fighters will square off not just against British authorities but also the Irish loyal to England.

ON APRIL 19, 1920, Virginia Woolf notes that she intends to begin *Jacob's Room*, the work that will finally live up to her own elevated expectations of the modern novel—one that will truly capture life. In the first entry of a new notebook, specifically dedicated to the subject, she writes: "I think the main point is that it should be free." Under this sentence, she jots down a sketch for the novel's first scene, in which the reader encounters the main character as a child at a seaside resort, together with his mother and his brother. Young Jacob wants to explore the sand and the ocean, the mussels and crabs, and marches off on his own much to the disapproval of his mother, who, worried and angry, sets off with his brother to look for him. The idyllic beach setting is full of ominous signs: frothy waves, black cliffs, and the white skull of a dead sheep. As the story progresses, Jacob's life is characterized as a never-ending series of restrictions—by his family, schools, and the military. Finally, in 1914, all trace of the young man, whose last name just happens to be Flanders, is lost in the war. In the novel's last scene, his mother grieves in his empty, cleared-out room, where all that remains of Jacob's existence is a pair of shoes. Throughout his entire life he never had any space of his own, and the various "rooms" he inhabited on his short journey proved to be nothing but cramped prison cells. Yet in the end, they outlive him.

IN EARLY MARCH 1920, Faisal I is crowned as the head of the Arab Kingdom of Syria in Damascus, after the Syrian National Congress declares the independence of the Arabian monarchy. Nonetheless, well-informed observers know that the window of hope for Syrian independence that opened after the agreements signed in Paris has already begun to close.

T. E. Lawrence is one of those observers. Shortly after his enthusiastic letter to the British prime minister, he realized that his own hopes were unlikely to come true. After leaving Paris, he returns to his hometown of Oxford, living for the most part with his mother. She is worried about him. Following the trials of war and the unsettled early days of peace, Lawrence is increasingly given to melancholy. After breakfast, he typically remains seated in one spot without moving even the smallest muscle in his face. In the library at All Souls College he repeatedly reads a lengthy poem by Charles Montagu Doughty entitled "Adam Cast Forth." The subject matter is the expulsion of Adam and Eve from the Garden of Eden.

It doesn't help Lawrence's unstable condition that after his father's death, his mother told him a carefully guarded family secret. Lawrence had always suspected the truth, but now he knows that his father wasn't the man he purported to be. His real name was Thomas Robert Tighe Chapman, and he came from a family of Anglo-Irish aristocrats who owned extensive property not far from Dublin. As the son and heir, Chapman had every reason to expect future wealth. He married a woman named Edith Sarah Hamilton, also from a good family, with whom he had four daughters. But theirs was an unhappy union. Edith came to terrorize the household with her religious fervor while Chapman turned to alcohol and became more and more sullen. The only time his face brightened was when the family's Scottish nanny, Sarah Lawrence, entered the room. The two had an affair, and in 1885 Sarah became pregnant. Chapman tried to keep this under wraps by renting a room for her and her newborn child in Dublin, where he frequently visited them. But when his wife learned of his infidelity and the illegitimate child, she issued him an ultimatum: her or me. Chapman chose to leave his elegant house to lead a simple life with the former nanny. They never married, although Chapman did adopt the name

Lawrence, and they lived inconspicuously in a variety of places. Sarah eventually gave birth to nine children, of whom six survived into adulthood. One of them was Thomas E. Lawrence, who in 1919 suddenly understood why his father rarely worked, enjoyed hunting, spoke fluent French, and was unusually well educated. His son now recognized the source of his own inner conflicts— the fact that he was both the child of aristocracy and a bastard.

This is his state of mind when shocking news from the Middle East reaches him in April 1920. Syria's fate has been sealed at the Conference of San Remo, called to determine the future structure of the eastern Mediterranean. Like other former Ottoman territories in the Middle East, Syria will be governed by one of the victorious colonial powers, under a mandate granted by the newly established League of Nations. This arrangement represents a compromise between Wilson's principle of national self-determination, which has been taken up by many peoples around the world, and the interests of the major imperial powers. On the one hand, the outcome protects these territories from simply being divided up among the victors; on the other, the territories are denied independence. Instead, they are to "mature" under the protection of the league until they are ready to function autonomously. France is given a mandate to control Syria and Lebanon, while Britain will govern Palestine and Mesopotamia, today's Iraq. The French have made no secret about how they intend to perform their protective task. A short time after the conference, France attacks the fledgling Arab Kingdom of Syria, which is illegitimate in the eyes of the international community, and achieves a decisive victory in the Battle of Maysalun. King Faisal is driven from his throne and forced to seek exile in Britain. If Lawrence still maintained any hopes that the Arabian dream could be fulfilled, they are now smashed completely.

SUMMER HAS ARRIVED on the Dutch island of Wieringen, and Wilhelm von Preussen remains a prisoner, living a hermit's life in his cottage. One hot and lazy day, bitter news arrives from his home in Potsdam. His younger brother Joachim has taken his life in Villa Liegnitz in the royal park of Sanssouci. With the failure of the Kapp Putsch, the young prince, who has always tended toward depression, lost all faith in a restoration of the Hohenzollern dynasty and saw no reason to carry on. On June 18, 1920, he shot himself with his revolver, wounding himself so seriously that he died a short time later. This is terrible news, but at the same time it convinces Wilhelm that he wants to live, that a life under the conditions of this new era is still better than throwing everything away. Even after Germany's republican revolution, not everything the Hohenzollerns once had is lost. The family retains possession of most of its hereditary estates, and deep inside, there is still a faint hope that the times will change. Perhaps 1918 won't be the final German revolution.

BY AUGUST 1920, Terence MacSwiney's closest associates can see that the new Lord Mayor of Cork is just about drained of energy. His work for the independent Irish parliament, together with his efforts on behalf of his home region and his constant fear of being arrested or assassinated, have worn him down. He hasn't slept in his own bed for months, and his office has to be protected by IRA guards. His daughter, Máire, only knows him as a voice on the telephone, although the little girl always reaches for the receiver when the bell rings. The threats against his life are becoming more serious. He even hears a rumor that he's already dead. His doctors advise him to take a vacation.

But there's no chance of that now. On August 12, 1920, British Army units with several hundred men surround Cork City Council, where MacSwiney has his office. He tries to escape through a back door but is arrested as he runs out of the building and taken to Victoria Barracks in the city. There he is stripped of his effects, which allegedly include a cipher key, an indication that he has been involved in illegal activities. Before long, Muriel MacSwiney is forced to witness her husband being transported in the back of an army truck to face a court-martial. She has heard from some freed IRA fighters that right after his arrest Terence tried to convince his fellow prisoners to join him in a hunger strike. She knows her husband well enough to be sure that he will refuse all nutrition regardless of whether anyone else joins him or not. It is terrible for her to watch helplessly as his face grows gaunter and gaunter. Even if she could manage to get him a piece of bread, he wouldn't eat it. "From the morning that I heard my husband was on a hunger strike, I believed that he would die," she said later.

On August 16, Terence MacSwiney's court-martial begins. He has become quite a well-known figure, and both the British and Irish press take enormous interest in the military trial. During the recesses, Muriel is allowed to speak with her husband in Gaelic. Although the first five days of his hunger strike have already sapped his physical strength, his will seems unbroken. When he stands up to answer accusations, he faces his judges without fear and makes it clear that he considers the trial illegitimate. The Irish

Republic exists, he argues. Thus, representatives of the old Irish regime have no right to try officials of the new government.

Ultimately MacSwiney is found guilty of sedition and sentenced to two years in prison. When the verdict is read, he responds: "Whatever your government may do, I have decided the term of my imprisonment. I shall be free, alive or dead, within the month as I will take no food for the period of my sentence."

ON AUGUST 18, 1920, Moina Michael sees a report in the *Atlanta Constitution* that galvanizes her life anew. Eighteen months have passed since she left New York and her remembrance poppies achieved some success. In that time she has worked tirelessly, but despite her efforts and the commitment of her designer, who invested considerable sums of money to start a national campaign, the poppies haven't bloomed to their full potential. Discouraged, she's about to give up and focus on her career rather than on the veterans of the war gone by.

But what she reads in the paper revives her spirits. Unbeknownst to her, while they were still stationed in France, some soon-to-be US veterans had begun organizing the American Legion, a veterans service organization. Now she learns that the legion's Georgia Department will be meeting in Augusta, over a hundred kilometers from where she lives, in Athens. Could this be a sign? She doesn't hesitate for a minute in packing a crate of cloth poppies and an illustrated edition of John McCrae's poetry and traveling to Atlanta where three legion delegates are readying for their trip to the convention. She prepares a resolution and succeeds in convincing one of them to present it at the meeting.

Moina waits restlessly in the days that follow until finally some staggering news arrives from Augusta: the Georgia Department of the American Legion has adopted the poppy as its official symbol of remembrance for those who fell in the Great War. In addition, the department has decided to file a motion at the American Legion's national convention to make the poppy the symbol for the group's activities across the country. At the same time, connections are being established elsewhere in the world. A Frenchwoman named Anna Guérin—the founder of the American-French Children's League who has been collecting donations from the United States for children in war-torn parts of France—attended the Georgia meeting and immediately recognized the poppy's potential. She now plans to have French children make lapel pins with the insignia to be sold in America. The profits will go to needy people in France.

Thanks to Guérin, the poppy campaign becomes a global success. The following year, she sends a group of Frenchwomen to London to sell lapel pins and convinces the chairman of the Royal British Legion and former British Army commander in chief Douglas Haig, to have his people adopt the poppy symbol, too. Via representatives, she also succeeds in mobilizing some of the nations of the British Empire—Canada, Australia, and New Zealand—to promote the flowers that blossomed in the fields of Flanders. By 1921, the vast majority of the English-speaking world is united by the poppy symbol, at least during the annual Armistice Day commemorations. The vision Moina had in November 1918 has become reality.

TERENCE MACSWINEY IS transported via Wales to London's Brixton Prison, where as inmate 6,794 he is immediately admit-

ted to the prison hospital. The trip has taken its toll after a week
in which he has consumed only water. No sooner has MacSwiney
arrived in prison when a newspaper reports that he may not survive the night. Prison guards regularly leave appetizing food on
his bed, but MacSwiney refuses to eat a bite. He spends most of
his time in bed to conserve his strength. He wants to stay alive
as long as possible. The British government may relent, but if not,
he'd like to keep the media and public attention focused on his
cause for as long as he can.

Nevertheless the lack of nutrition is starting to have gruesome
effects. MacSwiney's skin becomes hypersensitive and begins to
split and crack. His joints ache and swell, while his body begins
to break down muscle tissue. A priest is summoned to pray with
him and anoint his hands and forehead.

The Irishman, however, is far tougher than the doctors think.
It's now September 1920, and after four weeks in prison he's still
alive. Every day the Irish, English, and North American press run
new headlines about him. From Dublin, Michael Collins begins
to smuggle IRA fighters across the Irish Sea and make preparations to liberate MacSwiney from captivity. By this point, eye-
witnesses report that the prisoner is unable to move and that he
rarely speaks in a further attempt to conserve energy. Every day
is a life-or-death struggle. King George V is besieged with peti-
tions urging him to pardon MacSwiney, but the British government will not hear of it. It's not the first time an Irish liberation
fighter has gone on a hunger strike, and if the country relents,
Great Britain would open itself to extortion, since MacSwiney
has made it clear that he will only resume eating if he is immediately released from prison. The British government is far more
concerned with the general situation in Ireland than with the

welfare of a lone man who has devoted his life to fighting the empire. Still, the authorities fear that if MacSwiney dies, open rebellion will break out in the south of the island. Already in early September, four thousand workers march through Dublin and attend a mass held in MacSwiney's honor. In death, the Lord Mayor of Cork would surely become a martyr. On the other hand, the authorities fear that if he is released, loyalist forces in Ireland might lose faith, refuse to work for the crown and the empire, and might even organize their own violent acts of protest. By the middle of the month, MacSwiney's condition has deteriorated to such an extent that he can no longer be kept alive by force feeding, as has been done previously with men who went on hunger strikes.

ON OCTOBER 11, 1920, after painful years of separation and months of negotiations between attorneys, Walter Gropius and Alma Mahler are finally divorced. In order to give the court a clear reason for a quick annulment of the marriage, a private detective is hired to report that he has caught Gropius "in flagrante delicto" with a prostitute. The detective's testimony represents more like the opposite of what is going on, but the court falls for the charade. The bitter marriage between Alma and Gropius, which has existed primarily on paper, comes to an end.

The divorce, which entails for Gropius the loss of custody for their daughter, Manon, leaves its marks on him. Although he has started a long-distance romance with a young married artist, he feels lonely and suffers from wild mood swings. In his correspondence he repeatedly describes himself as a shooting star. "Again I have made a long curve around the universe and corkscrewed up several eons further," he writes. "I have by now exploded 10

times, but the scraps of my soul are still alive and are even growing in strength. I have gotten divorced, full of love, from my
wife . . . Now more than ever I am a nomad star in the heavens
with no fixed position."

At the same time, the Bauhaus is commanding all of Gropius's attention. He travels throughout Germany soliciting donations so he can build his campus. But even the founding of the
new school of art is riddled with internal conflicts, specifically
between Jewish faculty members like Franz Singer and Bruno
Adler and their allies, who are perceived as pushy, and their gen-
tile colleagues. One such ally, the Swiss painter Johannes Itten,
has attracted a group of devoted students and begins to style
himself a charismatic leader, introducing the teachings of
Nietzsche's *Zarathustra* into his artistic work. He also subjects
his students to strict daily regimens of garlic, meditation, and
eurythmy and orders them to shave their heads and wear a special cowl of his own design. Backed by his followers, Itten seeks
to become the most prominent figure at Bauhaus—at the expense
of other teachers. This stirs up resentment, and Gropius is forced
to mediate. "The brilliant Jewish group Singer-Adler has gotten
too presumptuous, and unfortunately Itten has been seriously
influenced by it as well," Gropius writes. "They want to use him
as a lever to gain total control over the Bauhaus. Understandably,
the Aryans have rebelled against that." "Jews" against "Aryans"—
even at the progressive Bauhaus! For the time being, though,
Gropius is able to quell the discord.

IN EARLY OCTOBER 1920, after Terence MacSwiney somehow
survives six weeks of his hunger strike, his supporters are

beginning to believe in miracles, while his enemies speculate that someone is secretly slipping him food. But as doctors note, his bed pan is always empty. His physical condition is fatal, and yet he's still alive. He can move a bit, and his mind is alert, so he's probably conscious of his body taking leave of this world. Fluid has accumulated all over his back, and his heart is barely beating. He complains of feeling pins and needles in his arms. His doctors offer a further diagnosis of tuberculosis.

On October 17, the sixty-sixth day of his protest, MacSwiney receives the news of the death of a fellow inmate who has also refused to eat. In Ireland, violent clashes between rebels and police are on the rise, and casualties on both sides are mounting.

MacSwiney is by now slipping in and out of consciousness, which allows prison doctors to pour some broth down his throat. On October 24, day seventy-three of his hunger strike, his brother, Seán, and a priest are allowed to spend the night in his cell. When they approach MacSwiney's bed early the following morning, he is lying there motionless and unconscious, with his eyes open. The priest whispers a prayer in his ear. Doctors try to reanimate the dying man with an injection of strychnine, but his wasted body doesn't react, and after several minutes his shallow breathing ceases. MacSwiney's last recorded words are: "I want you to bear witness that I die as a soldier of the Irish Republic."

THE DEATH OF the Lord Mayor of Cork reverberates around the world. Parades are held in his honor in several North American cities and in Paris and Belfast. On November 1, 1920, he is buried in Saint Finbarr's Cemetery in Cork with a crowd of his supporters in attendance. Comrades in Cork, who also refused food to protest his arrest, continue with hunger strikes of their own.

Nguyen Ai Quoc is also shocked by MacSwiney's death, even as he admires the Irishman's unshakable dedication to his convictions. Nguyen's path as an independence fighter is a different one, however. After failing to get himself heard in Versailles, he becomes an increasingly devoted follower of Marxist-Leninist ideology and declares, after joining the Socialist Party in France, that colonialism is a form of capitalist exploitation. In Paris Nguyen's activity is limited since the French secret police are always right behind him. They have taken away his passport so that he can't leave the country, and a number of spies have infiltrated Vietnamese independence circles. French intelligence officials are reliable purchasers of the revolutionary pamphlets Nguyen and his comrades have printed up. Closely watched, isolated, and far from the land to which he is so committed, Nguyen places all his hopes on the global revolution that ideologues in Communist Russia and on the French left are always talking about. If the downtrodden peoples in all the countries of the world rise up, he thinks, then surely Vietnam will also gain its freedom.

In December 1920, after spending some time in Paris and stopping in Geneva, Soghomon Tehlirian arrives in Berlin. As he will later testify in court, he moves in with a fellow countryman on Augsburger Strasse 51. Registering with the police, he says he intends to study applied mechanics.

In February 1921, on his way back from the zoo, he suddenly

hears voices talking in Turkish. The name "Pascha" is mentioned. When Tehlirian swivels round, he recognizes the former interior minister of the Ottoman Empire, Talât Pascha, the man considered responsible for the Armenian genocide. He follows the group of Turkish speakers to a movie theater. Once inside, Tehlirian feel nauseous and can't help reliving scenes from the massacre in his imagination. He hastily leaves the cinema. At least this time he's not seized by the cramps that accompanied earlier dizzy spells. He's able to stay on his feet. Several weeks ago he passed out on the street. Since then he's been treated by a professor of medicine named Cassirer.

In the early days of March, Tehlirian is again overwhelmed by insistent memories, which make him feel worse than ever before. He writes: "The pictures of the massacre kept appearing before my eyes. I saw the corpse of my mother. It got up and approached me and said: 'You've seen Talât here with your own eyes, and you're indifferent? You're no son of mine!'" That was the moment, Tehlirian will later say at his trial, that he decided to kill Pascha, the man he blamed for the annihilation of his family. He moves into a room on Hardenbergstrasse 37, directly across from the building where Pascha lives. But now that he can look his victim directly in the eye, he begins to have doubts. "I started turning it over in my mind. I asked myself: How can you kill a human being . . . I told myself I wasn't capable of killing another human being." So he drops his plans for killing and devotes himself to his former pursuits—German lessons with a Miss Beilenson, occasional visits to the theater and cinema, and reading the papers. At least, this is the story Tehlirian will tell when everything is over.

UPON HER ARRIVAL in Prague, Louise Weiss rents some rooms from a Jewish antiques dealer. The new regime has assigned an officer to protect her and serve as her guide, a man of the Belle Epoque, who greets her with a gallant kiss of the hand and is determined to introduce the Parisian lady to the natural beauties of his homeland. But after several weeks of wandering around Czech forests and hunting estates, Louise has had enough of his tutelage. She wants to start what she came to Prague to do—report about the heady infancy of the new Czechoslovakian state.

The new government throws open its doors to the correspondent from Paris, an early supporter when the government was still in exile and the former intimate of Milan Štefánik, who, now that he's dead, no longer stands in anyone's way. President Tomáš Masaryk receives her in his official residence, the Koloděje Palace, whose walls have been freshly whitewashed and stripped of all the Habsburg trappings. To Louise, the building looks like a "democratic monastery," and Masaryk is the embodiment of the new sobriety, still every inch the professor he was when he fled to Paris in 1915. Leading the new nation, however, is anything but an academic exercise, and in exile, Masaryk had no idea of how complex it would be. "He only knew Czechoslovakia theoretically," Weiss writes. Now he's trying frantically to get an overview of countless numbers, figures, and facts. An army of new state administrators needs to be hired, and a budget designed for a nation made up of very different parts: Bohemia, Moravia, Slovakia, and Ruthenia, which used to belong to Hungary. Ruthenia in particular is full of desperately poor farmers as well as Jews and "gypsies," who will be difficult to integrate into the new republic. At the time of the armistice, Masaryk tells Weiss, there was a famine in Ruthenia, and he had sent trainloads of food east, including some American cocoa powder. The local farmers, having never heard of cocoa, used the brown powder to paint the walls of their wooden huts. Wherever he goes, he complains, he runs into resistance from the old bureaucracy, which seems not to have changed since the Middle Ages. Louise had not imagined that the exciting early days of Czechoslovakia would be anything like this.

The reports the journalist files from Prague are the talk of Paris. Philouze wants at all costs for her to return to *L'Europe nouvelle*. Louise, on a visit home, is willing, but only if he agrees to pay her the salary she was originally promised, change her title to editor-in-chief, and allow her to monitor subscriptions and check the books. In addition, he must appoint her a voting member of the paper's advisory board and make her father its chairman. Philouze, whose face blanches at Louise's demands, perks up a bit at this final condition. Paul Louis Weiss is a wealthy man. He will certainly use private funds to help *L'Europe nouvelle* out of its financial difficulties. Readership has dropped off since the end of the negotiations in Versailles.

Thus it happens that Louise Weiss moves back into her blue-painted office, determined that no one is ever again going to tell her what to do. She takes a stiff broom to the premises, organizes the chaotic files lying around everywhere, reviews the paper's desperate financial situation, makes sure that the books are kept correctly, and instills discipline in a team of reporters who have grown used to working as little as possible. She soon realizes that funds are being diverted from the accounts. Philouze tries to retain control from behind the scenes, but Louise is determined not to let her authority be undermined by his petty intrigues. When conflict once again threatens to break out in the editorial department, she has had enough. She knows very well that the future of the paper depends on investors, including her father, and she has a lot of negative evidence against its founder, who has bossed her around for too long. This time he loses the power struggle. In a scene worthy of the cinema, she shows him the door.

Later Louise returns to Prague and then travels on to Budapest, Vienna, and Bucharest. But everywhere she comes to the same conclusion. The idea of launching young, free nations into a better future, as she envisioned it from Paris, is upon closer inspection a farce—or even a tragedy. The new states that have been created aren't shiny new edifices, but rather war-torn, fragile constructions. By the fall of 1919, the enthusiasm she helped to spread during the period of negotiations has given way to an embittered, at times almost cynical realism.

SOGHOMON TEHLIRIAN IS torn between the commanding voice of his mother, which he constantly hears whenever his mind wanders, and the voice of his conscience. On March 15, 1921, he paces his room, reading a book, when he sees the former interior minister of the Ottoman Empire leave his building across the street. In this moment Tehlirian is once again flooded by memories: the columns of soldiers, the shots, his sister, the ax, and the image of his mother and the sound of her demanding, admonishing, almost threatening words. Tehlirian had purchased a revolver back in Tbilisi in 1919 in order to defend himself, he later claimed, against further Turkish attacks. In Berlin, he takes it out of the trunk where he had stashed it among his clothes, puts it in his pocket, and rushes out onto the street, where he sees Talât Pascha disappearing in the direction of the zoo. Tehlirian runs after him on the other side of the street until he's level with his target. He then crosses Hardenbergstrasse, approaches Pascha from behind, puts the barrel of the pistol to the back of his victim's head, and pulls the trigger.

The shot rips open the top of the man's skull, and he pitches forward to the ground, blood streaming down his face. As people rush in from all sides, Tehlirian tosses the pistol to one side and, as though in a daze, tries to run away. He doesn't get far. An eye-witness stops him on Fasanenstrasse, and he is soon encircled by a crowd who restrain him. A man raps him on the head with a large metal key, while another searches his pockets for weapons. Someone else tries to get him to talk. All Tehlirian says, in broken German, is: "I Armenian, he Turk, no harm to Germany." Later when he is taken to the police station near the zoo, he lights a cigarette and is able to regain some composure. He thinks about what he has just done and feels "satisfaction in his heart." He had always dreamt of vengeance. Now he has it.

IN JUNE 1921, Arnold Schönberg travels to the Austrian town of Mattsee to enjoy the fresh summer air. Although he does hike around a bit exploring the region, the main purpose of the trip is to find the peace and quiet he lacks in Vienna so that he can compose. Guests report that Schönberg is enjoying his working holiday.

What he seems not to know is that Mattsee is one of a number of Austrian vacation spots that boast of not accommodating Jews. The restriction was first imposed in 1920, when the community decreed that in the future only "German Aryan" holiday guests would be allowed to reside there. The Salzburg city chronicle of July 1921 reports that the ordinance has been a success and that Mattsee is being kept "Jew-free" although "it takes effort . . . due to the notorious pushiness of Jews." Perhaps Schönberg has heard of the restrictions but thinks they don't apply to him because he converted to Christianity some time ago. In any case, his-sister-in-law booked his accommodation, and her father used to be the mayor of Salzburg.

The Schönbergs and their guests enjoying Mattsee's fresh summer breezes pose an affront to several of the community's leading citizens. There's no legal way to banish the unwanted visitors from Vienna, so they decide to apply public pressure and post announcements in town about a meeting of the civic council in which the issue of Jewish tourists was discussed. The posters read: "The town's representatives appeal urgently to the entire population of Mattsee to abide . . . voluntarily by the restriction so that our beautiful town of Mattsee is spared the consequences of possible Jewification and renters and landlords aren't subject to harassments by the German Aryan population."

When Schönberg sees the posters, he is dumbstruck and decides to leave Mattsee—a decision reinforced by an official letter from the community asking him to prove that he is not a Jew. Schönberg would like to depart immediately, but he wants to do so without kicking up a fuss and creating a public scandal. It's only after his sister-in-law's father intervenes and smoothes the waves that he puts off his departure. It almost looks as though the Schönbergs will end up spending their entire vacation in

Mattsee, but then the Viennese newspaper *Neue Freie Presse* reports that the composer intends to leave. The paper takes his side in the affair, asking how a small holiday town is able to contravene Austrian national law. That in turn stirs up interest in the right-wing press. The Salzburg newspaper *Volksruf* runs an article with the headline "The Jew Colony of Mattsee," which contains a barely concealed threat of violence against Jewish vacationers. Similar articles follow, and on July 5, Schönberg receives a postcard addressed to "the famous composer A. Schönberg residing right now in Mattsee—unfortunately."

Under the circumstances, Schönberg can hardly remain in the community where he had hoped to enjoy a bit of peace and quiet with his family. They had planned to stay in Mattsee for months, so a lot of suitcases need to be packed. On July 14, the Schönbergs and some of the composer's students, who have accompanied him, move to the town of Traunkirchen, where the composer stays until the fall, trying to overcome the shock of being driven out of Mattsee.

DURING THE SUMMER of 1921, Matthias Erzberger is also traveling. Together with his wife and daughter Gabriele, he wants to catch his breath before returning to politics following his lengthy break. After his lawsuit against Helfferich and a temporary retreat from government responsibility, he staged a determined campaign for his political rehabilitation. In a series of further legal actions, he was able to disprove many of the accusations leveled against him. Now he feels strong enough to resume a leading role in German politics, but first he wants to spend a few peaceful weeks with his family.

In the Black Forest town of Bad Griesbach, the Erzbergers
rent rooms in a Catholic spa, which serves as their home base
for long walks in the region. On August 26, Erzberger receives a
visit from his Center Party ally Carl Diez from Konstanz. The
family is eating breakfast when he arrives. It is the second-to-last
day of their vacation, and Mrs. Erzberger starts packing their
belongings while the two men decide to take a walk despite the
poor weather. On a country road to the Kniebis Hills Diez notices
two well-dressed young men who come up from behind and
overtake them without any greeting.

The two politicians have no way of knowing that these men
are members of the right-wing "Organization Consul," which has
dedicated itself to fighting "everything anti-national and international, Jewry, social democracy and radical left-wing parties"
as well as "the anti-national Weimar constitution." The men's
names are Heinrich Tillessen and Heinrich Schulz, and they
were members of the Freikorps until the paramilitary groups
were dissolved in the wake of the failed Kapp Putsch. Like many
of the street fighters, they joined the radical right-wing underground, and since then they have officially been employed by a
nonexistent timber company. The two are convinced not only
that Erzberger is a "repulsive traitor" and an opportunist making a career by fulfilling enemy demands, but also a "freemason
under Jewish control, hitched to Judas's wagon." One day they
received a letter from their superior, the former navy captain lieutenant Manfred von Killinger, which said—as Tillessen would
later recall—"After a drawing of lots in the directorship you
have . . . been chosen to do away with the former Reich finance
minister Erzberger. It is up to you how you choose to carry this
out. You are not to report the fulfillment of your mission . . .

Brothers, you can rest assured you will receive support from our order in case you are discovered."

When Erzberger and Diez start on their way back to the spa, the two men also turn around and overtake them again, before pivoting so they are face-to-face with the politicians. One of them pulls a revolver from his jacket, points it at Erzberger's forehead, and fires. A second shot hits Erzberger in the chest, and the heavy-set man crumples. Diez attacks the shooter with his umbrella and takes a bullet himself. Lying on the ground, Diez hears more shots, this time muffled, as though the barrel of the gun had been placed up against clothing. Then all is silent. Diez has been shot in the upper arm: the bone is shattered, and the bullet is lodged in one of his lungs, close to his spine. Diez manages to lift his head but he can't see Erzberger. With great effort, he gets up and follows a wide trail of blood about thirty meters across the path and down an embankment to a pine tree, where he finds Erzberger lying on the ground, his face covered in blood, no longer breathing.

Diez drags himself along the country road back to the village. On the way he meets a woman. He tells her what has happened and asks her for help, but she refuses him, exclaiming, "How could you go for a walk with Erzberger?" With his final ounce of strength, he reaches Bad Griesbach and informs a friend of the Erzberger family, who sets off to break the news to the murdered man's widow. Only then does Diez himself go to the doctor.

Erzberger is buried in his hometown of Biberach, but that same day memorial ceremonies are held throughout Germany. Thousands of people turn out to show their sympathy and to protest against right-wing terror. Despite all their criticism many people recognize that Erzberger, a realist, had tried to represent

German interests in the world as an honest broker and reliable partner. But the mourning of his supporters is drowned out by the rage of his enemies, who make no secret of their glee that the man has been gunned down. An article in the *Oletzkoer Zeitung* reads: "Erzberger, who negotiated the shameful peace of Versailles, has gotten his just desserts as a traitor to the fatherland."

FOR THE FIRST months after it opens, Harry S. Truman's haberdashery shows a decent profit, and when someone offers to buy the business Truman turns him down. But by January 1920, the short upswing in the American economy following the armistice is over. The return of huge numbers of able-bodied men who had been deployed on the battlefields of Europe, for whom there aren't enough jobs, as well as the abrupt cessation of demand for war products make themselves felt. For the next eighteen months, the United States will be rocked by a major economic crisis, and the country's GDP will shrink severely. Prices drop by 30 percent, which for a retailer like Truman, means having to sell his wares for less than he bought them. His old war buddies still come to the store to chew the fat, but they no longer splurge on a silk shirt or tie. And even if they do, Truman takes a loss on every sale.

He tries to stir up business by exploiting personal contacts and taking out ads. He also devotes considerable time to founding the first American Legion post in his home state of Missouri. In November 1921 he helps organize a huge ceremony inaugurating a war memorial in Kansas. Even Marshal Foch, currently on a speaking tour of the United States, shows up. Hundreds of thousands of Kansans turn out to watch the veterans parade. Truman receives the honor of presenting the Allied commanders who have made the trip with American Legion flags.

By then the worst of the economic crisis is over; nevertheless in September 1922 Truman & Jacobson has to close its doors. Truman, the war hero, is now saddled with twelve thousand dollars of debt. But he refuses to declare bankruptcy. Instead, he works like a dog to pay back the monthly installments of his exorbitant loans to various creditors. It will take ten years until Truman is debt-free. At least for the time being his dream of a family, a home, and traveling around in his own Ford is over.

HER VISITS TO Prague and Budapest were very disillusioning for the idealistic Louise Weiss. She believed so fervently in the future of national revolutions and in the freedom and autonomy they would bring to the nations of the former Habsburg Empire. But now she's forced to acknowledge how difficult this undertaking actually is. And no place is more disenchanting than Moscow, which she visits in 1921 in one final stint as correspondent for *Le Petit Parisien*, after arranging for a temporary acting editor at *L'Europe nouvelle*. In the "tortured city," ruled by mistrust, she finally loses her faith in the power of revolution. From the Czech embassy, the Parisian journalist tries to assess the situation in the Russian metropolis. Despite numerous warnings to the contrary, she's convinced that the Soviet secret police, the Cheka, aren't interested in her.

One evening she ventures out to visit a woman named Vera B., whom she met on the train from Riga to Moscow. Vera lives in a plain room separated into halves by a curtain. Behind the divider, a child can be heard wailing. "The poor little thing can't get used to the food in Moscow," Vera says. "Just look at this." She holds up a container full of lukewarm fluid that smells like cabbage.

As they sit down around the kettle, the phone rings constantly, and Vera announces that she's expecting friends. It is already late in the evening, but Vera is sure that they will come because they know she's brought back food from Latvia. Soon people begin to fill the room. Vera introduces one of them as a good Communist. Louise knows some of them from Paris.

From one minute to the next, however, the mood changes. The conversation is no longer about topics of general interest, but rather about the reasons for Louise's presence in Moscow. She suddenly feels as though she's on trial, and she realizes that it's not by chance that she or these other people are here. The air is thick with tension, and for the first time since her arrival in Moscow, she senses that her liberty might be endangered.

"Comrade," says a woman Louise met in France.

"I'm not your comrade, Madame," Louise shoots back. "Please address me the way you did in Paris."

Then she turns to a certain Moghilevsky from the Russian consulate in Riga.

"Please tell these people why I'm here. You saw my passport in Riga. We talked about my work. You know who I am."

Moghilevsky says she should tell them herself.

"Very well, if you think that's what I should do. Ladies and gentlemen, you see before you a bourgeoise who also represents an important bourgeois newspaper, *Le Petit Parisien*. You all know this paper because you all speak French."

"So you're our enemy, then," a woman hisses.

"Say what you want, but I respect your ideology and Russia's misery too much to lie to you," Louise says.

She stands up, demonstratively takes out a tube of bright red lipstick, and begins to apply it.

"I won't lie, Madame, as you do," she says to the woman who called her "comrade." Although the woman has just returned from Paris, Louise continues, she still spreads the impression in Moscow that France and the other countries of Europe are on the verge of revolution. She knows better, so why doesn't she tell the truth and admit that the bourgeoisie has emerged as the victor of the war in France and shows no signs of relinquishing the spoils of its triumph. It is risky business to give a false impression in Moscow and raise hopes that half the world will soon be joining Russia's cause.

Although she was just accused of being a spy, Louise has touched a sore spot among the Communist activists. People shift uneasily on their chairs, and a heated discussion commences about whether and how a world revolution can be launched. For, according to Lenin's theories, the Russian Revolution will only attain its goal if the proletariat seizes power the world over. Louise's strategy of defending herself by attacking the others is bold but it works, turning her from defendant into plaintiff. It also allows her to divert the others' attention. At some point another "comrade" offers to drive her home. On the way back, her heart stops for a moment when the driver halts his vehicle in front of a building that Louise knows all too well is the head-quarters of the Cheka. "This is the end of our excursion," he says with a sadistic grin. He drinks in her fear before again stepping on the accelerator.

Upon returning to Paris, Louise meets a colleague at Latin-ville, a popular patisserie in the Saint-Augustin district. Over hot chocolate, she can't hold back unbearable memories and images from her long journey through Eastern Europe, and she bursts into tears. The other patrons assume the young woman is suffering from a broken heart, and they're not entirely incorrect. "I saw unforgettable men battling terrible privation, a wonderful people I loved for their courage and nobility, a doctrine whose ideals fill me with an incurable nostalgia," Louise will write. She is weeping for her dreams of revolution, of a new Europe and a new world of peace and freedom, which reality has left in tatters. It is little consolation that Élie Joseph Bois has run the articles she sent back to Paris on the front page of the *Petit Parisien* every day.

ON FEBRUARY 8, 1922, Gandhi, who is in the city of Bardoli, receives news that causes him physical and mental anguish. From the very beginning, the noncooperation movement had many followers in the provincial city of Chauri Chaura, and it called for a demonstration to protest the arrest of some of its activists. A crowd gathered in front of the municipal jail demanding the release of the political prisoners. Then they marched through the city center chanting antigovernment slogans. The local security forces lost their nerve and started shooting into the masses. But the protestors were undeterred by the small numbers of police and went on the offensive, driving them back into their station. The building was set on fire, and twenty-three people perished in the flames. Again Gandhi is at a loss as to how his strategy of noncooperation could lead to such catastrophic results. Again he is confronted with doubts that the Indian people are ready for such a demanding form of resistance. He demonstrates his disapproval of what has happened by fasting for six days. A short time later, the Indian National Congress decides to suspend the noncooperation movement. The colonial government declares a state of emergency in Chauri Chaura, and one month later Gandhi is arrested and sentenced to six years in prison for sedition. His dream of leading a peaceful resistance to the British colonial regime recedes into the distant future.

ON MAY 1, 1922, the Monument to the March Dead—designed by Walter Gropius to commemorate the ten workers who lost their lives in the fight against Freikorps paramilitaries in the city during the Kapp Putsch—is unveiled at Weimar's Historical Cemetery. The term "March Dead" recalls an incident from Germany's failed democratic revolution in 1848, in which royal troops shot down rebellious civilians in Berlin. The monument reminds many visitors of a lightning bolt, but Gropius has something different in mind with his zigzagging lines. The sculpture points not from above to below but from the ground to the heavens and is intended to symbolize mankind's striving for something higher. Gropius rejects all attempts by the Left to interpret the monument as a symbol of the dynamism of socialism. He wants this to be a monument to human beings, not ideologies. In the winter of 1918, he had burned with passion for a revolution in politics, society, architecture, and art. And despite his own bitter personal, professional, and political experiences, he has nev-

ertheless retained his faith in humankind's striving for goodness, and in its search for new forms of a new society.

IN SUMMER 1922, George Grosz travels to the Soviet Union in
the company of the Danish writer Martin Andersen-Nexø, who
has been commissioned to write extolling the greatness of Soviet
Russia. Grosz, who enjoys a reputation as a revolutionary spirit,
is supposed to furnish the illustrations. Art is being drawn into
the incipient tug-of-war between the West and the Soviet Union—
by both sides. A short time before, a film entitled *The New Moon*
hit cinemas in the United States. Based on little more than
rumors, it told the story of Princess Maria Pavlovna, who fought
for her freedom and that of thousands of Russian women during
the chaos of the revolution. The women were supposedly forced
to register as "property of the state" and became the helpless
playthings of the *nomenklatura*.

The two artists, who have been chosen to heap praise on the
Soviet Union, meet in Denmark and embark for the town of
Vardø on the Barents Sea in Norway. Nexø has agreed with the
new Soviet government that a motorboat will be sent to take
them to Murmansk in the northern Soviet Union. But the two
men wait several weeks on the edge of Europe without seeing
the lights of any likely vessel. At one point they grow tired of
waiting and decide to make their way on their own, finding a
fisherman headed east who is willing, for a price, to take them
on board and make a detour on their behalf. Loaded up with
chocolate, knackebröd, and schnapps, they set off.

The fishing boat reaches Murmansk's Kola Bay in the middle

of the night and ties up in the harbor. No one in the city takes even the slightest interest in the arrival of the two artists. When morning dawns, Grosz and Nexø realize what a surreal place they've wound up in. Construction has begun on a new port but has been abandoned with the facility only half-finished. "Boats rested partially sunk or with their keels sticking up from the water," Grosz writes.

> A half-finished breakwater could be made out, and sacks of cement and bent, rusted pieces of iron stuck up everywhere. A bell buoy lay tipped over on its side, as did the crane that was supposed to place it in the water. Further back a whole submarine lay belly-up like a huge fish, covered with mussels and seaweed and with its paint peeling. Half-sunken wooden boats were stranded in water that smelled like manure. Alongside miles of empty petroleum drums were piled up, and there were whole rows of train cars, most without wheels, in which people were living. It was a massive garbage dump.

This was the bizarre backdrop for an equally bizarre spectacle that began to unfold as soon as the sun rose. Suddenly a large number of people converge on the fishing boat that had transported the two artists and where they had spent an uncomfortable night. Taking the lead are two men in leather jackets, jackboots, and military caps embellished with hammers and sickles. The two are accompanied by a seaman with wildly glancing eyes who keeps a revolver trained on the two new arrivals.

The pair of commissars interview the fisherman and then withdraw, entrusting the sailor to guard the suspicious interlopers. They take Grosz and Nexø's papers with them. Nothing happens for what seems ages. "In Russia you always have to wait forever," Grosz will write in his memoirs. At some point an interpreter shows up, but that's no great cause for hope. It can take days for their case to be reviewed. As it turns out, several hours later the news arrives that the artists are expected at the local worker's council.

"I admit that it was difficult to discover anything positive about Russia back then," Grosz writes. "In 1922, it was all immediately after a long war. Wherever we went, the entire country was, by Western European standards, falling apart terribly."

The two artists are finally put on a train and sent on their way through forests of pine and fir. In Leningrad, Grosz is given a more cordial reception. He has an appointment to meet with an international group of artists who are about to found a journal that will make the superiority of Soviet art known throughout Europe. At a restaurant, Grosz observes the luxury enjoyed by functionaries of the regime. It stands in stark contrast to the living conditions among the ordinary people Grosz encountered on his journey.

In Leningrad, Grosz also meets Vladimir Tatlin, one of the leading figures in constructivist Soviet art, who shows him a five-meter-tall model of a tower. The "Monument to the Third International," if built, will be taller than the Eiffel Tower, taller even than the Woolworth Building in New York, the world's tallest skyscraper. As a monument to the revolution, it's designed to rotate, symbolizing the energy of change. The only person who's not convinced by the project is Leon Trotsky, the most popular of the Russian revolutionary leaders. When he inspects the model, instead of expressing his admiration, he asks pointed questions: Why should the thing move and why does it circle around itself, always in one spot? Why should such a structure be a symbol of the continually progressing revolution? The gigantic project along with its proponent and his colossal visions for Soviet art are quickly condemned to obscurity.

One experience particularly clouds Grosz's view of the young Soviet Union: a reception in the Kremlin to which he's been invited as a foreign visitor. Lenin himself attends, greeting all those present without any formalities and speaking his words of welcome in German. Grosz notices that the people around Lenin are constantly whispering. He can't imagine why this should be the case until a journalist tells him that the great revolutionary leader has grown somewhat frail and forgetful of late. Men from his inner circle have adopted the habit of prompting him during his speeches whenever he threatens to lose his train of thought.

"My trip to the Soviet Union was not a success," Grosz writes, summarizing his experiences in Russia. It's not just that the book he was supposed to publish with Nexø never gets written. For Grosz, what counts as unsuccessful are his experiences with the Soviet Union and, ultimately, the Soviet Union itself. In 1921, the American journalist Lincoln Steffens had gone to Russia and reported back enthusiastically: "I have seen the future, and it works." Grosz, too, has seen the future, but it consists of a ships' graveyard with threatening commissars, a restaurant for wealthy apparatchiks, a senseless, megalomaniacal construction project, and a sickly dictator. For Grosz, the Soviet future—to be truthful, the future in general—doesn't work. But what else can one expect from a Dadaist? Had he ever truly believed in the Revolution?

In October 1922, Virginia Woolf's novel *Jacob's Room* appears in her own publishing house, the Hogarth Press. Nervously, the author awaits the first public reactions, writing:

> As for my views about the success of Jacob, what are they? I think we shall sell 500: it will then go on slowly, & reach 800 by June. It will be highly praised in some places for 'beauty'; will be crabbed by people who want human character. The only review I am anxious about is the one in the Supt.: not that it will be the most intelligent, but it will be the most read & I cant bear people to see me downed in public. The W[estminster] G[azette] will be hostile; so, very likely, the Nation. But I am perfectly serious in saying that nothing budges me from my determination to go on, or alters my pleasure, so whatever happens, though the surface may be agitated, the centre is secure.

Woolf underestimates her sales figures, and the reception in the press is also less ambiguous than she anticipated. The novel is almost universally panned. Still, the judgment of her literary friends is positive, and avant-garde insiders encourage her hopes that *Jacob's Room* represents a breakthrough. Unsurprisingly, Woolf becomes the toast of London society.

Together with her literary success, a personal encounter will soon change her life. Woolf writes: "I am too muzzy headed to make out anything. This is partly the result of dining to meet the lovely gifted aristocratic [Vita] Sackville West last night at Clive's. Not much to my severer taste—florid, moustached, parakeet coloured, with all the supple ease of the aristocracy, but not the wit of the artist." She describes Sackville-West as "a grenadier; hard; handsome, manly; inclined to double chin," while she herself feels "virgin, shy, & schoolgirlish." This new acquaintance is another breakthrough, another step into a new sphere for Woolf the artist and renewer of the novel, as well as another step toward a passion that couldn't be more different from the one she feels for Leonard Woolf. The relationship between the two women will go through extreme highs and lows and will last for many years. In opening herself to it, Virginia will once and for all leave the "rooms" of what is socially approved that have thus far hemmed in her life.

NGUYEN AI QUOC reaches the Soviet Union in June 1923. Avoiding the watchful eyes of the French secret police has not been easy. It is only with the help of the international leftist network that he's been able to steal away from Paris and then travel by train through Germany and by boat across the Baltic Sea. He has left letters of farewell with his friends in the French capital that make it clear he has no intention of returning. To the children of a friend, his "nieces" and "nephews," who have grown close to his heart, he writes: "You will not see your uncle Nguyen for a very long time. You won't be able to climb on my lap or my back as you've always done, and many years will pass until I see my Alice and my Paul again. When we meet again, I will probably be old and you will be as big as your Mama and Papa . . . When you're big, you will fight for your country like your parents, like Uncle Nguyen and your other uncles."

The Vietnamese independence fighter pictured his arrival in post-revolutionary Russia very differently. Upon entering the country, he's detained by the Bolsheviks, and it takes weeks for

them to check him out. He can't travel to Moscow until it's established that he can be trusted. He originally planned to stay in
the capital of the Russian Revolution for only a few months, but
it ends up being more than a year. During that time he learns to
survive the fierce, often deadly conflicts within the Communist
Party, and he cements his own ideological position. Little by little,
he rises through the inner circles of the party and gets to know
Lenin. Ngyuen never tires of reminding his party comrades that
the Vietnamese people are doubly subjugated: as a people of
laborers who are exploited as workers are all over the world, but
also as members of a race considered inferior by white people.
For Ngyuen, the battle for Vietnamese independence is one of
many national revolutions that will precede a global Communist
revolution. In 1924, Nguyen finally succeeds in convincing the
party in the Soviet Union that he should be sent on a mission to
China. Equipped with a ticket for the Trans-Siberian Railway
and a bit of money, he sets off for Canton.

IN APRIL 1923, Arnold Schönberg receives an invitation from
the painter Vasily Kandinsky, who has moved from Moscow to
Weimar, to apply for the directorship of the city's Academy of
Music, which is about to become vacant. But Schönberg has
heard—most probably from Alma Mahler and his student
Erwin Ratz—that anti-Semitism is rife in academy circles and
that Kandinsky himself has made disrespectful remarks about
Jews. In the wake of the Mattsee episode, Schönberg has not
written about his experience of anti-Semitism, but he now goes
on an explosive counterattack. On April 20 he answers Kandinsky: "I have at last learnt the lesson that has been forced upon

me during this year, and I shall not ever forget it. It is that I am not a German, not a European, indeed perhaps scarcely even a human being (at least, the Europeans prefer the worst of their race to me), but I am a Jew . . . I have heard that even a Kandinsky sees only evil in the actions of Jews and in their evil actions only Jewishness, and at this point I give up the hope of reaching any understanding. It was a dream. We are two kinds of people. Definitively!"

Kandinsky responds promptly, attempting to mollify Schönberg by saying that he is "shattered," but his reply shows that the accusation of anti-Semitism isn't entirely wrong. In it, Kandinsky raises the "Jewish problem" and characterizes Jews as a "nation possessed" by the devil. "That is an illness that can be cured," the artist writes. "During this illness, 2 terrible traits come to the fore: the negative (destructive) power and the lie, which also has destructive effects." He says he would have liked to talk over the matter with Schönberg, who should have written as soon as he heard about the "remarks" in Weimar. Kandinsky also reassures him that nothing anyone could think and say in general about Jewry applied to the extraordinary Viennese composer and his friend. Schönberg pens a second response in which he attacks the artist's thinking even more vigorously. "How can a Kandinsky . . . refrain from combating a view of the world whose aim is St. Bartholomew's nights in the darkness of which no one will be able to read the little placard saying that I'm exempt!" Schönberg writes. "What is anti-Semitism to lead to if not to acts of violence? Is it so difficult to imagine that? You are perhaps satisfied with depriving Jews of their civil rights. Then certainly Einstein, Mahler, I and many others have to be gotten rid of." Schönberg does not travel to Weimar. The experience of war and the end of the fighting that led him to a new religiosity culminates in his social exclusion as a member of a religious community upon which he in fact has long turned his back.

That very year, 1923, when he rejects the prospect of moving to Weimar, Schönberg publishes his epochal "Composition with Twelve Tones." In it he argues for his version of twelve-tone music, which he anticipated in the *Jakobsleiter* oratorio and which he applied more consistently in his *Five Piano Pieces*. It is the attempt to liberate atonal music from the objection that it is arbitrary. The series of twelve tones and their systematic variation over the course of a composition provide an anchor for Schönberg's music, challenging to the ear as it is, within a compositional framework that opens every measure, every note to analysis and explanation. Schönberg is convinced that he has created something revolutionary, that he has established a new foundation for writing music. As early as July 1921 he had written to his student Josef Rufer about twelve-tone composition, proclaiming: "Today I have discovered something that will ensure the superiority of German music for the next hundred years."

ON THE NIGHT of May 31, 1923, Rudolf Höss and some comrades are on the move in the town of Parchim in northeastern Germany. The men from the Working Group Rossbach, as they now call themselves, are half-drunk and full of rage. A few days earlier, one of their number, Albert Leo Schlageter, was sentenced to death by the French occupation army in the Rhineland and executed. He was accused of acts of sabotage, in particular

bombings, against the occupational forces. The German paramilitaries think that they have discovered the man who betrayed
Schlageter to the French: an unpopular fellow member of the
Working Group named Walther Kadow, whom Höss and his
comrades believe is a spy. These veteran street fighters feel
nothing but contempt for the newly founded German republic
and its authorities. They are convinced that the new German
government, which cooperates with the French, has no interest
in getting to the bottom of the Schlageter case. So they decide to
"take justice into their own hands in the traditional German
fashion."

Kadow is out drinking with some buddies in a Parchim pub—
the perfect opportunity for Höss and his comrades to give the
traitor what he deserves. When the men arrive at the establishment, Kadow is passed out on a sofa. Höss is armed with a
revolver, while the others carry brass knuckles and rubber trun-
cheons. They grab the heavily intoxicated man and toss him in
their car. They drive down a country road into the forest where
they shove Kadow out of the vehicle. He tries to flee, but a warning shot from Höss freezes him in his tracks. Now the men
begin to beat Kadow. Höss even snaps a young tree in half and
uses it to bash the victim's head.

What should they do with the bloody, half-dead man? Should
they wash him up and take him to the hospital? Höss has a different idea and orders that he be buried in the forest. The victim
is wrapped up in a rain cape, hoisted atop the car's baggage rack,
and driven deeper into the forest. When they reach a suitable
spot, Kadow is laid out on the ground, and one of Höss's men
slits his throat with a knife. Kadow's body is still twitching, so
Höss puts a bullet in his head. The murderers then haphazardly

cover the body and clean the car. The next morning they'll return to the scene of their crime to bury Kadow and conceal the traces of what they've done. After 1945, in the memoirs he wrote in prison, Höss explains his motivation for the murder. "Back then, I was convinced, as I still am today, that this traitor deserved death. Since in all likelihood, no German court would have come back with a conviction, we executed him on the basis of an unwritten law, born from the necessity of the times, which we imposed on ourselves."

EPILOGUE

Death is not an event in life: we do not live to experience death.

—Ludwig Wittgenstein,
Tractatus logico-philosophicus, 1918

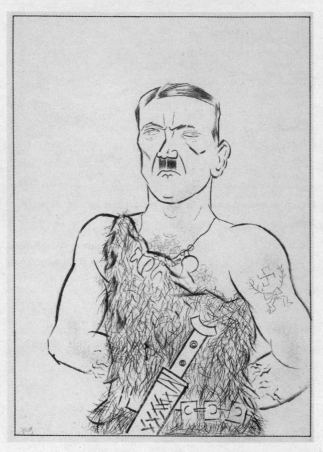

George Grosz, *Hitler, the Savior*, 1923

IN THE FALL of 1919, Marina Yurlova finally escapes the Russian civil war, which the Bolsheviks won't win until 1922. From the deck of a ship, she watches the roofs of Vladivostok, the final eastern stop of the Trans-Siberian Railway, disappear on the horizon. Yurlova's destination is Japan, where she soon arrives. There she is transformed from a soldier back into a young woman who does traditional "women's work," first as a nanny, then serving as a secretary, and eventually discovering her true calling after taking dance lessons from a Japanese master. As a dancer, she gains recognition at private soirees and is granted an artist's visa to the United States, achieving a certain degree of fame in San Francisco and New York. She dies in 1984.

TERENCE MACSWINEY IS one of more than a thousand victims of the Irish struggle for independence. While Sinn Féin is laying the foundations for a new state in the Irish shadow parliament, the Irish Republican Army wages a guerrilla war against the British authorities. It is a conflict without clear boundaries or front lines, and which spills out onto the civilian population. Ambushes, robberies, and assassinations spark a vicious cycle of reprisals. In November 1920, a few weeks after MacSwiney's death, the violence rises to a new level on "Bloody Sunday" in Dublin. The Irish independence fighters aren't able to deliver a knockout blow to the British and the loyalists, nor can the British Empire contain the separatist movement. By July 1921, people have begun to realize that the war could go on for years with neither side achieving victory. A cease-fire is declared, and preparations are made for an independent Republic of Ireland in the south of the island. Terence MacSwiney becomes a national hero. In 1964, a bronze bust of him is put on permanent display in front of Cork Town Hall.

IN JUNE 1921, a Berlin jury hears the case of the Armenian assassin Soghomon Tehlirian. The trial sets off an intense discussion concerning the treatment of Armenians by the Ottoman Empire, Germany's recent ally. Sympathy with the victims of the massacre and with Tehlirian dominates media reports, and the trial ends with an acquittal, based primarily on the testimony of neurologist and psychiatrist Richard Cassirer. Cassirer found it credible that the defendant had not planned the shooting, but had acted on impulse and under the aftereffects of a trauma.

Only later does it emerge that Tehlirian was a member of Operation Nemesis, a secret organization with a special commando unit charged with killing everyone responsible for the Turkish massacre of the Armenians. The shooting of Talât Pascha wasn't Tehlirian's first murder—he had already killed in the name of Armenia back in Constantinople. In contrast to what he told the court, he had not witnessed the massacre of his family. In the months and years following Tehlirian's spectacular trial,

Operation Nemesis will carry out further assassinations in Berlin, Tbilisi, and Constantinople.

IN AUGUST 1921, after murdering Matthias Erzberger, Heinrich Schulz and Heinrich Tillessen flee abroad. They stay outside Germany until Hitler's assumption of power in 1933, when they return and make careers for themselves. They are put on trial only after 1945, in the Federal Republic of Germany, where Erzberger is recognized as an architect of parliamentary rule and honored as a "martyr of German democracy." In 2017, one of the buildings of the German Bundestag in Berlin is renamed Matthias-Erzberger-Haus.

AFTER THE FAILURE of his campaign for an independent Arabia, Thomas E. Lawrence decides that he will no longer seek to play a role in world politics. Beginning in 1923, two years after the British appointed his friend Faisal king of Iraq, he enlists under a false name as an ordinary soldier in the Royal Air Force. On May 13, 1935, he dies from injuries sustained in a motorcycle crash.

FERDINAND FOCH DIES on March 20, 1929, after a long illness. At his state funeral, his remains are interred near Napoleon's tomb at Les Invalides in Paris. Such national honors, however, cannot obscure the fact that Foch's star declined quickly after his triumph in November 1918. After leaving the military, he served as an advisor to various French governments, but the opinions of the hardline former marshal increasingly deviated from the official French position, which worked toward a step-by-step reconciliation with the former enemy Germany. At the end of the war Foch may have been a hero, but in the battle over the peace he emerged a loser.

HENRY JOHNSON ALSO dies in 1929, alone in a Washington, DC, hospital, having been granted no more than an invalid's pension in 1927. After the war, Johnson never regained a footing in civilian life, and alcohol, poverty, loneliness, and tuberculosis put him in an early grave. It won't be until 2015 that President Barack Obama will posthumously award Johnson the national Medal of Honor.

HARRY S. TRUMAN will need until the early 1930s to pay off the debts from his haberdashery. Shortly after the failure of that business, however, he begins his political career, for which he also exploits his military contacts. At first he serves as a county judge and then works his way up the ladder rung by rung. In 1945, Truman becomes the thirty-third president of the United States, eventually serving two terms in office. One of the decisions the former artillery officer makes as America's commander in chief is to drop atomic bombs on Hiroshima and Nagasaki. In 1918 he swore he would never fire another shot as long as he lived.

ON MARCH 21, 1933, the so-called Day of Potsdam, former crown prince Wilhelm of Prussia stands alongside Adolf Hitler in that city's Garrison Church. Wilhelm has been living in Germany as a private citizen since late 1923, and a few weeks after the Nazis' assumption of power, it looks as though Hitler may keep his promise and restore the Hohenzollerns to their ancestral throne. But this fond dream doesn't last long. In reality, Hitler has little time for Germany's former rulers, whom he viewed as too weak to stave off revolution; as far as he's concerned the former kaiser can see out his days in Dutch exile. Nor does Hitler put any stock in the talk that the Kaiser's eldest son, Wilhelm, who he thinks is interested only in women and horses, could assume the crown. Thus despite the symbolic show of unity between the royal family and the Nazi leader, Potsdam Day does not improve the Hohenzollerns' situation. The former crown prince won't play a role in the higher spheres of power during the Third Reich, and his father, the last German kaiser, will never return home. Friedrich Wilhelm von Hohenzollern, as he has been legally known since his abdication, will die in Dutch exile in 1941.

RUDOLF HÖSS IS convicted of murdering Walter Kadow and sentenced to ten years in prison, of which he serves only four before he is released as part of a general amnesty. A free man, the former paramilitary makes ends meet with agricultural work and again becomes active in radical right-wing circles. His life takes a decisive turn when Hitler comes to power on January 30, 1933. Höss joins the SS and becomes a member of that organization's Totenkopfverbände (Death's Head Units). He works in various concentration camps before being made commandant of Auschwitz in 1940, where he is responsible for implementing the "final solution to the Jewish question" and oversees the construction of the gas chambers in which more than a million people, most of them Jews, are murdered with the poison gas Zyklon B.

After the war, Höss goes underground using an alias, but in 1946 he is apprehended and sent to Poland to face justice. The following year, he is tried in Warsaw and sentenced to death. Fourteen days after the verdict is rendered, the ex-commandant of Auschwitz is hanged in front of his former house, overlooking the death camp.

BY THE TIME the Nazis take power in Germany, George Grosz is in the United States. Having already been a fellow of an art association in New York, Grosz decided on January 12, 1933, to turn his back on his homeland for good. A few weeks later, Hitler is named Reich chancellor, and the new regime orders the police to raid Grosz's studio and arrest the artist. But the studio is empty and the raid is unsuccessful. A short time later, Grosz is stripped of his German citizenship, and his works are declared "decadent art." However, he is as successful in America as he has been in Germany. It isn't until 1959, at the insistence of his wife, Eva, that he decides to return to his home country. But only a few weeks after his arrival, Grosz—who suffers from depression and alcoholism—falls down a flight of stairs and dies.

ARNOLD SCHÖNBERG SPENDS the 1920s as a professor of musical composition in Berlin and leaves Germany in 1933. In Paris he converts back to Judaism before fleeing to the United States.

After spending time in Boston and New York, he succeeds in procuring a professorship in California, where he lives not far from Alma Mahler and Franz Werfel in Beverly Hills. In 1941 he becomes an American citizen. He dies of a heart attack in 1951.

WHEN MOINA MICHAEL retires at the age of sixty-nine in 1938, she can look back on an impressive career. Not only had she worked her way up from being a village school teacher to a college professor at a time when it was unusual for women even to attend university, but her idea of selling paper poppies to benefit the veterans of the Great War had become a success throughout the English-speaking world and beyond. Many people continue to sell poppies and wear them on their lapels every November 11 in the United States, Britain, and fifty-two other countries. Until 1940, the sale of the red blossoms brings in an annual seven million dollars, which is then distributed to needy veterans. But what must this once stout, now sickly elderly lady think during her final years when the Second World War breaks out and once again millions of young people lose their lives or health on the battlefields of Europe? Michael doesn't live to see the end of this latest paroxysm of mass murder. She dies on May 10, 1944.

IN 1941, AFTER completing her novel *Between the Acts*, Virginia Woolf once again falls into an acute depression, and Leonard takes her to see a doctor in Brighton. But Virginia no longer has the strength to withstand another bout of all-consuming darkness. On March 28, she commits suicide in the river Ouse, filling her pockets with stones and drowning, although she is a fine swimmer. In her farewell note to Leonard, she writes: "If anybody could have saved me it would have been you. Everything has gone from me but the certainty of your goodness. I can't go on spoiling your life any longer. I don't think two people could have been happier than we have been."

IN 1933, KÄTHE Kollwitz watches as the Nazis, who will later classify her art, too, as "decadent," assume power. In 1940, her beloved husband, Karl, dies. A committed pacifist, Kollwitz suffers through the Second World War, but doesn't live to see another peace. Having been bombed out of her apartment, she moves to the town of Moritzburg, near Dresden, where she dies on April 22, 1945, a few days before Nazi Germany's capitulation.

AFTER LEAVING MOSCOW, Nguyen Ai Quoc spends several years in China, teaching young Vietnamese exiles the basics of socialism at a progressive academy. Like his activities in Paris and Moscow, this activity, too, is preparation for his life's work: securing the independence of Vietnam. But the chance to achieve that end will not come until the Second World War, when Vietnamese rebels succeed in defeating Vichy France and its ally Japan. In the country's August Revolution, Vietnam finally gains its independence as a democratic republic. Nguyen, who has adopted the name Ho Chi Minh, goes on to lead his country against the United States in the Vietnam War.

MOHANDAS GANDHI HAS to wait for two more years to see his life's work fulfilled. India declares its independence in 1947, accepting the partition of the country Gandhi sought to avoid. The result is a majority Hindu India and a predominantly Muslim Pakistan. A few months after the establishment of India, the seventy-eight-year-old politician is killed by a bullet fired by the assassin Nathuram Godse. The Hindu nationalist blames Gandhi for the division of India and is convinced that the Mahatma sold out the interests of Hindus.

LIKE SCHÖNBERG AND Grosz, Walter Gropius has to flee the Nazis, who attack the Bauhaus as a "church of Marxism." Via England he emigrates to the United States, where he becomes a professor of architecture at Harvard University and remarries. It isn't until the 1950s that Gropius will once again be involved in projects in Germany. In 1957, he takes part in the International Building Exhibition (Interbau) with a nine-story, concave apartment house in Berlin's Hansaviertel neighborhood. Gropius dies in 1969 in Boston.

BY THAT TIME, Gropius's ex wife, Alma Mahler, has been dead for five years. In 1938, shortly before Nazi Germany annexed Austria, she left her home city of Vienna, her love for Franz Werfel inspiring her to join him in exile. The couple was able to cross the Pyrenees on foot to Barcelona and then continue on via Lisbon to Los Angeles, where a colony of German-speaking refugees was already living. Alma Mahler remained married to Werfel until his death in 1945. In 1951, she moved to New York, where the multiple widow lived out her final years, her beauty ravaged by time and alcohol. She died in 1964.

AFTER THE END of the Second World War, Richard Stumpf lives in the eastern German town of Heiligenstadt in the Soviet occupation zone. Following the Great War, he eventually found work, married, and fathered four sons. He even continued writing, publishing essays on naval and political topics. In the wake of his experiences with the paramilitary Freikorps, he became a moderate leftist and a critic of the rising National Socialist movement. Consequently, he had a hard time getting a job as of 1933. The published version of his First World War diary, which attracted considerable attention in Weimar Germany, was banned by the Nazis. In 1953, as workers in Communist East Germany take to the streets to protest hikes in production quotas, Stumpf is with them. That lands him in jail, and he will live the rest of his life as a suspected enemy of the East German regime. He dies in 1958 as a citizen of the German Democratic Republic.

ALVIN C. YORK passes away in 1964 in Nashville's VA Hospital. The school he founded is now part of the Tennessee public education system. Tennessee State Highway 127, for whose construction York lobbied, bears his name to this day. York ultimately overcame his objections to a film based on his life story. In *Sergeant York* (1941), he was played by Gary Cooper, who won an Oscar for the role.

IN 1979, AFTER a lifetime as a journalist and as one of the earliest and most passionate activists for women's rights and a united Europe, Louise Weiss is elected as a deputy to the European Parliament for the French Gaullist Party. She is eighty-six years old. Until her death on May 26, 1983, she remained the eldest member of the European Parliament. The parliament building in Strasbourg has borne her name since 1999.

Acknowledgments

The initial impulse for this book came from the film producer Gunnar Dedio. Not only did he invite me to contribute a book to a major project on the history of the interwar period, but years of working together with him on film scripts led me to attempt a different, more scene-oriented way of writing. It was inspiring to exchange ideas with the team working on the eight-part television film *War of Drums*. My thanks to writer-director Jan Peter, writer Frédéric Goupil, and producer Regina Bouchehri.

Tobias Schönpflug offered inspiration and support as I explored the possibility of taking a different approach toward history writing. Céline Dauvergne opened my eyes to the reciprocal influence of history and the visual arts. My agent, Barbara Wenner, accompanied the creation of this book from beginning to end with particular sensitivity.

I would like to thank my German publisher, S. Fischer, for its trust in my work and the excellent guidance I received from the first draft to the finished product. My gratitude goes out to the whole team, editorial director Nina Sillem and my editor, Tánja Hommen.

I've had the privilege of working with many extraordinary minds at the Wissenschaftskolleg Berlin, and I would particularly like to thank the 2015–17 fellows as well as my colleagues for their help and encouragement, especially as I neared the end of my project. Our library provided me with valuable resources and services, quickly procuring even obscure publications and assisting my research.

I was able to write a large section of the manuscript with the help of a stipend from the Centre canadien d'études allemandes et européennes at the Université de Montréal, and this book owes much to fascinating conversations I had with the scholars there. I offer my heartfelt gratitude to the director of the center, Laurence McFalls, as well as scholars Till van Rahden and Barbara Thériault.

Some of my fellow historians read parts of the manuscript and offered suggestions and constructive criticism. Thanks are due to Stephan Malinowski, Barbara Kowalzig, and Torsten Riotte. Their comments were truly valuable and certainly improved the book. The same goes for the critical readings of the manuscript by Nicola Willenberg and Karin Hielscher. Any remaining shortcomings are the sole responsibility of the author. Finally, special thanks to my father, Wolfgang Schönpflug, who supported this book and the new direction it represents with his invaluable advice.

Last, but not least, I would like to sincerely thank my American editor, Sara Bershtel, and my translator, Jefferson Chase, for the care and competence invested in the English version. Thanks as well to Philip Boehm, for his useful comments and ingenious renderings of poetry, and to Prudence Crowther for her sensitive copyediting.

Bibliography

THE FIRST WORLD WAR

Beaupré, Nicolas, *Das Trauma des großen Krieges 1918 bis 1932/33*, Darmstadt 2009.

Becker, Jean-Jacques, and Serge Berstein, *Victoire et frustrations 1914–1929*, Paris 1990.

Best, Nicolas, *The Greatest Day in History: How, on the Eleventh Hour of the Eleventh Day of the Eleventh Month, the First World War Finally Came to an End*, London 2008.

Blom, Philipp, *Die zerrissenen Jahre. 1918 1939*, Munich 2014.

Boittin, Jennifer Anne, *Colonial Metropolis: The Urban Grounds of Feminism and Anti-Imperialism in Interwar Paris*, Lincoln 2010.

Burbank, Jane, *Intelligentsia and Revolution: Russian Views of Bolshevism 1917–1922*, New York 1989.

Churchill, Winston, *The World Crisis*, vol. 4: *The Aftermath 1918–1922*, London 1929.

Cooper, John Milton, *Breaking the Heart of the World: Woodrow Wilson and the Fight for the League of Nations*, New York 2001.

Englund, Peter, *Schönheit und Schrecken. Eine Geschichte des Ersten Weltkriegs, erzählt in neunzehn Schicksalen*, Reinbek 2011.

Fitzpatrick, Sheila, and Yuri Slezkine (eds.), *In the Shadow of Revolution: Life Stories of Russian Women from 1917 to the Second World War*, Princeton 2000.

Gerwarth, Robert, *The Vanquished: Why the First World War Failed to End*, New York 2016.

Hagedorn, Ann, *Savage Peace: Hope and Fear in America 1919*, New York 2007.

Hughes, Gordon, and Philipp Blom (eds.), *Nothing but the Clouds Unchanged: Artists in World War I*, Los Angeles 2014.

Jannik, Allan, and Stephen Toulmin, *Wittgenstein's Vienna*, Chicago 1996.

Janz, Oliver, *Das symbolische Kapital der Trauer. Nation, Religion und Familie im italienischen Gefallenenkult des Ersten Weltkriegs*, Tübingen 2009.

Jones, Mark, *Founding Weimar: Violence and the German Revolution of 1918–1919*, Cambridge 2016.

Julien, Elise, *Paris, Berlin. La mémoire de la guerre 1914–1933*, Rennes 2009.

Kershaw, Ian, *To Hell and Back: Europe 1914–1949*, London 2015.

Kyvig, David E., *Daily Life in the United States 1920–1939: Decades of Promise and Pain*, Westport 2002.

Leonhard, Jörn, *Die Büchse der Pandora. Die Geschichte des Ersten Weltkriegs*, Munich 2014.

Lowry, Bullitt, *Armistice 1918*, Ohio 1996.

Machtan, Lothar, *Die Abdankung. Wie Deutschlands gekrönte Häupter aus der Geschichte fielen*, Berlin 2008.

MacMillan, Margaret, *Paris 1919: Six Months That Changed the World*, New York 2002.

Malinowski, Stephan, *Vom König zum Führer. Deutscher Adel und Nationalsozialismus*, Frankfurt am Main 2010.

Manela, Erez, *The Wilsonian Moment: Self-Determination and the International Origins of Anticolonial Nationalism*, New York 2007.

Mondrian, Piet, et al., "Manifest I," in *De Stijl* 2:1 (Nov. 1918), pp. 4–5.

Müller, Tim B., *Nach dem Ersten Weltkrieg. Lebensversuche moderner Demokratien*, Bonn 2014.

Pedersen, Susan, *The Guardians: The League of Nations and the Crisis of Empire*, Oxford 2015.

Peukert, Detlef, *Die Weimarer Republik. Krisenjahre der Klassischen Moderne*, Frankfurt am Main 1987.

Pieper, Ernst, *Nacht über Europa. Kulturgeschichte des Ersten Weltkriegs*, Berlin 2013.

Radkau, Joachim, *Das Zeitalter der Nervosität. Deutschland zwischen Bismarck und Hitler*, Munich 1998.

Raphael, Lutz, *Imperiale Gewalt und mobilisierte Nation. Europa 1914–1945*, Munich 2011.

Reichardt, Sven, *Faschistische Kampfbünde. Gewalt und Gemeinschaft im italienischen Squadrismus und in der deutschen SA*, Vienna 2009.

Salomon, Ernst von, *Die Geächteten*, Berlin 1930.

Schlögel, Karl, *Petersburg. Das Laboratorium der Moderne 1909–1921*, Frankfurt am Main 2009.

Spengler, Oswald, *The Decline of the West*, New York 1947.

Tooze, Adam, *The Deluge: The Great War and the Remaking of the Global Order*, New York 2014.

Troeltsch, Ernst, *Kritische Gesamtausgabe*, vol. 14: *Spectator-Briefe und Berliner Briefe (1918–1922)*, Gangolf Hübinger (ed.), Berlin 2015.

Weipert, Axel, *Die Zweite Revolution. Rätebewegung in Berlin 1919/1920,* Berlin 2015.

Wirsching, Andreas, *Vom Weltkrieg zum Bürgerkrieg? Politischer Extremismus in Deutschland und Frankreich in Berlin und Paris im Vergleich,* Munich 1999.

MATTHIAS ERZBERGER

Domeier, Norman, "Der Sensationsprozess Erzberger–Helfferich: Die Verquickung politischer und wirtschaftlicher Interessen in der Weimarer Republik," in Christopher Dowe (ed.), *Matthias Erzberger. Ein Demokrat in Zeiten des Hasses,* Karlsruhe 2013, pp. 158–83.

Dowe, Christopher, *Matthias Erzberger. Ein Leben für die Demokratie,* Stuttgart 2011.

Erzberger, Matthias, *Erlebnisse im Weltkrieg,* Berlin 1920.

Erzberger-Prozess, Der, Stenographischer Bericht über die Verhandlungen im Beleidigungsprozess des Reichsfinanzministers Erzberger gegen den Staatsminister a. D. Dr. Karl Helfferich, Berlin 1920.

Haehling von Lanzenauer, Reiner, *Der Mord an Matthias Erzberger,* Karlsruhe 2008.

Helfferich, Karl, *Fort mit Erzberger!,* Berlin 1919.

Jasper, Gotthard, "Aus den Akten der Prozesse gegen die Erzberger-Mörder," in: *Vierteljahrshefte für Zeitgeschichte* 10 (1962), pp. 430–53.

Krausnick, Michael, and Günther Randecker, *Mord Erzberger. Matthias Erzberger: Konkursverwalter des Kaiserreichs und Wegbereiter der Demokratie,* Books on Demand 2005.

Marhefka, Edmund (ed.), *Der Waffenstillstand 1918–1919. Das Dokumentenmaterial der Waffenstillstandsverhandlungen von Compiègne, Spa, Trier und Brüssel*, Berlin 1928.

Sabrow, Martin, "Organisation Consul (O.C.) 1920–22," in Historisches Lexikon Bayerns: https://www.historisches-lexikon -bayerns.de/Lexikon/Organisation_ Consul_%28O.C.%29, _1920-1922 (accessed May 18, 2017).

FERDINAND FOCH

Foch, Ferdinand, *Mémoires pour servir à la mémoire de la guerre*, 2 vols., Paris 1931.

Greenhalgh, Elizabeth, *Foch in Command: The Forging of a First World War General*, Cambridge 2011.

Mordacq, Henri, *L'Armistice du 11 novembre 1918. Récit d'un témoin*, Paris 1937.

———, *Le ministère Clemenceau: journal d'un témoin*, vol. 2, Paris 1931.

Notin, Jean-Christophe, *Foch. Le mythe et ses réalités*, Paris 2008.

Weygand, Maxime, *Le onze novembre*, Paris 1958.

MOHANDAS KARAMCHAND GANDHI

Fischer, Louis, *Life of Mahatma Gandhi*, New York 2004.

Gandhi, Mohandas Karamchand, *An Autobiography: The Story of My Experiments with Truth*, Boston 1993.

Parvate, T. V., *Bal Gangadhar Tilak*, Ahmedabad 1958.

Rothermund, Dietmar, *Gandhi. Der gewaltlose Revolutionär*, Munich 2003.

Vidwans, M. D., *Letters of Lokamanya Tilak*, Poona 1966.

WALTER GROPIUS AND ALMA MAHLER

Gropius, Walter, *Idee und Aufbau des Staatlichen Bauhauses Weimar*, Munich 1923.

Hilmes, Oliver, *Witwe im Wahn. Das Leben der Alma Mahler-Werfel*, Munich 2004.

Isaacs, Reginald R., *Walter Gropius. Der Mensch und sein Werk*, Berlin 1983.

Mahler, Alma, *Mein Leben*, Frankfurt am Main 1963.

GEORGE GROSZ

Blumenfeld, Erwin, *Einbildungsroman*, Frankfurt am Main 1998.

Flavell, Mary Kay, *George Grosz: A Biography*, New Haven 1988.

Grosz, George, *Ein kleines Ja und ein großes Nein*, Hamburg 1955.

Hecht, Ben, *Revolution im Wasserglas: Geschichten aus Deutschland 1919*, Berlin 2006.

Hess, Hans, *George Grosz*, Dresden 1982.

Jentsch, Ralph, *George Grosz*, Cologne 2013.

Lewis, Beth Irwin, *George Grosz: Art and Politics in the Weimar Republic*, Princeton 1971.

THE HARLEM HELLFIGHTERS: ARTHUR LITTLE, HENRY JOHNSON, JAMES REESE EUROPE

Badger, Reid, *A Life in Ragtime: A Biography of James Reese Europe*, New York 1995.

Barbeau, Arthur E., and Florette Henri, *The Unknown Soldiers: Black American Troops in World War I*, Philadelphia 1974.

Gero, Anthony F., *Black Soldiers of New York State: A Proud Legacy*, Albany 2009.

Grant, Colin, *Negro with a Hat: The Rise and Fall of Marcus Garvey*, Oxford 2010.

Little, Arthur, *From Harlem to the Rhine: The Story of New York's Colored Volunteers*, New York 1936.

Sissle, Noble, *The Memoirs of Lieutenant Jim Europe*, typed manuscript, ca. 1942: http://memory.loc.gov/cgibin/ampage?collId =ody_musmisc&fileName=ody/ody0717/ody0717page .db&recNum=0&itemLink=r?ammem /aaodyssey :@field(NUMBER+@band(musmisc+ody0717))&linkText =0 (accessed May 18, 2017).

Slotkin, Richard, *Lost Battalions: The Great War and the Crisis of American Nationality*, New York 2005.

Williams, Chad L., *Torchbearers of Democracy: African American Soldiers in the World War I Era*, Chapel Hill 2010.

RUDOLF HÖSS

Höss, Rudolf, *Kommandant in Auschwitz. Autobiographische Aufzeichnungen*, Martin Broszat (ed.), Munich 2013.

Koop, Volker, *Rudolf Höss. Der Kommandant von Auschwitz. Eine Biographie*, Cologne 2014.

PAUL KLEE

Klee, Paul, *Das bildnerische Denken. Schriften zur Form und Gestaltungslehre*, Jürg Spiller (ed.), Stuttgart 1964.

———, *Tagebücher 1898–1918*, Felix Klee (ed.), Cologne 1957.

Schlumpf, Hans-Ulrich, *Das Gestirn über der Stadt. Ein Motiv im Werk von Paul Klee*, dissertation, Zürich 1969.

Trepesch, Christoph, and Shabab Sangestan (eds.), *Paul Klee. Mythos Fliegen*. Katalog zur gleichnamigen Ausstellung (23.11.2013–23.2.2014) im H2 Zentrum für Gegenwartskunst, Berlin 2013.

KÄTHE KOLLWITZ

Kollwitz, Käthe, *Die Tagebücher*, Jutta Bohnke-Kollwitz (ed.), Berlin 2007.

Winterberg, Jury and Sonya Winterberg, *Kollwitz—die Biographie*, Gütersloh 2015.

CROWN PRINCE WILHELM OF PRUSSIA

Cecilie, Kronprinzessin, *Erinnerungen an den Deutschen Kronprinzen*, Biberach 1952.

Jonas, Klaus W., *Der Kronprinz Wilhelm*, Frankfurt am Main 1962.

Rosner, Karl (ed.), *Erinnerungen des Kronprinzen Wilhelm. Aus den Aufzeichnungen, Dokumenten, Tagebüchern und Gesprächen*, Stuttgart 1922.

Wilhelm von Prussia, Kronprinz, *Meine Erinnerungen aus Deutschlands Heldenkampf*, Berlin 1923.

THOMAS E. LAWRENCE

Anderson, Scott, *Lawrence in Arabia. War: Deceit, Imperial Folly and the Making of the Modern Middle East*, New York 2013.

Brown, Malcolm (ed.), *Lawrence of Arabia, The Selected Letters*, London 2005.

Lawrence, Thomas E., *The Complete 1922 Seven Pillars of Wisdom*, Fordingbridge 2004.

Thomas, Lowell, *With Lawrence in Arabia*, New York 1924.

Wilson, Jeremy, *Lawrence of Arabia: The Authorized Biography of T. E. Lawrence*, New York 1990.

TERENCE MACSWINEY

Augusteijn, Joost, *From Public Defiance to Guerilla Warfare: The Experience of Ordinary Volunteers in the Irish War of Independence 1916–1921*, Dublin 1996.

Breen, Dan, *My Fight for Irish Freedom*, Dublin 1921.

Costello, Francis J., *Enduring the Most: The Life and Death of Terence MacSwiney*, Dingle 1995.

MacSwiney Brugha, Máire, *History's Daughter: A Memoir from the Only Child of Terence MacSwiney*, Dublin 2006.

MacSwiney, Terence, *Principles of Freedom*, Dublin 1921.

MOINA MICHAEL

Michael, Moina, *The Miracle Flower: The Story of the Flanders Fields Memorial Poppy*, Philadelphia 1941.

NGUYEN TAT THANH / NGUYEN AI QUOC / HO CHI MINH

Duiker, William J., *Ho Chi Minh: A Life*, New York 2000.

Großheim, Martin, *Ho Chi Minh. Der geheimnisvolle Revolutionär*, Munich 2011.

Lacouture, Jean, *Ho Chi Minh*, Paris 1967.

Quinn-Judge, Sophie, *Ho Chi Minh: The Missing Years 1919–1941*, Oakland 2003.

Tran Dân Tîen, *Glimpses of the Life of Ho Chi Minh, President of the Democratic Republic of Vietnam*, Hanoi 1958.

Trang-Gaspard, Thu, *Hô Chí Minh à Paris (1917–1923)*, Paris 1992.

ARNOLD SCHÖNBERG

Gervink, Manuel, *Arnold Schönberg in seiner Zeit*, Laaber 2000.

Nono-Schönberg, Nuria (ed.), *Arnold Schönberg 1874–1951. Lebensgeschichte in Begegnungen*, Klagenfurt 1998.

Ringer, Alexander L., *Arnold Schoenberg: The Composer as Jew*, Oxford 1990.

Schönberg, Arnold, *Die Jakobsleiter: Oratorium*, Vienna 1917.

———, *Letters*, Erwin Stein (ed.), New York 1965.

Staatliche Tretjatow Galerie and Goethe Institut Inter Nationes (eds.), *Arnold Schönberg und Wassily Kandinsky. Malerei und Musik im Dialog. Zum 50. Todestag von Arnold Schönberg*, Moskau 2001.

Tenner, Haide (ed.), *"Ich möchte solange leben, als ich Ihnen dankbar sein kann." Alma Mahler–Arnold Schönberg. Der Briefwechsel*, Salzburg 2012.

Theurich, Jutta (ed.), *Der Briefwechsel zwischen Arnold Schönberg und Ferruccio Busconi 1903–1919*, dissertation, HU Berlin 1979.

Waitzbauer, Harald, "Arnold Schönberg ist in Mattsee unerwünscht," in Robert Kriechbaumer (ed.), *Der Geschmack der Vergänglichkeit. Jüdische Sommerfrische in Salzburg*, Vienna 2002, pp. 153–73.

RICHARD STUMPF

Horn, Daniel (ed.), "The Diarist Revisited: The Papers of Seaman Stumpf," in *The Journal of the Rutgers University Libraries* 40:1 (1978), pp. 32–48.

———, *The Private War of Seaman Stumpf: The Unique Diaries of a Young German in the Great War*, London 1967.

Stumpf, Richard, *Warum die Flotte zerbrach. Kriegstagebuch eines christlichen Arbeiters*, Berlin 1927.

SOGHOMON TEHLIRIAN

Der Prozeß Talaat Pascha, Stenographischer Prozeßbericht mit einem Vorwort von Armin T. Wegner, Berlin 1921.

Hosfeld, Ralf, *Operation Nemesis. Die Türkei, Deutschland und der Völkermord an den Armeniern*, Cologne 2005.

HARRY S. TRUMAN

Ferrel, Robert H. (ed.), *Dear Bess. The Letters from Harry to Bess Truman 1910–1959*, New York 1983.

McCullough, David, *Truman*, New York 1992.

Miller, Merle, *Plain Speaking: An Oral Biography of Harry S. Truman*, New York 1974.

Truman, Margaret, *Harry S. Truman*, London 1973.

LOUISE WEISS

Bertin, Célia, *Louise Weiss*, Paris 1999.

Weiss, Louise, *Mémoires d'une Européenne*, Paris 1968.

————, *Milan Stefanik*, Paris 1920.

————, *La République tchéco-slovaque*, Paris 1919.

VIRGINIA WOOLF

Bell Anne-Olivier, *The Dairy of Virginia Woolf*, vols. 1 and 2, New York 1977–78.

DeSalvo, Louise, and Mitchell A. Leaska (eds.), *The Letters of Vita Sackville-West and Virginia Woolf*, New Jersey 2001.

Lee, Hermione, *Virginia Woolf*. New York 1999.

Nicolson, Nigel (ed.), *The Question of Things Happening: The Letters of Virginia Woolf*, vol. 2: *1912–1922*, London 1976.

Phillips, Kathy J., *Virginia Woolf Against Empire*, Knoxville 1994.

Spater, George, and Ian Parsons, *A Marriage of True Minds: An Intimate Portrait of Leonard and Virginia Woolf*, New York 1977.

Woolf, Virginia, *Jacob's Room*, Richmond 1922.

————, *Night and Day*, Richmond 1919.

————, *The Voyage Out*, London 1915.

ALVIN C. YORK

Lee, David D., *Sergeant York: An American Hero*, Lexington 1985.

Skeyhill, Tom (ed.), *Sergeant York: His Own Life Story and War Diary*, New York 1928.

MARINA YURLOVA

Yurlowa, Marina, *Cossack Girl*, Hamburg 1935.

————, *Russia, Farewell*, London 1936.

PICTURES

1 Paul Klee © ARTOTHEK

2 © IWM (Art.IWM ART 1146) / Bridgeman Images

3 © Private Collection / Bridgeman Images

4 © Digital image, The Museum of Modern Art, New York / Scala, Florence / VG Bild Kunst, Bonn 2017

5 © Philadelphia Museum of Art, Pennsylvania, PA, US / The Louise and Walter Arensberg Collection, 1950 / Bridgeman Images / VG Bild Kunst, Bonn 2017

6 © bpk / Nationalgalerie, Staatliche Museen zu Berlin / Andres Kilger

7 © akg-images / Bildarchiv Monheim / VG Bild Kunst, Bonn 2017

8 Art © Estate of George Grosz / VG Bild Kunst, Bonn 2017

Index

Page numbers in *italics* refer to illustrations.